Frommer's



# BRITAIN'S BEST-LOVED DRIVING TOURS

Simon & Schuster Macmillan

Written by Roy Woodcock, John McIlwain

Revised second edition 1995, published in this format 1997
First published January 1991

Edited, designed and produced by AA Publishing.



Published by AA Publishing

Published in the United States by Macmillan Travel
A Simon & Schuster Macmillan Company
1633 Broadway, New York, NY 10019

Macmillan is a registered trademark of Macmillan, Inc

ISBN 0-028615570-0

Cataloging-in-Publication Data is available from the Library of Congress.

Color separation: Daylight Colour Art, Singapore

Printed and bound by G. Canale & C. S.P.A., Torino, Italy

Right: *Woolsack Races, Tetbury, Gloucestershire*

# CONTENTS

# ABOUT THIS BOOK

This book is not only a practical touring guide for the independent traveller, but is also invaluable for those who would like to know more about the country.

It is divided into 6 regions, each containing between 4 and 6 tours which start and finish in major towns and cities which we consider to be the best centres for exploration.

Each tour has details of the most interesting places to visit en route. Panels catering for special interests follow some of the main entries – for those whose interest is in history, wildlife or walking, and those who have children. There are also panels which highlight scenic stretches of road and which give details of events, crafts and customs.

The simple route directions are accompanied by an easy-to-use map at the beginning of each tour, along with a chart showing how far it is from one town to the next in miles and kilometres. This can help you to decide where to take a break and stop overnight, for example. (All distances quoted are approximate.)

Before setting off it is advisable to check with the information centre at the start of the tour for recommendations on where to break your journey and for additional information on what to see and do, and when best to visit.

**Banks**
Banks are generally open between 9am and 4pm weekdays, though times do vary from bank to bank, and some are open on Saturday mornings until noon. In Scotland, times vary – some banks have different opening times and some close for lunch.

**Camping and Caravanning**
For information on camping and caravanning in Britain see pages 160–5.

**Credit Cards**
All major credit cards are widely accepted throughout Britain.

**Currency**
The unit of currency is the pound (£), divided into 100 pence. Coins are in denominations of 1, 2, 5, 10, 20 and 50 pence and one pound (£1); notes are in denominations of £5, 10, 20 and 50.

**Customs Regulations**
Visitors from EU countries are governed by EU regulations and can bring in items for their own personal use without paying duty. Limits apply to goods obtained at duty-free shops.

Visitors resident outside Europe are entitled to higher allowances, and amounts should be verified at the time of purchase.

**Electricity**
The standard electricity supply is 240 volts, 50 cycles AC. Plugs are three-pin. Shavers operate on 240 or 110 volts. Since most American appliances are designed to operate on 120 volts, 60 cycles, a transformer will be required. Visitors from Europe, Australia and New Zealand will need an adaptor. Most hotels have special razor sockets which will take both voltages.

**Embassies**
Australia: Australian High Commission, Australia House, Strand, London WC2 tel: 0171–379 4334.
Canada: Canadian High Commission, Canada House, Trafalgar Square, London SW1Y 5BJ tel: 0171–258 6600.
New Zealand: New Zealand High Commission, New Zealand House, Haymarket, London SW1 tel: 0171–930 8422.
US: American Embassy, 24 Grosvenor Square, London W1A 1AE tel: 0171–499 9000.

**Emergency Telephone Numbers**
Police, fire and ambulance tel: 999.

**Entry Regulations**
Passports are required by all visitors except citizens of EU countries, but they must be able to prove their identity and nationality. Visas are not required for entry into Britain by American citizens, nationals of the British Commonwealth and most European countries.

**Health**
Inoculations are not required for entry to Britain. Health insurance is recommended for non-EU citizens.

**Motoring**
For information on all aspects of motoring in Britain, including accidents, breakdowns and speed limits see pages 158–60.

**Post Offices**
Post offices open from 9am to 5.30pm or 6pm Monday to Friday and 9am to 12.30pm on Saturdays.

**Public Holidays**
1 January – New Year's Day
2 January – holiday in Scotland only
Good Friday
Easter Monday (not Scotland)
1st Monday in May – May Day (8 May in 1995)
Last Monday in May – Spring Bank Holiday
1st Monday in August – Bank

Holiday in Scotland only
Last Monday in August – August Bank Holiday (not Scotland)
25 December – Christmas Day
26 December – Boxing Day

**Telephones**
Insert coins after lifting the receiver; the dialling tone is a continuous tone.
Useful numbers:
Operator – 100
Directory Enquiries – 192
International Directory Enquiries – 153
International Operator – 155.

To make an international call, dial 00 (the international code), then the country code, followed by the area code and the local number.

Country codes are:
Australia 61;
Canada 1;
New Zealand 64;
Republic of Ireland 353;
UK and Northern Ireland 44;
US 1.

**Time**
The official time is (GMT) Greenwich Mean Time.

British Summer Time (BST) begins in late March when the clocks are put forward an hour. In late October, the clocks go back an hour to GMT. The official date is announced in the daily newspapers and is always at 2am on a Sunday.

**Tourist Offices**
England: English Tourist Board, Blacks Road, Hammersmith, London W6 9EL (tel: 0181 846 9000).
Scotland: Scottish Tourist Board, 23 Ravelston Terrace, Edinburgh EH4 3EU (tel: 031–332 2433).
Wales: Wales Tourist Board, Brunel House, 2 Fitzalan Road, Cardiff CF2 1UY (tel: 0222 499909).

Hever Castle, Kent: Henry VIII was a frequent visitor to Anne Boleyn's childhood home

# THE WEST

The rich, rural lands of the counties from Dorset and Wiltshire westwards contain some spectacular scenery. Soft chalklands around Salisbury give way to harder and older rocks, which create the steep and dramatic hills of the Quantocks, Exmoor and Dartmoor.

An alternating sequence of cliffs and beaches forms the western coastline: there are the precipitous granite cliffs near Land's End, and stupendous sandstone cliffs on the northern fringe of Exmoor. Steep roads are an indication of the resistance of the rocks. As a contrast to hills and cliffs, the flat fen lands of the Somerset Levels stretch away from the coast.

The pretty village of Selworthy in Somerset stands on the side of a wooded hill

The Levels are dotted with dairy cattle grazing on lush green meadows, many of which, thanks to conservation techniques, still contain buttercups and other wild flowers. West Country towns are situated round the edges of the high ground and in the river valleys. Many coastal towns which grew up as fishing ports have become holiday resorts, and traffic tends to be congested during the summer. Even the M5 motorway can become crowded at peak holiday weekends.

Early settlements left their mark on this area, too: Dartmoor probably has the greatest number of relics, but more famous and popular are the sites at Glastonbury, Stonehenge and Avebury. More recent evidence of human activity can be seen in many areas of mining, which is still practised near St Austell, where china clay is obtained for the paper industry.

Copper and tin were important minerals in Cornwall from the time of the Romans until earlier this century, when richer and larger deposits in other countries made the British mines uneconomic. The history of mining can be traced in the mining museums which are among the increasing number of the southwest's indoor centres, adding to the many attractions of this most scenic part of Britain.

St Michael's Mount – a place of mystery and magic

**Penzance**
The end of the railway line and the most westerly major town of England enjoys a mild climate which enables palm trees to grow along the coastline. Penzance was immortalised by Gilbert and Sullivan in *The Pirates of Penzance*. The National Trust's Trengwainton Gardens, just inland, contains magnolias and many delicate shrubs. A maritime museum and a natural history museum are among the other attractions, and there is plenty of activity in the harbour. The *Scillonian* makes regular sailings to the Isles of Scilly.

**St Austell**
Originally noted for tin mining, St Austell has recently become associated with the china clay industry, which is why the landscape to the north is scarred with hollows overlooked by lunar mounds of white debris. The Wheal Martyn Museum gives a fascinating depiction of mining history. This regional market centre grew up around the Market Hall, one of many local buildings built from granite, and other buildings of architectural interest include the parish church, the White Hart Hotel and the Quaker Meeting House.

**Lynton**
Steep tree-covered cliffs make up the northern edge of Exmoor, with Lynton at the top of the slope and Lynmouth down by the sea below. The Catholic church is an outstanding building with decorative marble work, and the Lyn and Exmoor Museum has interesting displays about the area. Joining Lynton with Lynmouth is the dramatic cliff railway, built by the Victorian lawyer Sir George Newnes out of the fortune he made by publishing the famous *Sherlock Holmes* stories.

**Salisbury**
This ancient town was originally at Old Sarum, 2 miles (3km) to the north, where there was an Iron Age settlement. In 1220 the foundations of the new cathedral were laid at New Sarum, now called Salisbury, and gradually the new town developed. The cathedral is beautiful, built in the shape of a double cross, with a graceful spire rising to 404 feet (123m). Among many features of interest are the Poultry Cross, St Thomas's Church, the Playhouse and the delightful River Avon.

**Bridgwater**
Situated on the edge of Sedgemoor, where James II defeated the Duke of Monmouth's rebellion in 1685 in the last battle fought on English soil, Bridgwater grew up as a port and still has a tidal river linking it to the sea. The church is a fine and imposing building, well worth a visit; Monmouth used the tower as a look-out while trying to locate the King's infantry. Another famous figure in the Bridgwater area was Admiral Blake, and his birthplace is now a museum which contains exhibits of his life, as well as a history of the town.

# Bays, Cliffs & Granite

Small bays, sandy beaches and steep rugged cliffs alternate around the Cornish coast on this tour, which then heads inland across undulating countryside, dotted with relics of the mining industry. Granite is everywhere, in the walls and in the villages.

**3 DAYS • 158 MILES • 255KM**

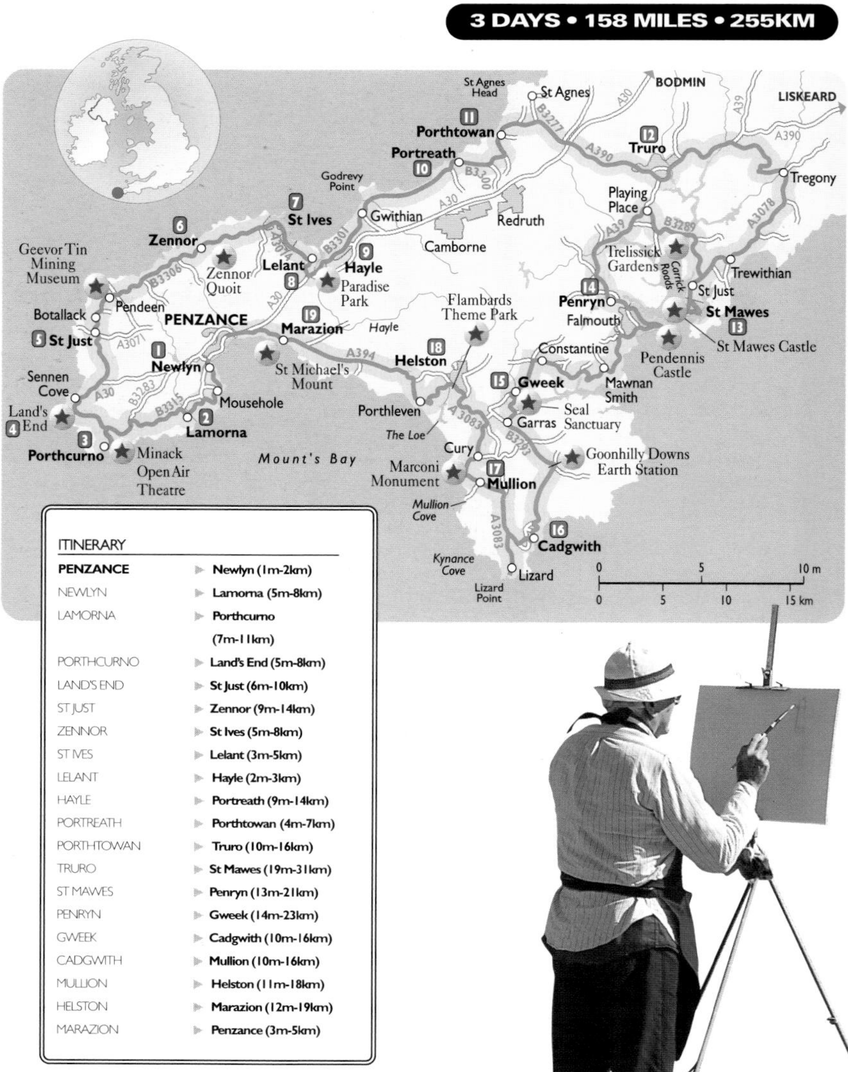


ITINERARY

| | |
|---|---|
| **PENZANCE** | ► **Newlyn (1m-2km)** |
| NEWLYN | ► **Lamorna (5m-8km)** |
| LAMORNA | ► **Porthcurno (7m-11km)** |
| PORTHCURNO | ► **Land's End (5m-8km)** |
| LAND'S END | ► **St Just (6m-10km)** |
| ST JUST | ► **Zennor (9m-14km)** |
| ZENNOR | ► **St Ives (5m-8km)** |
| ST IVES | ► **Lelant (3m-5km)** |
| LELANT | ► **Hayle (2m-3km)** |
| HAYLE | ► **Portreath (9m-14km)** |
| PORTREATH | ► **Porthtowan (4m-7km)** |
| PORTHTOWAN | ► **Truro (10m-16km)** |
| TRURO | ► **St Mawes (19m-31km)** |
| ST MAWES | ► **Penryn (13m-21km)** |
| PENRYN | ► **Gweek (14m-23km)** |
| GWEEK | ► **Cadgwith (10m-16km)** |
| CADGWITH | ► **Mullion (10m-16km)** |
| MULLION | ► **Helston (11m-18km)** |
| HELSTON | ► **Marazion (12m-19km)** |
| MARAZION | ► **Penzance (3m-5km)** |

*i* *Station Road, Penzance*

**SPECIAL TO...**

A 20-minute helicopter flight from Penzance takes you to St Mary's, the largest of the Isles of Scilly. There is now a summer service to Tresco, the second largest island. Tresco has several miles of deserted golden beaches, but no roads and cars.

*From Penzance, drive south along the coast for a mile (1.6km) to Newlyn, and a little further to Mousehole.*

**1 Newlyn,** Cornwall
Really a suburb of Penzance, this is a lively and colourful fishing port, once famous for its artist colony. The Passmore Orion Picture Gallery shows some of their work. Further along the coast is Mousehole. Pronounced 'mowzel', this delightful old fishing village consists of a semi-circle of colour-washed and granite houses round its harbour. Some of the roofs are specially weighted down to combat strong sea winds. Dolly Pentreath, supposedly the last person to speak Cornish as her native language, died here in 1777.

*Continue on unclassified road for 5 miles (8km) to Lamorna.*

**2 Lamorna,** Cornwall
Lamorna is a holiday centre. The tempting golden sand of its spectacular cove is surrounded by steep blocks of granite cliffs and rocky outcrops.

*Join the **B3315**, then at Trethewey turn left on to an unclassified road to Porthcurno.*

**3 Porthcurno,** Cornwall
Porthcurno's beach of almost-white sand is overlooked by a remarkable theatre in the cliffs. The Minack is Britain's equivalent to an ancient Greek theatre, set 200 feet (60m) above the waves. It was created by Miss Rowena Cade, who cut it out of the cliffs in 1931. The theatre has a 16-week season, and can seat 750 on its granite terraces.

*Return to the **B3315** and continue for another 4 miles (6km), then join the **A30** to Land's End.*

**4 Land's End,** Cornwall
England's most westerly point, Land's End is 873 miles (1,405km) from John O'Groats, Scotland's most northerly town. On a fine day the Isles of Scilly, 28 miles (45km) away, can be seen, along with Wolf Rock Lighthouse and the Longships Lighthouse, only a mile and a half (2km) offshore. Land's End is the setting for wild coastal walks and amazing rock formations. Further along is the small village of Sennen, the battleground of the last Cornish fight against invading Danes. Sennen Cove has a good sandy beach and excellent bathing.

The end of England – the haunting majesty of Land's End

*Continue with the **A30**, then left on to the **B3306** for 5 miles (8km) to St Just.*

**FOR CHILDREN**

The legendary Last Labyrinth at Land's End is a major attraction using electronic equipment and including a life-size galleon with scrambling nets and cabins. You can also watch the glass-blower or wood-carver at work, and there is a fascinating collection of shells.

St Ives' golden beaches attract many holidaymakers in summer

**5 St Just,** Cornwall
This enchanting village and its neighbourhood are rich in antiquities. St Just is noted for the contents of its large medieval church: a stone of the 5th or 6th century inscribed with XP, the first two letters of the Greek word for Christ, and the shaft of a 9th-century Hiberno-Saxon cross. Abandoned and ruined mines litter the countryside north of the town.

At Botallack, along the B3306, is a deep mine which extended out beneath the sea, and at the Geevor Tin Mining Museum at Pendeen, a little further on, you can take an underground tour of this working mine.

▶ *Keep going along the **B3306** to Zennor.*

**6 Zennor,** Cornwall
Zennor, named after St Senara, is a grey stone village huddled round its restored 12th-century church in a wild, bleak landscape. The Wayside Museum, the oldest private museum in Cornwall, recaptures the flavour of this area from 3000BC onwards, with displays on archaeology, tin mining and many other aspects of Cornish life. The writers D H Lawrence and Virginia Woolf both lived here in the 1920s. Zennor Quoit, to the southeast, is a chambered tomb from about 2000BC.

▶ *A further 5 miles (8km) along the **B3306** is St Ives.*

**7 St Ives,** Cornwall
St Ives was a prosperous pilchard port in the 19th century, but now is more noted for tourism, with its two fine sandy beaches and many excellent museums and galleries. The town has managed to preserve its old-world charm: quaint houses and narrow streets cluster round the 15th-century church. Be sure to visit the Barbara Hepworth Museum and Sculpture Garden, and the Model Railway Museum.

*i The Guildhall, Street-an-Pol*

▶ *Take the main **A3074** for 3 miles (5km) to Lelant.*

**8 Lelant,** Cornwall
Lelant has a fine Norman and Perpendicular style church with a 17th-century sundial, but is now noted for Merlin's Magic Land, which claims to provide a 'Funtastic' day out for the whole family, with bumper boats, motor bikes and many other attractions.

▶ *Follow the **A3074**, then the **B3301** to Hayle.*

**9 Hayle,** Cornwall
During the 18th century Hayle developed as a port for the copper trade, but now it is a small industrial town with a good sandy beach, though there are still a few boats to be seen in the harbour. Paradise Park, just off the road before entering Hayle, is a conservation theme park with otters and endangered species of birds. There is also a first-class falconry display.

▶ *The **B3301** runs along the coast to Portreath.*

**RECOMMENDED WALKS**

From the B3301 it is possible to walk to Godrevy Point and Navax Point on a circular walk of 3 miles (5km).

**10 Portreath,** Cornwall
Portreath's tiny harbour cottages cluster around the port and the 18th-century pier, at the foot of windswept cliffs. It is a marvellous place to go walking along the coast path and there are spectacular views from Reskajeage Downs, above.

▶ *Turn inland along the **B3300**, then left on unclassified roads for Porthtowan.*

**11 Porthtowan,** Cornwall
Porthtowan is a pleasant little place with a sandy beach and magnificent cliffs to north and south. If you have time, walk up on to the cliffs for fantastic views inland and over the Atlantic.

▶ *Follow unclassified roads, then the **B3277** and **A390** to Truro.*

**12 Truro,** Cornwall
Truro is a fascinating town with a mixture of old and new buildings. Lemon Street has many fine Georgian structures, and Walsingham Place is a beautiful early 19th-century crescent off Victoria Place. The whole town is dominated by the cathedral, which has three spires and was

built on the site of the 16th-century church of St Mary. The County Museum in Silver Street is considered to be the finest in Cornwall and now there is also a fine new art gallery.

*i Municipal Buildings, Boscawen Street*

▶ *Follow the **A39** eastwards, then turn right along the **A3078** for St Mawes.*

**13 St Mawes,** Cornwall
Smart shops and houses and many narrow old streets make this an interesting place to wander round. You should try to visit St Mawes Castle, built by Henry VIII in the 1540s to guard the mouth of the Fal estuary. The views across Carrick Roads, a stretch of sea, to Falmouth are particularly impressive.

Trelissick Gardens, north of St Mawes, boasts a fine collection of exotic plants from all over the world.

▶ *Turn north on the **A3078** then the **B3289**, using King Harry ferry, which closes before dusk, then join the **A39** to Penryn.*

**14 Penryn,** Cornwall
Almost everything in Penryn is built of granite – granite buildings, a granite port and granite blocks lying around everywhere waiting to be shipped out. The narrow streets of this old town stretch up the sides of the valley in an untidy but appealing way.

Further on is Falmouth, on one of the finest natural habours in the world. There are beaches to the south of the town, and on the northern side of the peninsula are the docks and 18th- and 19th-century buildings. Pendennis Castle was built at the same time as its twin, St Mawes Castle, to guard the harbour entrance.

*i 28 Killigrew Street, Falmouth*

▶ *Leave Falmouth on unclassified roads passing through Mawnan Smith, Porth Navas, Constantine and Brill to Gweek.*

**15 Gweek,** Cornwall
This lovely little stone village with two stone bridges across the channels of the Helford River is now better known as a seal sanctuary. Along the picturesque and tranquil banks of the Helford, sick and wounded seals and birds are treated. There are displays which show the work of the centre, and a safari bus will take you round the park to see the convalescent pool and nursery and exercise areas.

▶ *Travel to Garras on unclassified roads. Then take the **B3293** and unclassified roads across Goonhilly Downs, south to Cadgwith and on to Lizard Point on an unclassified road and the **A3083**.*

**16 Cadgwith,** Cornwall
Attractive thatched cottages clustered round the small beach and harbour create a beautiful setting for local fishermen and tourists. Sandy caves alternate with rugged cliffs along this stretch of coast, but the most dramatic feature is the noisy water of the Devil's Frying Pan, created when a vast sea cave collapsed.

Truro's cathedral was built on the site of a 16th-century church

Cadgwith, a busy fishing harbour
Opposite: Sir Francis Drake

Further on, Lizard Point is the southernmost point in England with dramatic 180-foot (55m) cliffs and a lighthouse, open to the public.

▶ *Head north from Lizard Point for 4 miles (6km) along the **A3083**, then the **B3296** to Mullion.*

> **RECOMMENDED WALKS**
>
> Among the most dramatic walks is the path from Cadgwith towards Landewednack. On the west coast of the Lizard, the coast near Kynance Cove can look most romantic and appealing.

**17 Mullion,** Cornwall
The village of Mullion boasts a fine 14th- and 15th-century church, whose carved oak bench-ends are worth inspecting. The church tower is partially built of the local multi-coloured serpentine. Nearby Mullion Cove is surrounded by steep cave-pocked cliffs and has splendid views.

▶ *Drive on unclassified roads via Poldhu and Cury to the **A3083** and on to Helston.*

**18 Helston,** Cornwall
Radio buffs should visit Poldhu Point before entering Helston, to see the Marconi Monument, which commemorates the first transatlantic transmitting station. The ancient Furry Dance takes place in Helston on 8 May, when there is dancing in the streets all day. In the past this town was a port, before the Loe Bar, a 600-foot (183m) ridge of shingle, blocked it off from the sea. Behind Loe Bar is The Loe, a pretty lake, into which, according to legend, Sir Bedivere threw King Arthur's sword Excalibur.

Nearby Flambards Theme Park provides entertainment for the whole family, open in the evenings in July and August. It features a Victorian village, a simulation of the World War II blitz and many other themes.

▶ *Take the **B3304** through Porthleven, then along the **A394** to Marazion. Take an unclassified road before the bypass into the village.*

**19 Marazion,** Cornwall
This ancient port is famous for St Michael's Mount, the granite island located offshore, but is a remarkable place in its own right. Cornwall's oldest chartered town, it has the safest beach in Cornwall and some of the best wind-surfing in Europe. Henry III granted the town a charter in 1257 and for hundreds of years tin and copper ores were exported from here. The small town still attracts visitors, in spite of the bypass, which has reduced the amount of through-traffic.

▶ *Return to Penzance via an unclassified road to the **A394**.*

> **FOR HISTORY BUFFS**
>
> St Michael's Mount is accessible by foot at low tide, and you should make time to get across to see the castle and priory, both founded by Edward the Confessor in the 11th century. This was the legendary home of the giant Cormoran, who was slain by Jack the Giant Killer.

> **BACK TO NATURE**
>
> The birdwatching hotspot of Marazion Marsh lies close to the sea just behind the coast road at Marazion. Autumns in previous years have produced regular sightings of aquatic warblers and spotted crakes, as well as occasional records of transatlantic vagrants such as white-rumped sandpipers and lesser yellowlegs.

# **Mining,** Moorland & Legends

This tour leads through granite scenery, market towns and green river valleys, before crossing the moorland expanse of Dartmoor, with its famous ponies and notorious prison, and finally descending to the farmlands around Tavistock.

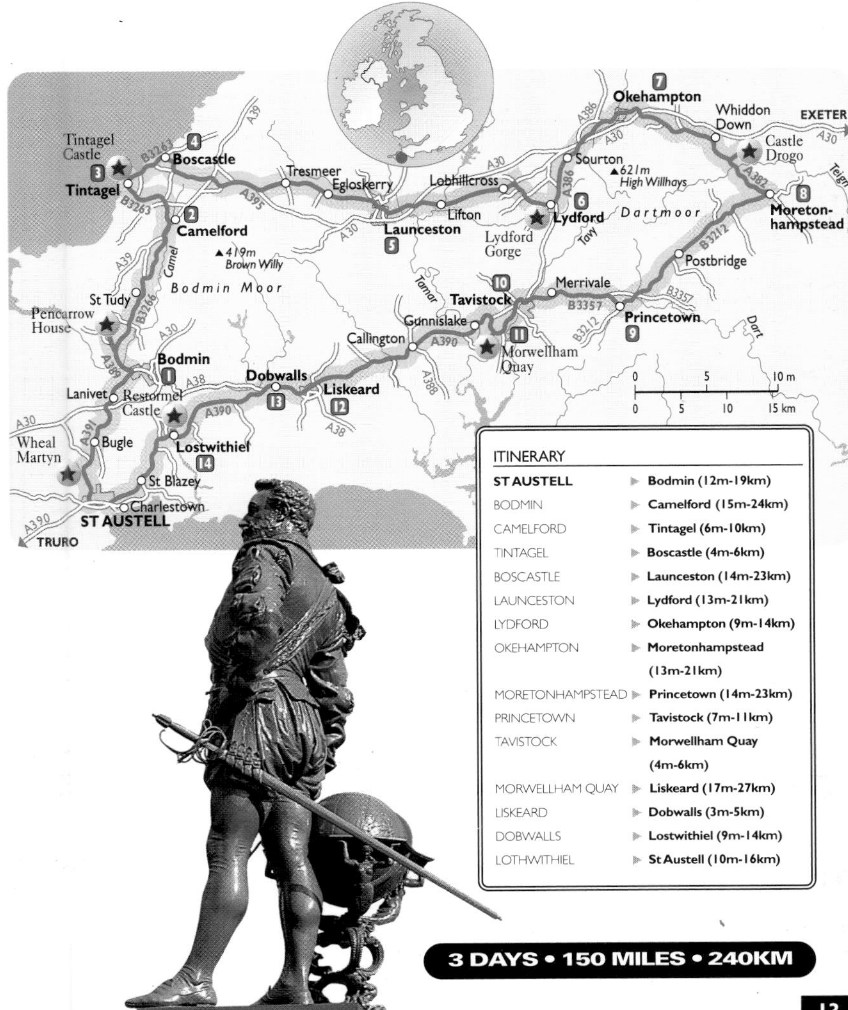


| ITINERARY | |
|---|---|
| **ST AUSTELL** | ▶ **Bodmin (12m-19km)** |
| BODMIN | ▶ **Camelford (15m-24km)** |
| CAMELFORD | ▶ **Tintagel (6m-10km)** |
| TINTAGEL | ▶ **Boscastle (4m-6km)** |
| BOSCASTLE | ▶ **Launceston (14m-23km)** |
| LAUNCESTON | ▶ **Lydford (13m-21km)** |
| LYDFORD | ▶ **Okehampton (9m-14km)** |
| OKEHAMPTON | ▶ **Moretonhampstead (13m-21km)** |
| MORETONHAMPSTEAD | ▶ **Princetown (14m-23km)** |
| PRINCETOWN | ▶ **Tavistock (7m-11km)** |
| TAVISTOCK | ▶ **Morwellham Quay (4m-6km)** |
| MORWELLHAM QUAY | ▶ **Liskeard (17m-27km)** |
| LISKEARD | ▶ **Dobwalls (3m-5km)** |
| DOBWALLS | ▶ **Lostwithiel (9m-14km)** |
| LOTHWITHIEL | ▶ **St Austell (10m-16km)** |

**3 DAYS • 150 MILES • 240KM**

TOUR 2

## **Mining,** Moorland & Legends

*i* *Bypass Service Station, St Austell*

*Leave St Austell and drive 12 miles (19km) north on the **A391**, then cross the **A389** to Bodmin.*

### 1 **Bodmin,** Cornwall

The only Cornish town recorded in the Domesday Book, Bodmin lies on the steep southwest edge of Bodmin Moor, which overlooks the town. The Celts, Romans and King Arthur have all had links with the town, and the parish church, the largest in Cornwall, is dedicated to St Petroc, the greatest of all Celtic saints.

Further north, just off the A389, is Pencarrow House, begun in the 1700s by Sir John Molesworth. In the grounds is an ancient Iron Age encampment, and there are walks through the flower gardens, a play area and a pets' corner.

*i* *80 Bradford Street, Shire House, Mount Folly Square*

*From Pencarrow return to the **A389**. Turn left, then after half a mile (0.8km), left again on to the **B3266** to Camelford.*

### 2 **Camelford,** Cornwall

Camelford is thought by some to have been Camelot, the fabulous city of King Arthur, and Slaughter Bridge, one mile (1.6km) to the north, is said to have been Arthur's last battleground. The North Cornwall Museum contains many items of rural life in Cornwall, with sections on agriculture and slate and granite quarrying.

*i* *80 Bradford Street, North Cornwall Museum, The Clease*

*From Camelford continue on the **B3266**, turning left on to the **B3314** and almost immediately right to join the **B3263** to Tintagel.*

### 3 **Tintagel,** Cornwall

Romance and legends connect this area strongly with King

Tintagel: the Old Post Office (left); weathered cliffs and caves (below)

Arthur. The dramatic cliffs of slate on 'the Island', which is really a peninsula, have caverns and a waterfall. The 12th-century ruins of Tintagel Castle are in a spectacular setting on a wild, wind-lashed promontory. In the small town the highlight for most visitors is the Old Post Office, a small 14th-century manor house built of local slate. Excellent and beautiful walks can be found along the coast paths near by and in the Rocky Valley, a few miles further north.

▶ *Follow the **B3263** along the coast to Boscastle.*

> RECOMMENDED WALKS
>
> **Trethevy car park, north of Tintagel, is a good starting point for walks in the Rocky Valley, especially to St Nectan, for beautiful woodland scenery.**

Okehampton Castle, now in ruins but open to the public

**4 Boscastle,** Cornwall
Boscastle is a picturesque harbour at the head of a deep S-shaped inlet between high cliffs. A few houses are actually built in to the side of the road and oak woods, river valleys and the sea combine to make this a classic beauty spot. The river and the tide occasionally meet with explosive collisions just beyond the outer breakwater.

▶ *From Boscastle take the **B3266** and unclassified roads east across the **A39** to join the **A395**. Turn left on to the **A395** and follow it for 3 miles (5km) before branching left on to unclassified roads again through Tresmeer and Egloskerry to Launceston.*

**5 Launceston,** Cornwall
Launceston is an ancient town standing on the hill top around the ruins of a castle. This was the only walled town in Cornwall and the South Gate, a narrow arch, remains. St Thomas's Church has the largest font in Cornwall, and the Church of St Mary is famed for the carvings completely covering its external walls. A nostalgic steam railway runs into the Kensey Valley through 3 miles (5km) of glorious countryside. At the station there is a model railway and a small museum. The Tamar Otter Park and Wild Wood has peacocks and golden pheasants strutting about, and deer roam the woods.

[i] *Market House Arcade, Market Street*

▶ *Continue eastwards on the old **A30**, now unclassified, then just past Lobhillcross turn right on to unclassified roads to Lydford.*

**6 Lydford,** Devon
Formerly a major centre for tin, this secluded village on the edge of Dartmoor is dominated by the remains of its 12th-century castle. Its old prison, a reminder of the harsh conditions of the past, was described as 'one of the most heinous, contagious and detestable places in the realm'. Lydford Gorge, scooped out by the River Lyd is a mile (1.6km) to the southwest, where the 90-foot (27m) high White Lady Falls and Devil's Cauldron are to be found.

> RECOMMENDED WALK
>
> **Follow the River Lyd into the famous Lydford Gorge, and you will see the whirlpools and tumbling water of the Devil's Cauldron.**

▶ *Follow the **A386** north from Lydford, then after a short stretch east on the **A30** take the **B3260** to Okehampton.*

One of England's finest clapper bridges can be seen at Postbridge

**7 Okehampton,** Devon

Okehampton is at the foot of the highest part of Dartmoor, accessible to walkers when the army is not using the firing range. An old ruined castle, one of Devon's largest, sits on a hill to the west. The Museum of Dartmoor Life is an innovative museum portraying life in the area for hundreds of years.

Southeast of the town is Okehampton Camp, the remains of an Iron Age hill-fort on a steep ridge.

*i* *3 West Street*

▶ *Return to the old* ***A30*** *(now an unclassified road) past Sticklepath and South Zeal. Just before Whiddon Down turn right on to the* ***A382*** *for Moretonhampstead, at which take the* ***B3212*** *to Postbridge.*

**8 Moretonhampstead,** Devon

Before reaching this town you will pass the remarkable Castle Drogo, a massive granite castle designed by Edward Lutyens, to the left of the road near Drewsteignton. Drive on across the heart of Dartmoor to Moretonhampstead, a small market town with some fine old buildings. At Postbridge you can see the finest of the clapper bridges. One of England's oldest man-made bridges, it was used by pack horses to carry ore from the mines.

**RECOMMENDED WALKS**

From Castle Drogo a circular tour leads through the delightful village of Drewsteignton, down to Fingle Bridge and then back along the wooded valley of the River Teign.

▶ *Drive across Dartmoor for 14 miles (23km) along the* ***B3212*** *to Princetown.*

**9 Princetown,** Devon

Princetown, the highest town in England, is noted for its prison, which was built for French prisoners-of-war brought to Dartmoor to work for Sir Thomas Tyrwhitt, who built a magnificent house near by.

**FOR CHILDREN**

The miniature pony centre at Moretonhampstead encourages visitors to touch the animals, and rides can be arranged on the tiny ponies. The ponies have been pure bred in pedigrees stretching back to about 1890, and other miniature animals here include bulls, pigs, goats and harvest mice.

▶ *Head west along the **B3357** to Tavistock.*

**FOR HISTORY BUFFS**

Dartmoor is rich in prehistoric remains; Bronze Age coffins are beside the road a mile (1.6km) northeast of Princetown, along with a row of standing stones. Two miles (3km) northwest, at Merrivale, are hut circles and one of Dartmoor's finest burial cists, while another group of Bronze Age hut circles overlooks the River Walkham at Great Mis Tor, a mile (1.6km) further northeast of Merrivale.

### 10 Tavistock, Devon

Famous for its October Goose Fair, Tavistock is also of considerable interest for its association with tin and copper mining. The town is largely Victorian, but there are many older buildings – the remains of a Benedictine abbey founded in the 10th century, and 15th-century St Eustace's Church. The statue of Francis Drake is a reminder that the Elizabethan sailor was born at nearby Crowndale Farm.

*[i] Town Hall Buildings, Bedford Square*

▶ *Leave Tavistock on the **A386** and just before crossing the river bridge, turn right along an unclassified road for 4 miles (6km) to Morwellham Quay.*

### 11 Morwellham Quay, Devon

Formerly a port, Morwellham, at 350 feet (107m) above water level, is linked to the river by a remarkable inclined plane. It was the greatest copper port in Victorian times, and the old harbour and quays have been repaired by the Morwellham Trust. Crafts and costumes of 100 years ago are on show and there are underground reconstructions of working conditions and early mining techniques.

▶ *Return to the **A390** and head westwards to Liskeard.*

### 12 Liskeard, Cornwall

Liskeard is a small, lively town with attractive buildings including Webb's Hotel and Stuart House, where Charles I slept for a week during 1644. Relics of the past can be found at St Keyne Station on the B3254 just outside town. Fair organs, street organs and a mighty Würlitzer are on show here in Paul Corin's Musical Collection.

▶ *A short drive along the **A390** brings you to Dobwalls.*

### 13 Dobwalls, Cornwall

The remarkable family theme park has eight adventure areas, with ropewalks, towers to climb and two railroads on a gauge of 7¼ inches (18cm). You can roar through tunnels and canyons on the *Queen of Wyoming*, or one of the other engines pulling the mini trains.

▶ *Continue with the **A390** for Lostwithiel.*

### 14 Losthwithiel, Cornwall

Lostwithiel sits at the highest point reached by the tide on the River Fowey. The old bridge dates from the 14th century, and Restormel Castle, overlooking the River Fowey, is even older, having first been built as a wooden fort in the 11th century.

At Charlestown, a few miles along the road, is the Shipwreck and Heritage Centre, with an assortment of treasures from the sea bed. Outside the museum is the unspoilt harbour, which still looks much as it did in the 1790s.

*[i] Lostwithiel Community Centre, Liddicoat Road*

▶ *Return to St Austell on the **A390**.*

**BACK TO NATURE**

The wilds of Dartmoor have a surprising variety of wildlife. Cottongrass, sundew, bog asphodel and bog bean grace many of the wetter areas, and birdlife includes curlews, dunlin, lapwings, kestrels and buzzards.
In winter, look for short-eared owls, merlins and hen harriers.

**SPECIAL TO...**

Dartmoor and Bodmin Moor are great lumps of granite covered with boggy vegetation, heather and grasses, all of which can thrive on the acidic soils. When the minerals of granite are weathered, kaolin or china clay is often left behind. It has been quarried in this area for many years.
The Wheal Martyn Museum, at Carthew, near St Austell, has a historic trail through the 19th-century clay workings.

TOUR 3

# **Where Exmoor** Meets the Sea

Bright bays, steep coasts, low coastlines, lonely moorland and delightful stone villages combine to make this a memorable and varied tour.

**3 DAYS • 133 MILES • 215KM**

ITINERARY

| | |
|---|---|
| **LYNTON** | ▶ **Lynmouth (1m-2km)** |
| LYNMOUTH | ▶ **Malmsmead (7m-11km)** |
| MALMSMEAD | ▶ **Porlock (7m-11km)** |
| PORLOCK | ▶ **Luccombe (5m-8km)** |
| LUCCOMBE | ▶ **Minehead (6m-10km)** |
| MINEHEAD | ▶ **Watchet (9m-14km)** |
| WATCHET | ▶ **Brendon Hills (14m-23km)** |
| BRENDON HILLS | ▶ **Winsford (8m-13km)** |
| WINSFORD | ▶ **Simonsbath (10m-16km)** |
| SIMONSBATH | ▶ **South Molton (11m-18km)** |
| SOUTH MOLTON | ▶ **Great Torrington (15m-24km)** |
| GREAT TORRINGTON | ▶ **Bideford (7m-11km)** |
| BIDEFORD | ▶ **Barnstaple (10m-16km)** |
| BARNSTAPLE | ▶ **Arlington (8m-13km)** |
| ARLINGTON | ▶ **Blackmoor Gate (3m-5km)** |
| BLACKMOOR GATE | ▶ **Lynton (12m-20km)** |

## **Where Exmoor** Meets the Sea

Top: Lynton's Cliff Railway
Left: the harbour at Lynmouth

*Town Hall, Lee Road, Lynton*

> **RECOMMENDED WALK**
>
> Many footpaths lead from Lynton, notably a coastal walk into the Valley of the Rocks. Take the narrow road between the parish church and the Valley of the Rocks Hotel, and follow a path carved out of solid rock on Hollerday Hill.

▶ *Take the **B3234**, dropping very steeply down into Lynmouth.*

### 1 **Lynmouth,** Devon

Lynmouth is on a junction where the East and West Lyn meet. The 1890 cliff railway still provides a link with Lynton by means of two railcars; the top car uses water ballast to haul the other one up from the bottom. The poet Shelley lived in Lynmouth for a time. The River Lyn is very strongly embanked now and on leaving the town you will see the gorge down which the flood water came with such devastation in 1952.

▶ *Leave on the **A39** towards Barnstaple, turn left on to the **B3223** signed Simonsbath and then immediately left again up a narrow steep road which leads through Rockford and Brendon to Malmsmead.*

> **BACK TO NATURE**
>
> The wooded valley of Watersmeet, near Lynmouth, is safeguarded by the National Trust. Along the paths, look for the bright yellow flowers of Welsh poppy, sometimes growing alongside clumps of the rare Irish spurge. Woodland birds are common and dippers and grey wagtails have become accustomed to human visitors.

### 2 **Malmsmead,** Somerset

This isolated village is set in idyllic scenery, and is reached along narrow roads with gradients of 1 in 4. The East Lyn is a rocky stream, and if you walk up the valley of the tributary Badgworthy Water, you will see some of the best of Exmoor. This is popularly assumed to be Doone country, though Blackmore, who wrote *Lorna Doone*, always refused to say where his tale of bandits was actually set. R D Blackmore, grandson of a 19th-century rector of Oare, further on from Malmsmead, named his characters after local people. The 500-year-old church here was the setting for Lorna Doone's violent wedding. At the Robber's Bridge further along the road there is a picturesque spot by the East Lyn, now only a tiny stream called Oare Water.

▶ *Take the unclassified road then join the **A39** to Porlock and eventually on to Selworthy.*

> **RECOMMENDED WALKS**
>
> Starting from Malmsmead, walk upstream along Badgworthy Water, where you might see a dipper or a kingfisher. From the memorial in Blackmore, walk on to the waterslide and Lank Combe, the probable location of Doone Valley.

### 3 **Porlock,** Somerset

Once down the notorious steep hill, and a descent of 1,350 feet (411m), pause to admire Porlock Weir, a small village of thatched cottages fringing a tiny harbour. Culbone Church is possibly the smallest surviving medieval church in England, and can only be reached on foot.

Farm Park at Bossington is a must for family outings, with donkey rides, a hay bounce and quiz sheet. Just off the A39 is Selworthy. Much of this pretty village is owned by the National Trust.

▶ *Return to the **A39** and turn left towards Minehead. Shortly, turn right on an unclassified road to Luccombe.*

### 4 **Luccombe,** Somerset

Pause in this secluded village to visit the fine church and churchyard, entered through a charming lychgate, and have a gentle stroll past the thatched cottages. At Wootton Courtenay, on the road to Minehead, the magnificent church has a saddleback roof.

▶ *From Wootton Courtenay, turn north to rejoin the **A39** and continue to Minehead, then further to Dunster, just south of the **A39**, up the **A396**.*

**5 Minehead,** Somerset
A large expanse of sand and an attractive harbour area have lured visitors to this bright and breezy town. Take a ride on the West Somerset Railway, which runs through 20 miles (32km) of superb scenery from the coast to the Quantocks. Just outside Minehead is Somerwest World, a large holiday camp with a cable car, monorail, and funfair.

A little further on, Dunster's Norman castle looks out over the village and at the opposite end of the main street is the Conygar Tower, built in 1775 as a landmark for shipping. There is a 16th-century yarn market, and you can see the working water mill, on the River Avill, which dates from 1680 and still produces flour for local bakeries. Blenheim Gardens are fine to sit and relax in.

*i* *17 Friday Street*

SPECIAL TO...

The Minehead Hobby Horse (or 'Obby 'Oss) procession takes place on the eve of May Day, and is said to have originated as an attempt to frighten off Danish invaders, using a strange, multi-coloured beast accompanied by musicians to create a fearsome sight and sound. There is also an 'Obby 'Oss procession in Padstow.

► *Follow the **A39**, then the **B3191** towards Blue Anchor and Watchet.*

**6 Watchet,** Somerset
Much of Watchet's early growth was due to iron mining in the Brendon Hills; paper-making is now the main industry. The poet Coleridge found the main character for his epic poem *The Rime of the Ancient Mariner* in this historic seaport.

Just outside Washford, 3 miles (5km) south of Watchet, is Tropiquaria, which has displays of fish and animals. South of Washford is Cleeve Abbey, founded by Cistercian monks in 1198, with a well-preserved refectory, gate house and chapter house. Further along the road is Combe Sydenham Country Park, in a hidden valley on the edge of the Brendons, where there is a restored 11th-century corn mill and a deer park.

► *From Washford, follow the unclassified road southwards to join the **B3188** via Monksilver to Elworthy, then take the **B3224** west through the Brendon Hills.*

**7 Brendon Hills,** Somerset
These undulating slopes, where Exmoor merges into the distinctive patchwork of Brendon Hills, are not high enough for moorland, but have lush fields and trees and long views across the countryside. In earlier times small mining towns grew up to work the local deposits of iron ore, but the last one closed down in 1883. You can still see Bronze Age round barrows along the Ridgeway.

► *Continue along the **B3224**, turn left on the **A396** and then follow an unclassified road to Winsford.*

**8 Winsford,** Somerset
Winsford is one of the best centres for tourism on Exmoor, with its church standing over the village. The mysteriously inscribed Caractacus Stone, a mile (1.6km) to the south, probably dates from between the 5th and 7th centuries.

► *From Winsford take the unclassified road to join the **B3223** and continue to Simonsbath.*

**9 Simonsbath,** Somerset
Situated 1,100 feet (335m) above sea level, Simonsbath is the highest village in Exmoor, in the centre of what used to be the Royal Exmoor Forest. Climb steeply out of the hamlet and on to the moors. In places the traditional old Exmoor hedges block the fabulous views.

► *Use unclassified roads to cross the moor southwards, and join the **A399**, then the **B3226** for South Molton.*

**10 South Molton,** Devon
Formerly important for the wool trade, but now a cattle market and tourist centre, South Molton is known to have existed as a Saxon colony. The square is given grandeur by the Guildhall and Assembly Rooms which overlook it, and the splendid church has a magnificent tower and a remarkable stone pulpit. On the road west, the Cobbaton Combat Collection recalls World War II with tanks, artillery and radio equipment.

*i* *1 East Street*

► *Follow the **B3227** for 15 miles (24km) to Great Torrington.*

**11 Great Torrington,** Devon
Great Torrington was a market town in Saxon times and the scene of fierce fighting in the Civil War. The original church was used as a gunpowder stores but an explosion blew it to pieces. At Dartington Glassworks you can watch fine crystal glass being blown, and just outside the town the Royal Horticultural Society has a garden at Rosemoor. The Gnome Reserve at West Putford boasts the world's largest population of gnomes.

*i* *Town Hall, High Street*

► *Take the **A386** to Bideford.*

**12 Bideford,** Devon
This interesting little town was a major port in the 16th and 17th centuries with a busy trade in tobacco. There is a new high bridge for the main road, but ships still move upstream to the old stone bridge across the estuary. The Royal Hotel, which dates from 1688, was where Charles Kingsley wrote part of his novel *Westward Ho*! Follow the old road to Barnstaple and you will pass Instow, a resort by the dunes with colourful views

across to the port of Appledore.

Tapeley Park, on the way to Instow, has medieval banquets and is the home of the Jousting Association.

*i* *The Quay*

▶ *Follow the coast road along the **B3233** for 10 miles (16km) to Barnstaple.*

**FOR CHILDREN**

At Abbotsham, 2 miles (3km) west of Bideford, is the Big Sheep, where you can watch the free demonstration of sheep milking and sheep shearing, and have a go at spinning. Other attractions include sheep racing, a nature trail and an adventure playground.

**FOR HISTORY BUFFS**

Like most towns on Devon's north coast, Bideford has strong maritime traditions. It was a busy port in England in the 16th century, with many links to the East Indies and the Americas. Smuggling as well as legal trading were part of the life in this area, and some of this history can be seen in the North Devon Maritime Museum in Appledore, north of Bideford.

### 13 Barnstaple, Devon

Barnstaple is one of North Devon's major market towns. It was once a busy ship-building town and a port trading with America, but the River Taw

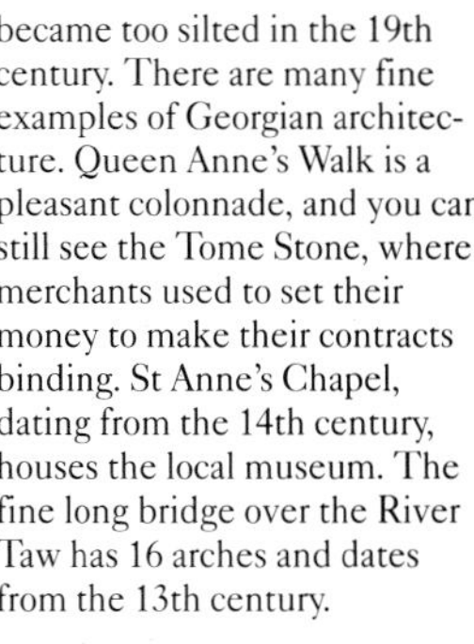

became too silted in the 19th century. There are many fine examples of Georgian architecture. Queen Anne's Walk is a pleasant colonnade, and you can still see the Tome Stone, where merchants used to set their money to make their contracts binding. St Anne's Chapel, dating from the 14th century, houses the local museum. The fine long bridge over the River Taw has 16 arches and dates from the 13th century.

*i* *North Devon Library, Tuly Street*

▶ *Continue northwards on the **A39** for Arlington.*

Quince Honey Farm, South Molton

### 14 Arlington, Devon

Arlington Court is one of the few great houses of North Devon. Formerly the home of the Chichester family, it has been owned by the National Trust since 1949. Sir Francis Chichester, the yachtsman, is the most famous descendant of this old family. The house contains a rich collection of model ships and there are walks in the park and woods. During the summer there are horse-and-carriage rides between the house and the collection of old carriages kept in the stables.

▶ *Continue along the **A39** to Blackmoor Gate.*

### 15 Blackmoor Gate, Devon

Blackmoor Gate is really a road junction, but the Exmoor Bird Gardens are near by along the B3226, and Tarzan Land provides entertainment for the children. For the next few miles the road is narrow, winding and very steep in places, with dramatic views of coastal cliffs. There is a short stretch of toll road, before entering the Valley of the Rocks, a gorge littered with enormous slabs of granite. Walk up to the top of Castle Rock, where the vertical drop is 800 feet (244m).

▶ *Take the **A399** and then an unclassified road via Trentishoe and Martinhoe back to Lynton.*

# Somerset's Hamstone Towns

Wooded hills and rich valleys combine with the mellow dignity of country towns in golden stone to make South Somerset and Dorset one of the least spoiled parts of England. Add to this a splendid sea view and you have a tour to linger long in the memory.

**3 DAYS • 130 MILES • 209KM**

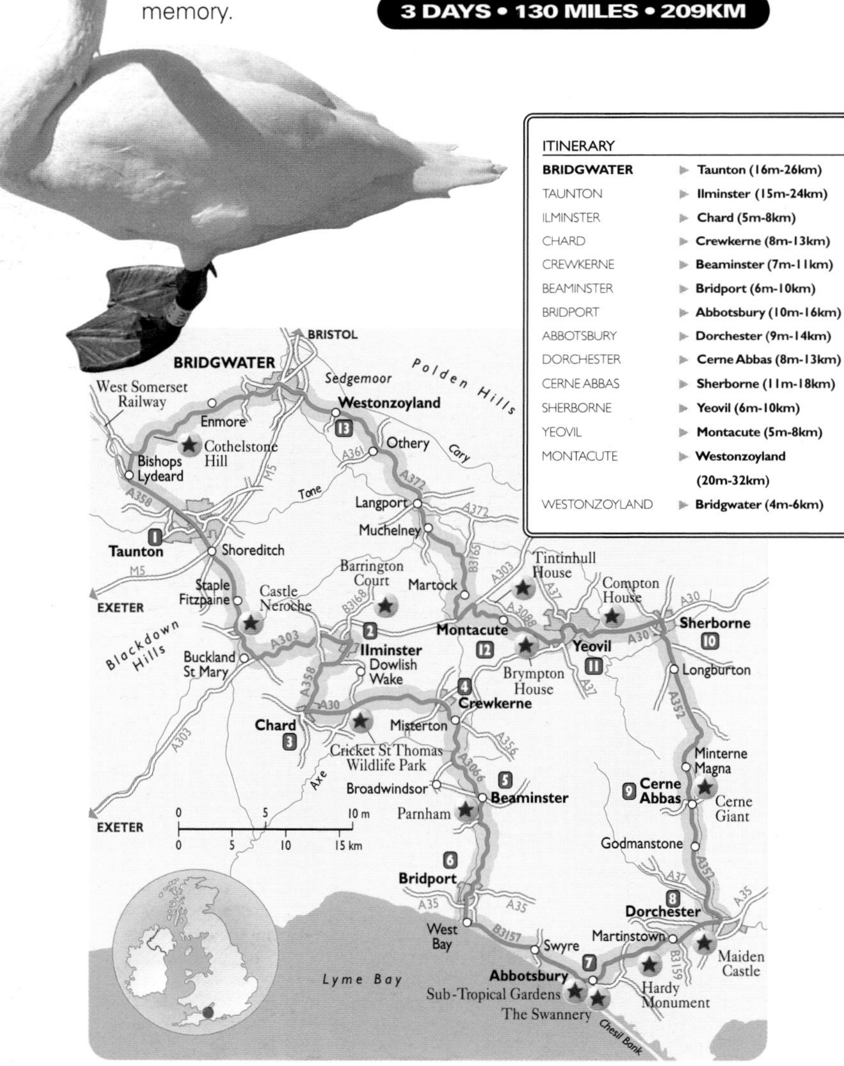


| ITINERARY | |
|---|---|
| **BRIDGWATER** | ▶ **Taunton (16m-26km)** |
| TAUNTON | ▶ **Ilminster (15m-24km)** |
| ILMINSTER | ▶ **Chard (5m-8km)** |
| CHARD | ▶ **Crewkerne (8m-13km)** |
| CREWKERNE | ▶ **Beaminster (7m-11km)** |
| BEAMINSTER | ▶ **Bridport (6m-10km)** |
| BRIDPORT | ▶ **Abbotsbury (10m-16km)** |
| ABBOTSBURY | ▶ **Dorchester (9m-14km)** |
| DORCHESTER | ▶ **Cerne Abbas (8m-13km)** |
| CERNE ABBAS | ▶ **Sherborne (11m-18km)** |
| SHERBORNE | ▶ **Yeovil (6m-10km)** |
| YEOVIL | ▶ **Montacute (5m-8km)** |
| MONTACUTE | ▶ **Westonzoyland (20m-32km)** |
| WESTONZOYLAND | ▶ **Bridgwater (4m-6km)** |

[i] *High Street, Bridgwater*

▶ *Leave Bridgwater on an unclassified road to Enmore. Continue to Bishops Lydeard then turn left on to the* ***A358*** *to Taunton.*

**1 Taunton,** Somerset
As you drop steeply down from the Quantock Hills, a stunning view of the Vale of Taunton Deane opens up, with the undulating ridge of the Blackdown Hills in the distance. Taunton lies in the heart of this rich vale. The largest town between Bristol and Exeter, it has one of the biggest livestock markets in the southwest. In the Great Hall of Taunton Castle, the infamous Judge Jeffreys sent over 500 rebels to their deaths at his 'Bloody Assize'. A walk down Hammet Street gives the best view of the Perpendicular tower of 15th-century St Mary's Church. The town is a mecca for cricket lovers, and next to the County Ground is Somerset's Cricket Museum, in the 13th-century Priory Barn.

[i] *The Library, Corporation Street*

SPECIAL TO...

The West Somerset Railway is the longest preserved line in Britain, running through some of the finest scenery in the West Country. Starting off at Bishops Lydeard, at the foot of the Quantocks near Taunton, it runs 20 miles (32km) down to the coastal plain and beaches of the Bristol Channel.

▶ *Leave Taunton on the* ***B3170*** *heading south. Shortly after crossing the* ***M5****, turn left for Staple Fitzpaine. Continue on unclassified roads towards Buckland St Mary and the* ***A303****. Turn left on to the* ***A303****, then right on to the* ***B3168*** *to Ilminster.*

**2 Ilminster,** Somerset
Dabinetts, Brownsnouts, Kingston Blacks and Red Streaks are all local varieties of apples. Somerset is cider country, and near Ilminster, at Dowlish Wake, are Perry's Cider Mills, where this powerful apple brew has been made for centuries. Visitors can wander through the farm to see how it is done and afterwards sample some 'scrumpy' for themselves. Ilminster has a lovely little shopping centre, built in the local Hamstone (a golden limestone). Of particular note are the pillared market house and the 15th-century minster Church of St Mary. Herne Hill is a local beauty spot and vantage point to the southwest of the town. One of the earliest National Trust properties, Barrington Court, lies to the north – an intriguing model estate with Tudor manor house and gardens.

Leaving Bishop's Lydeard on the West Somerset Railway
Opposite: Abbotsbury swan

[i] *Shudrick Lane*

▶ *From Ilminster go south on an unclassified road, turning left on to the* ***A358*** *for Chard.*

### 3 **Chard,** Somerset

This handsome market town astride the busy A30 claims to be the birthplace of flight. To find out why, visit the Chard Museum in High Street. Besides flight, you can find out more about blacksmiths, early funerals, historic costumes and even artificial limbs – they were invented here too!

*i The Guildhall, Fore Street*

▶ *Leave Chard on the **A30** for Crewkerne (8miles/13km).*

> **FOR CHILDREN**
>
> The Wildlife Park at Cricket St Thomas is set in a deep, wooded valley just off the A30 between Chard and Crewkerne. The park is home to a great variety of animals and birds – from wild deer to penguins, elephants and parrots. There are plenty of leisure park features, including a scenic railway and an adventure playground.

### 4 **Crewkerne,** Somerset

Crewkerne is an ancient market town whose wealth was founded on minting coins, and in later centuries on flax-weaving and sail-making. It was here that HMS *Victory*'s sails were made, and more recently the sails for several contenders for the Americas Cup. Captain Hardy, Nelson's flag captain on the *Victory*, was a pupil at the ancient grammar school.

▶ *From Crewkerne on the **A356**, signposted Dorchester/Bridport, turn right on to the **A3066** for Beaminster.*

### 5 **Beaminster,** Dorset

'The forgotten county' and 'the hidden valley' are two of the epithets ascribed to the scenery around Beaminster. This town, in the Brit Valley, is virtually unspoilt. Three fires in 200 years once rendered the town 'the pityfullest spectacle that Man can behold' but the mellow honey-coloured hamstone houses testify to the healing power of time. Most streets offer a view of the fine pinnacled tower of the golden church, built in 1503. The Tudor manor house at Parnham, near Beaminster, enjoys world renown as a centre for craftsmanship in wood, and is open to the public on certain days of the week.

Parnham House, Beaminster

▶ *Continue south on the **A3066** to Bridport.*

### 6 **Bridport,** Dorset

In olden times, the term 'Bridport dagger' used to strike fear in to the heart of many a criminal, for that was the nickname for the hangman's noose. Ropes and nets have been made here for a thousand years now, and this is still Europe's biggest netmaking centre. The unusual width of the streets allowed for rope-walks, where the flax strands were laid out to be twisted into shape. In South Street, look out for St Mary's Church with its hamstone tower and 13th-century knight's tomb.

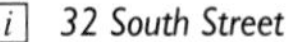

*i 32 South Street*

▶ *Leave Bridport heading for West Bay, then turn on to the **B3157** for 8 miles (13km) to Abbotsbury.*

### 7 **Abbotsbury,** Dorset

Abbotsbury shelters in a valley between high chalk downs and the shingle coast of Chesil Bank, that sweeps round to the 'Isle' of Portland. A long main street of thatched limestone cottages heralds your approach to the village centre, clustered round the 15th-century church and the Ilchester Arms public house. From opposite here a narrow, unsignposted road leads high up over Black Down Hill to the Hardy Monument, an obelisk commemorating Vice-Admiral Hardy. St Catherine's Chapel, built for seamen in the 15th century, looks down from its grassy knoll near by, and near the church are the remains of an 11th-century Benedictine abbey. The one surviving feature is a fine thatched tithe barn, the largest in England.

> **BACK TO NATURE**
>
> The Fleet is a large brackish lagoon which lies behind the shelter of Chesil Beach. Towards the western end, the swannery at Abbotsbury is worth visiting, while at the eastern end, the mudflats revealed at low tide support thousands of birds such as waders, gulls and other wildfowl. The shingle flora of Chesil Beach is worth studying, and in the heart of nearby Weymouth lies Radipole Lake, an RSPB reserve.

The Giant of Cerne Abbas

▶ *Leave Abbotsbury uphill on an unclassified road to Martinstown; then turn left and on to the **B3159**, then left again for Dorchester.*

**8 Dorchester,** Dorset
The county town of Dorset is in the heart of Thomas Hardy country and is still the busy market town portrayed in *The Mayor of Casterbridge*. Hardy's statue stands near the top of High West Street. Founded as *Durnovaria* by the Romans in AD70, Dorchester has many fine Georgian buildings. Judge Jeffreys was sent here by King James to punish rebels after the Battle of Sedgemoor in 1685. At Old Crown Court, six local farm-workers were sentenced in 1834 to be transported to Australia for forming a trades union: they became known as the Tolpuddle Martyrs. There are numerous sites of interest, including the floor of a Roman town house and Maumbury Rings, a Roman amphitheatre. The town boasts three museums: the Dinosaur Museum; the Military Museum, which is the unlikely location for Hitler's desk; and the Dorset County Museum.

*i 7 Acland Road*

**FOR HISTORY BUFFS**

Maiden Castle, 2 miles (3km) southwest of Dorchester, is the finest prehistoric hill-fort in Britain. The massive oval earth-works can be seen for miles around. Three huge ditches were dug by Iron Age men to protect some 5,000 inhabitants. Archaeological excavations have revealed a history stretching back to the Stone Age, and among the finds have been the skeletons of 34 people.

▶ *From Dorchester head north on the **A352** for Cerne Abbas.*

**9 Cerne Abbas,** Dorset
Before entering Cerne Abbas, as you pass through Godmanstone, look out for the smallest pub in England, the Smith's Arms, just 20 by 10 feet (6 by 3m). Cerne Abbas itself is a charming village and its main source of interest is not difficult to spot. Cut into the steep chalk hillside behind the village, the Cerne Giant, a well-endowed figure 180 foot (55m) high, is a fertility symbol dating from Roman times.

▶ *Continue north on the **A352** for Sherborne.*

**10 Sherborne,** Dorset
Sherborne claims, with some justification, to be one of the most beautiful towns in England. Set in a gentle valley among wooded hills, it has a charming stone-built centre. Two kings of Wessex were buried in Sherborne's Saxon abbey, the mother cathedral of the Southwest until 1075. Sherborne Old Castle dates from the 12th century, and Sherborne New Castle was built by Sir

Walter Raleigh in the 1590s. It was here that Sir Walter was 'extinguished' by a servant who first saw him smoking the tobacco he brought back from the New World.

At Compton House near by is Worldwide Butterflies where exotic species can be seen in 'tropical' surroundings. You can also see Britain's only silk farm, where many royal wedding dresses were made.

*i* *3 Digby Road*

▶ *Leave Sherborne on the **A30** heading west for Yeovil.*

**11 Yeovil,** Somerset

Yeovil is a thriving industrial and administrative centre, nationally known for its gloves and helicopters. It suffered disastrous fires in 1499, 1623 and 1640, and during World War II air raids destroyed many of its oldest buildings. One to survive was the 14th-century stone church, impressive for its simplicity and size.

*i* *Petter's House, Petter's Way*

▶ *Leave Yeovil on the **A30** and turn right on to the **A3088**, turning left for Montacute.*

**12 Montacute,** Somerset

This is yet another delightful hamstone village. In a corner of the square is the entrance to its showpiece, Montacute House, a splendid Tudor mansion in formal, landscaped gardens. It was built by Sir Edward Phelips, chief prosecutor of Guy Fawkes in 1605. Although on a smaller scale than Montacute, nearby Brympton House and Tintinhull House attract many visitors each year.

▶ *From Montacute take the **A3088** to Stoke-sub-Hamdon, then the **A303** and right on to the **B3165**. Join the **A372** heading for Westonzoyland.*

**RECOMMENDED WALKS**

There are several enjoyable walks from Montacute, notably the woodland Ladies' Walk, or the paths that lead to the folly of St Michael's Hill near by.

**13 Westonzoyland,** Somerset

Westonzoyland's 100-foot (30m) church tower looks boldly over Sedgemoor, once covered by sea and now a vast expanse of fenland – the largest wetland of its type anywhere in Britain. A map in the church porch will show you how to explore the historical connection, for near here the last battle on English soil was fought. A granite monument on this quiet open land is all that marks the spot for posterity.

▶ *From Westonzoyland continue on the **A372** for 4 miles (6km) to Bridgwater.*

Below: the charming hamstone town of Montacute
Right: Wells Cathedral's clock

# Hills & Vales of West Wessex

From Wiltshire's gentle valleys and downlands to the rugged hills and expansive wetlands of Somerset, the Wessex scenery constantly changes. This tour takes in one of Britain's finest cathedrals, one of Europe's loveliest gardens and the world's most famous prehistoric temple.

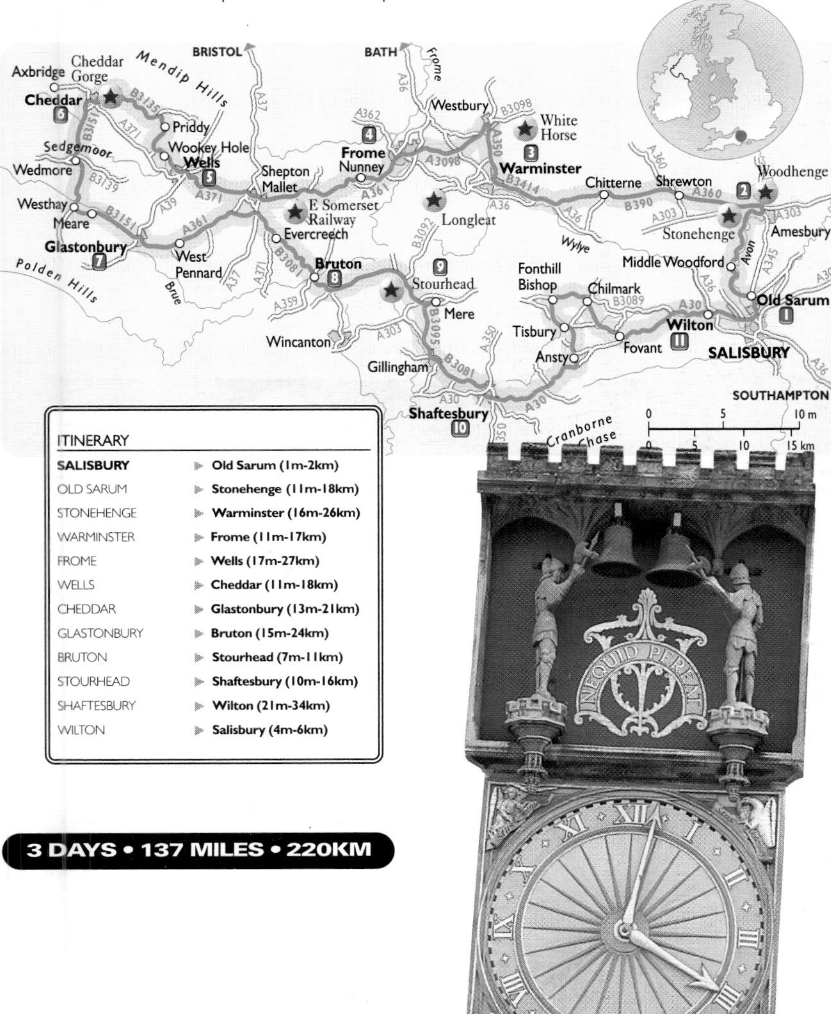


| ITINERARY | |
|---|---|
| SALISBURY | ▶ **Old Sarum (1m-2km)** |
| OLD SARUM | ▶ **Stonehenge (11m-18km)** |
| STONEHENGE | ▶ **Warminster (16m-26km)** |
| WARMINSTER | ▶ **Frome (11m-17km)** |
| FROME | ▶ **Wells (17m-27km)** |
| WELLS | ▶ **Cheddar (11m-18km)** |
| CHEDDAR | ▶ **Glastonbury (13m-21km)** |
| GLASTONBURY | ▶ **Bruton (15m-24km)** |
| BRUTON | ▶ **Stourhead (7m-11km)** |
| STOURHEAD | ▶ **Shaftesbury (10m-16km)** |
| SHAFTESBURY | ▶ **Wilton (21m-34km)** |
| WILTON | ▶ **Salisbury (4m-6km)** |

**3 DAYS • 137 MILES • 220KM**

Built for ceremonies long forgotten, Stonehenge remains a mystery

*i* *Fish Row, Salisbury*

▶ *Leave Salisbury on the* ***A345*** *signed Amesbury and in 1 mile (1.6km) reach Old Sarum.*

**1 Old Sarum,** Wiltshire
Iron Age men, Romans, Saxons, Danes and Normans in turn chose this windy hilltop for their settlements. Within a huge circular mound are the foundations of the Norman cathedral and castle that once stood here. Bishops Osmund and Roger built the cathedral, but cathedral life wasn't easy, and castle and clergy did not get on. In 1220 the bishop chose a new site in the valley, known today as Salisbury, and materials from the demolished cathedral were then used for Salisbury's new glory.

▶ *Continue on the* ***A345****, then take the first left on to unclassified roads for the Woodfords. In 5 miles (8km) reach Amesbury and 1 mile (2km) further north on the* ***A345*** *is Woodhenge. Return to the* ***A303*** *and head west signed Honiton, then right on to the* ***A360*** *to Stonehenge.*

**2 Stonehenge and Woodhenge,** Wiltshire
A henge is a prehistoric monument, usually of religious significance. Woodhenge, the neolithic precursor of Stonehenge, had six concentric rings of timber posts, surrounded by a ditch. The holes marking the site are now marked by concrete posts.

At Stonehenge huge stones 15 to 20 feet (4.5 to 6m) high have been the subject of enormous speculation. Is it a temple for Romans or Druids? How were 26-ton stones brought here? One thing is certain – the axis is aligned with the midwinter and midsummer sun; perhaps this revered monument is a giant calendar.

▶ *From Stonehenge continue on the* ***A360****, turning left on to the* ***B390*** *just past Shrewton. On reaching the* ***A36*** *turn right, then right again after 1 mile (1.6km) on to the* ***B3414*** *to Warminster.*

**3 Warminster,** Wiltshire
Warminster was formerly a wool town and corn market; today it is the home of the Army School of Infantry and the REME (Royal Electrical and Mechanical Engineers) workshops. Four miles (6km) to the west is Longleat, seat of the Marquess of Bath and nationally famous as a wildlife park.

*i* *Central Car Park, Three Horseshoes Mall, Warminster*

▶ *Take the* ***A350*** *for Westbury. Leave by the* ***A3098*** *for 7 miles (11km) to Frome.*

**RECOMMENDED WALK**

Westbury's White Horse, cut into the chalk escarpment of Salisbury Plain in the 18th century, is said to replace one carved in AD879 to commemorate King Alfred's victory over the Danes at Ethandun. Climb from the church at Bratton on the B3098, east of Westbury, or drive up to Westbury Hill, turning right from the B3098, just before the cemetery.

### 4 Frome, Somerset

'Friendly Frome' (say Froom), on the River Frome, is an attractive market town which grew rich on trade in woollen cloth. Its steep narrow streets are scattered with medieval and Tudor buildings. Cheap Street, with its ancient shops and leat gutter is a must, as are the 1726 Blue House, the bridge with its integral shops, and St John's Church.

Three miles (4.8km) from Frome, on the A361, is Nunney, with its romantic moated 14th-century castle.

*i* *Cattle Market Car Park*

*Leave Frome to join the **A361** for Shepton Mallet, 11 miles (16km), then by the **A371** to Wells (6 miles/10km).*

> **SPECIAL TO...**
>
> The Royal Bath and Wells Show, on the first weekend in June, attracts huge crowds from far and wide to the show-ground near Shepton Mallet, 11 miles (16km) from Frome. As well as the agricultural activities, attractions include aerobatics, show-jumping and motorcycle displays.

### 5 Wells, Somerset

Wells is England's smallest city, lying in the shadow of the Mendip Hills, and gets its name from the springs that bubble in to a pool in the bishop's garden. The splendid cathedral was begun in the 12th century and finished in the 15th, and its astronomical clock in the north transept is one of the oldest working clocks in the world. South of the cathedral is the moated Bishop's Palace, where the swans used to ring the bell by the bridge for food. St Cuthbert's Parish Church in High Street is the largest in Somerset, with a 122-foot (37m) tower.

*i* *Town Hall, Market Place*

> **FOR CHILDREN**
>
> Stalactites and stalagmites, soaring caverns and bottomless pits are all to be found at Wookey Hole Caves near Wells, first inhabited 50,000 years ago. On the surface, visitors can walk around a mill which still produces watermarked paper from rags, distort themselves in the mirrors of the old fairground and change new pence for old to play original one-arm bandits at the Penny Pier Arcade.

*Leave Wells on an unclassified road to Wookey Hole, and shortly after the Wookey Hole Caves fork right for Priddy, then left on the **B3135** for Cheddar (5 miles/8km).*

Elizabethan Longleat House, seat of the Marquess of Bath

BACK TO NATURE

Ebbor Gorge, on the route between Wookey Hole and Priddy, is thought by many to be the loveliest and most unspoilt Mendip gorge.

**6 Cheddar,** Somerset
The rugged grandeur of Cheddar Gorge unfolds slowly and magically as you descend a meandering road. Cliffs tower to a height of 450 feet (137m) here, and the 'Beware of falling rocks' sign is no idle warning. Climb the 274 steps of Jacob's Ladder at the south end for the best views, or rest in the Garden of Fragrance, especially created for the blind. At the bottom of the gorge, Gough's and Cox's Caves offer a chance to go subterranean in search of the lost Yeo.

Cheddar would not be Cheddar without its cheese, but the product outgrew the place and has largely gone elsewhere. A 1990 replica of a 1920s factory shows how it used to be made.

*i The Gorge*

FOR HISTORY BUFFS

Axbridge, near Cheddar, is a fine example of a close-knit winding medieval town. The jewel is King John's Hunting Lodge, at the corner of High Street and The Square. This handsome three-storeyed building has nothing to do with either King John or with hunting, but has been exquisitely restored by the National Trust, and now houses the Axbridge Museum, open on summer afternoons.

► *Leave Cheddar on the* ***B3151*** *for Glastonbury (12 miles/9km).*

**7 Glastonbury,** Somerset
Said to be the 'cradle of English Christianity', Glastonbury is a town steeped in Christian and Arthurian legends. The focal point is the ruined abbey, which may have originated in the 1st century, but was sacked at the Dissolution in 1539. Joseph of Arimathea is reputed to have come here as a missionary in AD63, and a thorn in the Abbot's kitchen is said to derive from his wooden staff, which turned into a thorn bush. The chapel on the Tor dates from AD179. Through the ages, writers have speculated that this is the site of Avalon, King Arthur's final resting place. The chalice which Christ used at the Last Supper is said to be beneath the Chalice Spring on the Tor. Of particular note in the town are the Abbey Barn, now housing the Somerset Rural Life Museum, the fine 14th-century George and Pilgrims Hotel, and The Tribunal, once a courthouse and now a museum.

*i The Tribunal*

► *Leave Glastonbury on the* ***A361*** *and in 7 miles (12km) turn left on to the* ***A37****, then right on to the* ***A371*** *signposted Castle Cary. Shortly, fork left on to the* ***B3081*** *for Bruton, (4 miles/6km).*

**8 Bruton,** Somerset
Little Bruton, on the River Brue, has a charm of its own. Be sure to explore The Bartons, narrow alleys leading down to the river, which is crossed by an unusual packhorse bridge. St Mary's Church, with its twin towers, is particularly fine, and prominent in the town is King's School, established in the 16th century. The tall building on the hill as you leave is the Bruton Dovecote, formerly belonging to the abbey which once existed here.

► *Leave Bruton by the* ***B3081****, signposted Wincanton. In Redlynch turn left at cross-*

Nature tamed: the classical order and opulence of Stourhead

*roads and in 3 miles (5km) right, and shortly right again to join the **B3092** to Stourhead (½mile/1km).*

**9 Stourhead,** Wiltshire
Henry Hoare, an eminent banker, decided to landscape his Palladian Wiltshire home, Stourhead, in the grand manner. He began in 1740 by damming springs of the Stour to create a sweeping lake with wooded islands. This is one of the finest gardens in the world, now in the care of the National Trust. An unmistakable landmark on the border of the Stourhead estate is Alfred's Tower, a triangular brick structure 160 feet (49m) high, built in 1772. It marks the spot where King Alfred rallied his troops to fight the Danes in AD879.

▶ *Leave Stourhead on the **B3092** for Mere (2 miles/3km). Take the **B3095**, then turn left on to the **B3092** to Gillingham (2½ miles/4km), then Shaftesbury (3 miles/5km) via the **B3081**.*

**10 Shaftesbury,** Dorset
Perched on a hill 700 feet (213m) above sea-level, the pretty town of Shaftesbury commands marvellous views across Dorset's Blackmoor Vale. The Local History Museum near St Peter's Church contains the Byzant, a strange ornamental relic, formerly carried by townsfolk in a ceremony confirming their rights to draw water from wells at the foot of the hill.

*i* *8 Bell Street*

▶ *Leave Shaftesbury on the **A30** signposted Salisbury. In 6 miles (10km) turn left for Ansty and Tisbury. Continue north, then turn right on the **B3089** at Fonthill Bishop. In 2 miles (3km) turn at Chilmark to Fovant (3 miles/5km). Go left on the **A30** to Wilton.*

**11 Wilton,** Wiltshire
In Saxon times, Wilton was capital of Wessex. Thousands now flock here each year to visit Wilton House, built in the 1540s and remodelled by Inigo Jones in the 17th century. The Double Cube Room, recently restored, is especially ornate. There is a world-famous collection of paintings by Rubens, Van Dyck and Tintoretto, among others.

▶ *Leave Wilton by the **A36** for Salisbury (4 miles/6km).*

Shaftesbury's most famous street, cobbled Gold Hill

### SCENIC ROUTES

On the B3151 south of Cheddar, it is worth stopping as you approach Wedmore to look back over Sedgemoor, one of England's few wetlands, stretching away to the marvellous backdrop of the Mendip limestone ridge.
As you ascend the steep hill to enter Shaftesbury, look back over the rich farmland of Dorset's lovely Blackmoor Vale, with the wooded ridge of Stourhead and Alfred's Tower beyond.

# THE SOUTH & SOUTHEAST

Despite being well populated, the five counties of Surrey, Sussex, Kent, Hampshire and Dorset have retained large areas of rich farmland, commons and heaths and forested areas. Perhaps the most famous area is the New Forest in Hampshire, much of which is heathland; 'forest' was originally a term for hunting ground.

Architectural styles are especially distinctive in the Weald of Sussex and Kent, where tile-hung houses can be seen in many villages, as well as thatched houses and oasthouses – though most of these are now residences, having ceased production of beer from locally grown hops. Further west is Hardy Country: many of Dorset's attractive towns and villages can be related to the writings of Thomas Hardy and his views of life in the 18th century.

The scenery varies from gentle, undulating landscapes to steep escarpments on the edges of the North and South Downs and dramatic coastal cliffs, notably at Beachy Head, where the South Downs reach the sea. At the foot of the white cliffs of Dover, where the North Downs reach the coast, the Channel Tunnel dives beneath the sea on its way to France.

The historic West Gate, Canterbury

Seaside resorts such as Bournemouth and Folkestone attract large numbers of visitors, especially in the summer months and at weekends, although many of the beaches are not very sandy in the south-eastern part of England.

Religion plays an important part in the life of this region, where Winchester and Canterbury are at opposite ends of the Pilgrim's Way. Fine cathedrals can be seen in both these towns, and a great many impressive churches are hidden away in small villages. These were often financed from agricultural profits and competition was fierce, with villages trying to outdo their neighbours with bigger or better churches. Near the chalk hills, many of these churches are built of this soft rock, but are faced with a layer of resistant flint.

New Alresford's ancient fulling mill on the River Alre

### Winchester

There is so much to see in this City of Kings that it is worth taking a guided walking or driving tour. Winchester is a place of history and legend. The Round Table in the castle's Great Hall is actually a medieval creation which celebrates the King Arthur legend. From here you can walk past the old Butter Cross in the centre of town and make a diversion to the fine cathedral – before taking a look at the statue of King Alfred, which recalls Winchester's past status as his kingdom's capital.

### Bournemouth

This town developed along with the Victorian enthusiasm for the seaside, when a few rich families built villas on what used to be a fairly desolate heath. An attractive beach stretches for miles along the coast, and windsurfing, swimming and boating are popular. There are beautiful gardens to visit with sub-tropical vegetation which thrives in the mild climate. Quiet, wooded walks can be taken in the steep valleys called chines, which slope down from the cliff tops to the shore.

### Royal Tunbridge Wells

This spa town has been a fashionable market and trading centre for many years; even in the 17th century, the Pantiles was an established shopping centre. The town first developed as a spa when its chalybeate spring was discovered in 1606; it can still be seen, in Bath Square. The surrounding countryside consists of miles of common, on which stand the spectacular High Rocks.

### Canterbury

Canterbury's cathedral dominates the landscape for miles around, but there is much more to see in this ancient city, often thought of as the birthplace of English Christianity. A walk round the streets is a walk through history, and a visit to the Canterbury Heritage Exhibition is a good way to start a tour. The city walls, St Martin's church, the ruins of St Augustine's Abbey, the Royal Museum and the Old Weavers' House are among the buildings you must not miss. There are also modern entertainments, including two theatres and an excellent pedestrianised area for shopping.

TOUR
6

# A Journey Across the Weald

**3 DAYS • 122 MILES • 197KM**

Over undulating sandstone hills, through the orchards of the 'Garden of England', and the once vast Forest of Anderida, this is an area of delightful villages, superb castles and immaculate gardens. Church spires and towers and tile-hung Wealden houses all add to its beauty, as the buildings and countryside compete with each other to provide the most delightful views.

| ITINERARY | |
|---|---|
| **ROYAL TUNBRIDGE WELLS** | ▶ **Penshurst (7m-11km)** |
| PENSHURST | ▶ **Hever (6m-10km)** |
| HEVER | ▶ **Limpsfield (10m-16km)** |
| LIMPSFIELD | ▶ **Sevenoaks (9m-14km)** |
| SEVENOAKS | ▶ **Ightham (6m-10km)** |
| IGHTHAM | ▶ **Mereworth (6m-10km)** |
| MEREWORTH | ▶ **Lamberhurst (14m-23km)** |
| LAMBERHURST | ▶ **Cranbrook (10m-16km)** |
| CRANBROOK | ▶ **Tenterden (11m-18km)** |
| TENTERDEN | ▶ **Northiam (8m-13km)** |
| NORTHIAM | ▶ **Bodiam (5m-8km)** |
| BODIAM | ▶ **Burwash (10m-16km)** |
| BURWASH | ▶ **Rotherfield (13m-21km)** |
| ROTHERFIELD | ▶ **Royal Tunbridge Wells (7m-11km)** |

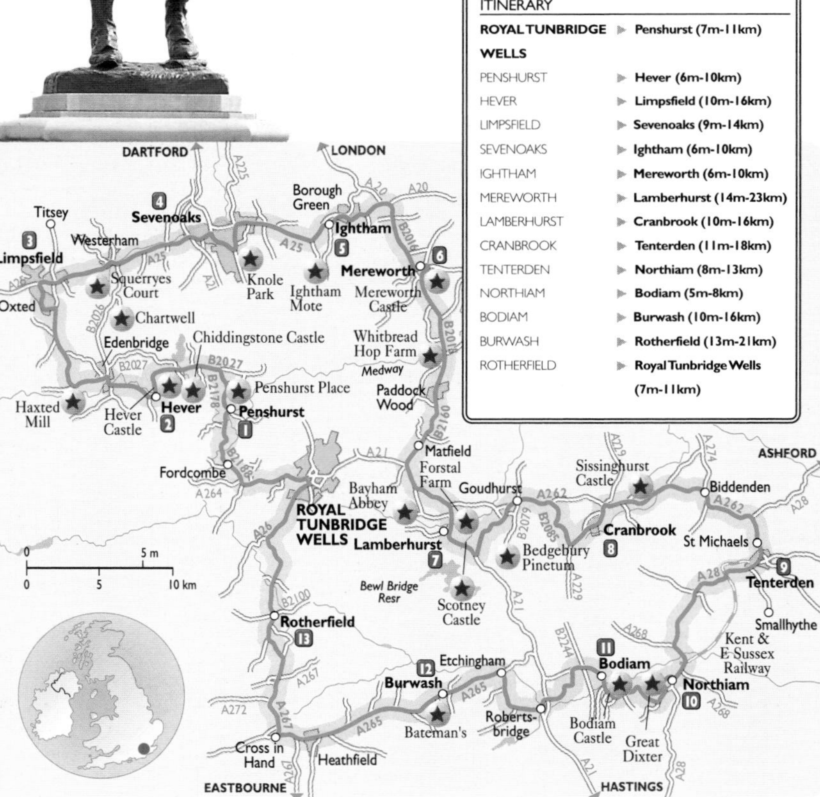

*[i] Monson House, Monson Way, Royal Tunbridge Wells*

▶ *Leave Tunbridge Wells on the **A264**, then take the **B2188** north to Penshurst.*

### 1 Penshurst, Kent

Penshurst is a small village with stone houses and a magnificent church, but the main attraction is 14th-century Penshurst Place, one of the outstanding stately homes of Britain, set in superb Tudor gardens. The famous chestnut-beamed Great Hall dominates the manor with its medieval splendour, and its scale and grandeur are almost beyond belief. It also houses a fascinating toy museum. The Elizabethan poet, Sir Philip Sidney, was born here in 1554, and the Sidney family still lives in the manor. The family became Earls of Leicester, and the village has the original Leicester Square – named after a favourite of Elizabeth 1. The Church of St Michael the Archangel dates from the 13th century and contains impressive memorials to the Sidney family.

▶ *Take the road past the church and follow the **B2176**, **B2027** and unclassified roads for 6 miles (10km) to Hever.*

### 2 Hever, Kent

Hever is known for its associations with Anne Boleyn, Henry VIII's second wife. The village inn is called King Henry VIII, and the fine church has a memorial to Sir Thomas Bullen, Anne's father, who is buried here. Hever Castle was the family home, and it was here that Henry VIII courted her. This fine, moated manor house was acquired by William Waldorf Astor in 1903, who did much work restoring it. He created the modern lake and superb Tudor-style gardens, including a spectacular Italian Garden, and built a mock-Tudor village behind the house. The house itself contains a superb collection of furniture and paintings, and the Tudor Long Gallery features a fascinating exhibition of scenes from the life and times of Anne Boleyn.

Just east of Hever is Chiddingstone. The entire village is owned by the National Trust, including Chiddingstone Castle, a late 18th-century Gothic manor house. The main street is lined with beautifully preserved half-timbered 16th- and 17th-century houses. The Chiding Stone, after which the village is named, is a piece of local sandstone where nagging wives were publicly chided by the assembled village population.

Three miles (5km) west of Hever is Edenbridge. The 16th-century Crown Hotel is noteworthy. The 13th-century church here has a massive tower crowned with a spire of a later date.

Near by, at Haxted, is a late 16th-century watermill, now a museum which contains mill machinery, two working waterwheels and a picture gallery.

▶ *From Haxted Mill take unclassified roads north to Limpsfield.*

The gardens at Penshurst Place
Left: General Wolfe, Westerham

### 3 Limpsfield, Surrey

This small town nestles at the foot of the North Downs in wooded countryside. The composer Frederick Delius is buried among the yews in the churchyard here. De Tillens is a fine 15th-century Wealden Hall House with a splendid king-post roof. Built by the yeomen of the weald, it contains a collection of furniture, porcelain and military items.

A little further is the village of Westerham. General Wolfe, who beat the French in Quebec in 1759, was born here. His boyhood home, 17th-century Quebec House, is near the green. Near by is Squerryes Court, a William and Mary manor house built in 1681 and owned by the Warde family for over 250 years. Wolfe received his commission here, and a room is set aside for Wolfe memorabilia. The house also contains fine paintings, tapestries and furniture, and the magnificent garden has lakes, spring flowers and shrubs. There is a statue of Wolfe in the High Street, and on the tiny green one of Sir Winston Churchill, who lived at Chartwell, just south of town, from 1924 until his death. The interior of the house is preserved as a museum, with many souvenirs of the great man's life, including some of his paintings.

► *Follow the **A25** to Sevenoaks.*

Chartwell was Winston Churchill's country home until his death

### RECOMMENDED WALKS

Many excellent walks can be found near Titsey, to the north of Limpsfield, southwards towards Edenbridge along the Vanguard Way, and east and west along the North Downs Way, which follows much of the old Pilgrim's Way from Winchester to Canterbury, giving fine views of southern England.

### 4 Sevenoaks, Kent

The traditional seven fine oaks which gave the town its name were reduced to only one in the great storm of October 1987, but new trees have been planted. Sevenoaks is notable for Knole Park, which dates from 1456 and is the largest private house in England. Thomas Sackville, the 1st Earl of Dorset, was granted the house by Elizabeth I. Set in a wide-rolling deer park, it contains an important collection of 17th-century furniture, fine staircases and fireplaces, two state beds of James II and galleries hung with original tapestries. Beer has been brewed in the area for centuries, and you can sample one of the wines from an increasing number of local vineyards.

*i Buckhurst Lane*

► *Leave Sevenoaks on the **A225**, and rejoin the **A25** to Ightham.*

### 5 Ightham, Kent

Visiting Ightham is like stepping back in time. Ightham Mote is an unspoilt, medieval, moated manor house surrounded by beautiful Wealden scenery. Undisturbed by time, the great hall, chapel and crypt have survived in fine condition. There are many fine old half-timbered medieval buildings in the village, including an oast house and the Old Coaching Inn. The Church of St Peter is mainly 14th- and 15th-century and contains some splendid stained glass and several brasses and sculptures.

► *Continue west on the **A25**, which joins and becomes the **A20**. Turn south on to the **B2016** to the turning east for Mereworth.*

### 6 Mereworth, Kent

This is the heart of the 'Garden of England'. The unusual church was rebuilt in 18th-century neo-Classical style, like nearby Mereworth Castle, and has a remarkable large steeple. The castle was built in the early 18th century as a copy of the Villa La Rotunda, near Vicenza in Italy. It has the appearance of an ancient temple, and contains some impressive ceiling paintings, as well as period furniture designed by William Kent. The present village was built by Lord Westmoreland, who destroyed the original in order to use the site for the extravagant and exotic castle.

On the road to Lamberhurst you will pass the Whitbread Hop Farm at Beltring, well worth a visit. The farm has the finest collection of Victorian oast houses in the world, now turned into craftsmen's workshops and a hop museum, recapturing the life of hop farmers in the past.

► *From Mereworth return to the **B2016** via the **A26**. Continue south on the **B2016**, **B2015**, **B2160** and **A21** for 14 miles (23km) to Lamberhurst.*

### 7 Lamberhurst, Kent

This village was the centre of the Wealden iron industry and at one time produced railings for St Paul's Cathedral in London. The Owl House is a small half-timbered, tile-hung house which was a noted haunt of wool smugglers. It stands in the middle of beautiful grounds and gardens of azaleas, roses and camellias. Bayham Abbey, 2 miles (3km) west of the village, is said to be the most impressive group of monastic remains in Kent, with church, monastery and a former

### FOR CHILDREN

Forstal Farm is situated on the A262, just ¼ mile (½km) off the A21 near Lamberhurst. This Model Museum and Craft Village is the result of 10 years' work by one man. There are model scenes which light up and can be brought to life at the touch of a button. Nursery scenes, Victorian London, World War II, science fiction and many other subjects are represented in a unique collection. In addition to the models there are shops and houses lining an old-fashioned village street. You can take a stroll round the nature trail or enjoy a home-made cake in the Oast Tea Rooms.

The gardens at Sissinghurst

### BACK TO NATURE

South of Goudhurst is Bedgebury Pinetum, an attractive place to visit at any time of the year. It is set in a big park surrounding a Louis XIV-style mansion. Rhododendrons and azaleas are specialities, but there are numerous varieties of fungi and its conifers. The mansion is now a girls' school, but most of the park is open. The Pinetum contains a nationally important collection of pine trees – several of the plants came originally from Kew Gardens, but the Forestry Commission now manages these woodlands. Birdwatchers come to Bedgebury, especially during the winter months,to see interesting species such as hawfinch, crossbill and firecrest.

gatehouse all well preserved.

Scotney Castle, south of Lamberhurst, is a ruined 14th-century castle with a moat, set in fine gardens.

▶ *Continue southeast on the **A21**, taking the unclassified road on the left after 1½ miles (2km), through Kilndown to the **A262** and Goudhurst. About 1½ miles (2km) after Goudhurst, turn right on to the **B2085**, then left to Cranbrook on meeting the **A229**.*

### 8 Cranbrook, Kent

Cranbrook is a pleasant town with many 18th-century buildings. In the centre is Union Mill, the finest working smock windmill in England. Often called the 'Capital of the Weald', Cranbrook was built from the profits of the wool trade in the 15th century. The fine medieval church, 'the Cathedral of the Weald', has a porch built in 1291, and the local museum recaptures much of the history of the area.

Three miles (5km) from the town is Sissinghurst Castle. The popular and colourful gardens were created in the 1930s by Vita Sackville-West and her husband, Sir Harold Nicolson. Derelict buildings and wild vegetation were transformed into this beautiful series of gardens with orchards, herbs and the famous 'white garden' where only white or grey flowers grow. Visitors can look at the quaint tower room where Vita wrote her novels.

[i] *Vestry Hall, Stone Street, Cranbrook*

▶ *Continue on the **A262**, then the **A28** to Tenterden.*

**9 Tenterden,** Kent
Described as the 'Jewel of the Weald', the centre of this Wealden market town is dominated by the marble tower of St Mildred's Church. It is worth the climb up the tower because of the fine views across the Weald and, on a clear day, as far as France. The high street has shops and houses, many with original Georgian fronts. William Caxton, the father of English printing, is believed to have been born in Tenterden, and at the western edge of the town is the William Caxton Inn. Pub signs are often quite revealing about the past, and near the church is the Woolpack Inn, a reminder that much of the town's wealth came from sheep during the 15th and 16th centuries.

Woollen cloth was traded overseas, using Smallhythe as a port. It is difficult to visualise this countryside location, now far removed from the sea, as a thriving port and shipbuilding centre. Dame Ellen Terry lived in Smallhythe Place, an early 16th-century timbered harbour master's house, from 1899 until she died in 1928, and the house is open to visitors during the summer months. Spots Farm, at Smallhythe, has 20 acres (8 hectares) of vineyards you can walk through, as well as an amazing herb garden containing over 500 varieties, possibly the largest collection in the UK.

A stretch of line on the Kent and East Sussex Railway, Tenterden

**SPECIAL TO...**

Tenterden is the main station for the Kent and East Sussex Steam Railway, and it handles thousands of passengers every year. A stretch of the line from Tenterden through the beautiful Rother Valley was reopened in 1974 by volunteer steam enthusiasts. An extension was opened to Northiam in 1990, making a total journey of 7 miles (11km), but the highlight for steam lovers is the thrill of the engine working hard to climb the steep hill into Tenterden.

[i] *Town Hall, High Street*

▶ *Follow the **A28** to Northiam.*

**10 Northiam,** East Sussex
The gnarled old oak tree on the village green achieved fame when Elizabeth I dined beneath it in 1573, while on her way to Rye. She is said to have taken her shoes off during the occasion and left them to the villagers when she continued her journey.

Great Dixter, half-a-mile (1km) away, is a large 15th-century manor house with a half-timbered and plastered front. The house was enlarged and restored by Sir Edward Lutyens in 1910. Its gardens are specially noted for their clematis.

▶ *Return towards the main road, taking the narrow road, first on the right, and follow country lanes to Bodiam.*

**11 Bodiam,** East Sussex
Bodiam Castle, on the edge of the village, is a magnificent moated fortress, built in the 1380s to stop French raiders coming up the Rother Valley. The castle survived the French, who did not attack, but could not survive Cromwell's armies, who destroyed it. The outside walls are still intact, but it is now an empty shell. Life in a medieval castle is shown on a video, and there are 'Activity Days', when school children can dress up in medieval costumes for living history lessons. It was voted one of the top six castles for children in 1989, and in May it hosts a longbow competition.

Five miles (8km) southwest of Bodiam is Robertsbridge. Its half-timbered and weather-boarded cottages, a feature of the area, line the High Street, and it is the home of Gray-Nicolls, makers of cricket bats since 1875. A mile (1.6km) east, a no-through road leads to the ruins of a Cistercian abbey, founded in 1176.

► *Follow the unclassified road past the station to Etchingham, then the* ***A265*** *to Burwash.*

**12 Burwash,** East Sussex
Burwash is an outstandingly attractive village of 16th- and 17th-century houses. Inside St Bartholomew's Church is a cast-iron grave slab which is thought to be the oldest in the country.

Bateman's, half-a-mile (1km) away, was the home of Rudyard Kipling from 1902 until 1936, providing the inspiration for much of his work. His study has been kept as it was during his lifetime, and the enormous 10-foot (3m) long desk has a few untidy pieces left standing on it. Much of the neighbourhood is featured in his novel *Puck of Pook's Hill.* Upstream there is a watermill which has been restored to working order, and near by is the waterdriven turbine Kipling had installed in 1902 to provide his house with electricity.

► *Take the* ***A265****, turning right on to the* ***A267*** *past Heathfield. Turn left on to unclassified roads shortly after Five Ashes and follow signs to Rotherfield.*

**13 Rotherfield,** East Sussex
On the edge of the Ashdown Forest, Rotherfield sits in the heart of beautiful countryside. It is a delightful place to stop off and walk about. There is a fine church dedicated to St Denys, which contains 13th-century wall-paintings including Doom, and St Michael weighing souls, and in the east window is some splendid stained glass by Edward Burne-Jones and William Morris.

► *Return via unclassified roads to the* ***A26****. Turn right and return to Tunbridge Wells.*

### FOR HISTORY BUFFS

The 'Heart of Kent' was formerly a vast forest, and the abundance of oak in medieval times gave rise to the characteristic timber-framed and half-timbered houses of the area. The houses often included a central hall and projecting upper storeys.

### SCENIC ROUTES

The roads leading into Mereworth, Lamberhurst, Scotney and Bodiam are particularly memorable. The combination of villages, old Wealden buildings, hills, valleys and woods create a picturesque landscape. Villages such as Ightham are very photogenic, as are the North Downs.

Bodiam Castle's moat could not protect it from Cromwell's army

TOUR
7

# From
# Cathedral to Cliffs

**2/3 DAYS • 107 MILES • 172KM**

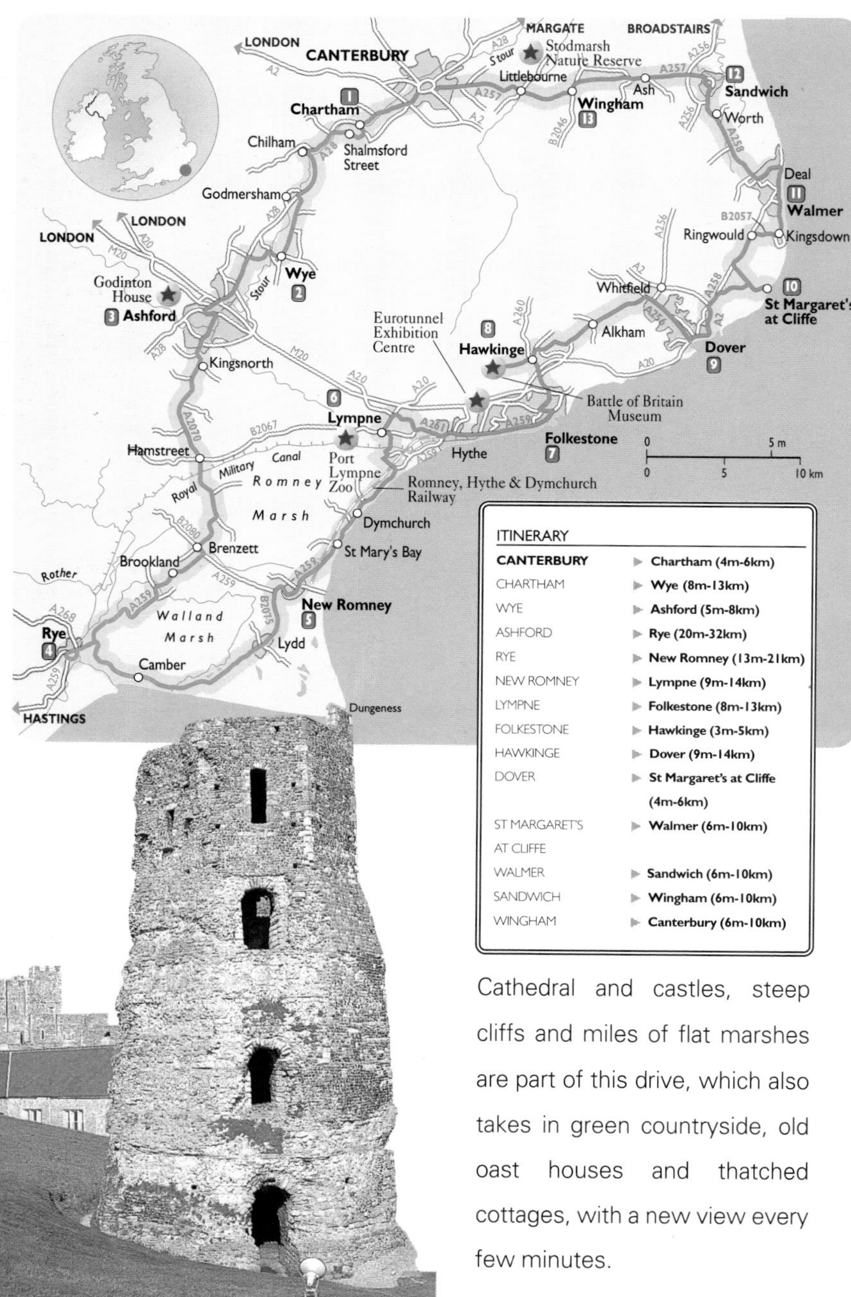


ITINERARY

| | |
|---|---|
| **CANTERBURY** | ▶ **Chartham (4m-6km)** |
| CHARTHAM | ▶ **Wye (8m-13km)** |
| WYE | ▶ **Ashford (5m-8km)** |
| ASHFORD | ▶ **Rye (20m-32km)** |
| RYE | ▶ **New Romney (13m-21km)** |
| NEW ROMNEY | ▶ **Lympne (9m-14km)** |
| LYMPNE | ▶ **Folkestone (8m-13km)** |
| FOLKESTONE | ▶ **Hawkinge (3m-5km)** |
| HAWKINGE | ▶ **Dover (9m-14km)** |
| DOVER | ▶ **St Margaret's at Cliffe (4m-6km)** |
| ST MARGARET'S AT CLIFFE | ▶ **Walmer (6m-10km)** |
| WALMER | ▶ **Sandwich (6m-10km)** |
| SANDWICH | ▶ **Wingham (6m-10km)** |
| WINGHAM | ▶ **Canterbury (6m-10km)** |

Cathedral and castles, steep cliffs and miles of flat marshes are part of this drive, which also takes in green countryside, old oast houses and thatched cottages, with a new view every few minutes.

Picturesque timbered Chilham
Left: Dover Castle and Pharos

[i] *34 St Margaret's Street, Canterbury*

**BACK TO NATURE**

Stodmarsh National Nature Reserve lies a few miles to the east of Canterbury. Vast reedbeds and areas of open water attract huge numbers of wildfowl. Reed warblers, Cetti's warblers and bearded tits can be found in the winter, sometimes in the company of short-eared owls.

▶ *Take the **A28** to Chartham.*

**1 Chartham,** Kent
The valley of the Great Stour, with gravel pits and small lakes, is noted for fishing and bird life, and Chartham is a well-known angling centre. St Mary's Church dates from the 13th century and has one of the oldest sets of bells in the country. Chartham Hatch Craft Centre is just down the road, set in delightful countryside.

Further along is Chilham, where the village square is set at the gateway to Chilham Castle, built for Henry II in 1174. The castle is not open to the public, but you can visit the gardens. There are usually medieval jousting tournaments on Sundays and Bank Holidays. The church has a stone and flint tower, and the largely unspoilt houses around the square are of Tudor and Jacobean style.

▶ *From Chilham return to the **A28**, travel south for 2 miles (3km) then turn off on to unclassified roads to Wye.*

**2 Wye,** Kent
This village, in its rural setting, is the location of the famous Agriculture School of London University, housed in a college first set up in the mid-15th century by John Kempe, a native of the town, who became Archbishop of Canterbury. The town also has a racecourse, a Georgian mill house and 18th-century Olantigh Hall.

▶ *Return to the **A28** for 5 miles (8km) to Ashford.*

**3 Ashford,** Kent
This old market centre for Romney Marsh and the Weald of Kent is now a thriving shopping and touring centre. Medieval, Tudor and Georgian houses still survive and the 14th- and 15th-century parish church retains much of its old character.

Godington House, northwest of town, was built in the 17th century. The rooms are full of Chippendale and Sheraton furniture, and there is fine topiary work in the garden.

[i] *18 The Churchyard*

▶ *Follow the **A2070**, then the **A259** across Romney Marsh for 20 miles (32km) to Rye.*

**4 Rye,** East Sussex
Rye is one of the Cinque Ports, a group of maritime towns which

were originally responsible for providing ships and men to guard against invasion. At one time Rye was almost encircled by the sea, but the harbour silted up in the 16th century and the water receded. In the winter, when mists roll in across the countryside, Romney Marsh can be sinister and mysterious – a fitting background to tales of the infamous parson and smuggler, Dr Syn.

*i The Heritage Centre, Strand Quay*

▶ *Head back on the **A259** to East Guldeford, then take an unclassified road through Camber to Lydd to join the **B2075** to New Romney.*

**5 New Romney,** Kent
Another ancient Cinque Port, now inland from the sea, New Romney was destroyed in 1287 by a violent storm which changed the course of the River Rother. The Romney, Hythe and Dymchurch narrow gauge railway opened in 1927, with locomotives and carriages which are one-third full size. Toys and models can be seen at New Romney station.

Getting up steam on the Romney, Hythe and Dymchurch Railway

*i Light Railway Car Park, 2 Littlestone Road*

FOR HISTORY BUFFS

There are as many as 74 Martello towers along the south coast. A noted survivor is at Dymchurch, near New Romney. Martello towers were built to resist an invasion by Napoleon which never happened. Many were used to control smuggling. The Dymchurch tower has been fully restored and has one of the original 24-pounder guns on the roof.

▶ *Take the **A259** again, then unclassified roads for 9 miles (14km) to Lympne, then via the **B2067** to the **A261** which leads eastwards to Hythe.*

**6 Lympne,** Kent
The 11th-century castle at Lympne (pronounced *Lim*) stands on top of a cliff which was once a coastline. Views from here extend across the Channel to the French coast on a clear day. From the castle, the remains of a Roman fort can be seen.

Just outside town is Port Lympne Zoo Park, set in 300 acres (121 hectares) of gardens surrounding a mansion. East of Lympne is Hythe, another Cinque Port which is now a popular seaside resort and the terminus for the Romney, Hythe and Dymchurch Railway. The town has several historic buildings and summer boating along the old Royal Military Canal.

*i Prospect Road Car Park, Hythe*

▶ *Follow the **A259** from Hythe to Folkestone.*

**7 Folkestone,** Kent
The harbour of this resort handles cross-Channel ferries, and still has a fishing fleet and a fish market. A Museum and Art Gallery in Grace Hill has displays on the town's maritime history, and the Eurotunnel Exhibition Centre explains, with the use of videos, models and displays, this huge project which has been talked about for 200 years. Spade House was the former home of the author H G Wells. The Leas, a wide grassy promenade along the cliff top, has fine views and provides an excellent walk through wooded slopes down to the beach.

*i Harbour Street*

FOR CHILDREN

The Rotunda Amusement Park in Folkestone is open seven days a week throughout summer. Ride on the southeast's only log flume or have a gentle round of crazy golf. There are indoor amusements, and on Sundays there is a huge outdoor market.

▶ *Head inland along the **A260** as far as Hawkinge.*

**8 Hawkinge,** Kent
Set in the heart of the Downland west of Hawkinge is the Kent Battle of Britain Museum, which conjures up visions of World War II. It houses the largest collection of fragments of British and German aircraft involved in the fighting.

St Margaret's Bay is a popular start for cross-Channel swimmers

▶ *Take unclassified roads eastwards from Hawkinge, eventually running south on to the **A256** for Dover.*

### 9 Dover, Kent

Dover, famous for its White Cliffs, was the chief Cinque Port. It was known to the Romans as *Dubris*, and the Painted House, discovered in 1970, dates from about AD200. Among the paintings are several references to the theme of Bacchus, the god of wine. More recent is the Old Town Gaol, which has been restored to show the dismal conditions of Victorian prison life. On Snargate Street you can see the Grand Shaft, a 140-foot (43m) staircase cut into the white cliffs, built in Napoleonic times as a short cut to the town for troops stationed on the Western Heights. The views across to France can be best seen from Dover Castle, which overlooks the town. The Pharos, a Roman lighthouse, stands within its walls near the fine Saxon Church of St Mary de Castro.

[i] *Townwall Street*

▶ *Take the **A258**, then an unclassified road to St Margaret's at Cliffe.*

### 10 St Margaret's at Cliffe, Kent

The flint-faced church in the upper part of this village is typical of chalkland buildings.

Massive chalk cliffs dominate the scene, and sheltered beneath them is the Pines Garden, created in the 1970s with trees, shrubs, a lake and waterfall, and a statue of Sir Winston Churchill.

Three miles (5km) further is Ringwould, which has another fine church, with an attractive 17th-century tower. Bronze Age barrows can be seen at nearby Free Down, and at Kingsdown there is a lot of flint, both on the buildings and on the shore.

▶ *Rejoin the **A258**, then take the **B2057** from Ringwould to Walmer.*

Sandwich is one of the oldest Cinque ports
Opposite: Winchester's Round Table

### 11 Walmer, Kent

Henry VIII built the castle here, along with over 20 other forts to defend the coast of southeast England. This fine coastal fortress, shaped like a Tudor rose, has been transformed into an elegant stately home with beautiful gardens, and is the official residence of the Lord Warden of the Cinque Ports. Lord Wellington was Warden from 1829 to 1852, and his famous boots are on display.

Further on, Deal Castle, also built by Henry VIII, is in the shape of a six-petalled flower, and tells the full story of the Tudor castles in the exhibition room. The Timeball Tower, which used to give time signals to shipping is a unique four-storey museum of time and maritime communication on the sea front. The museum in St George's Street has a collection of old photographs, model sailing ships and maps.

*i Town Hall, High Street, Deal*

**RECOMMENDED WALKS**

The North Downs Way can provide a long walk; there are clearly marked trails from Dover to Deal along the coast, or along an inland route. The route from Deal to Sandwich on the coast or inland will provide fabulous views.

► *Take the **A258** to Sandwich.*

### 12 Sandwich, Kent

The oldest of the medieval Cinque Ports, Sandwich is separated from the sea by 2 miles (3km) of sand dunes. Its white windmill dates from about 1760, and now houses a folk museum with domestic and farming exhibits. Sandwich Golf Course, between the town and Sandwich Bay, is a world-class championship course.

*i St Peter's Church, Market Street*

► *Follow the **A257 for 6 miles (10km)** to Wingham.*

### 13 Wingham, Kent

This picturesque village contains a magnificent church with a green spire, caused by oxidisation. The Bird Park has cockatoos, macaws, owls and waterfowl, all with plenty of flying space, as well as rare farm animals and pets. Valuable research work takes place here to help endangered species, and to overcome man's destruction of natural habitats. A little further out of town is the village of Littlebourne. Fruit and hops are grown around here, and there is an ancient thatched barn near the flint-faced church.

► *Continue along the **A257** for the return to Canterbury (6 miles/10km).*

**SCENIC ROUTES**

Romney Marsh and the Downs are a delight, and the inland countryside, with fields, orchards and crops, is very attractive. Along the coast there are dramatic cliffs and sea views between Folkestone, Dover and Sandwich.

**SPECIAL TO...**

The original Cinque Ports were Hastings, Romney, Hythe, Dover and Sandwich, with Rye and Winchelsea. They were given charters by Edward I in 1278 and were really trading and fishing ports which worked together to defend the coast and fight sea battles. In return they were granted royal charters and privileges.

# **The Downs &** Valleys of Hampshire

The Hampshire Downs provide a gentle interlude between harsh sandy heaths near London and the valleys of the Southwest. From Winchester this tour takes you through lush valleys to panoramic views of where battle fleets throughout history set sail.

**1/2 DAYS • 99 MILES • 158KM**

| ITINERARY | |
|---|---|
| **WINCHESTER** | ▶ **Stockbridge (9m-14km)** |
| STOCKBRIDGE | ▶ **Middle Wallop (6m-10km)** |
| MIDDLE WALLOP | ▶ **Mottisfont (12m-19km)** |
| MOTTISFONT | ▶ **Romsey (4m-6km)** |
| ROMSEY | ▶ **Marwell (11m-18km)** |
| MARWELL | ▶ **Bishop's Waltham (4m-6km)** |
| BISHOP'S WALTHAM | ▶ **Portsdown Hill (10m-16km)** |
| PORTSDOWN HILL | ▶ **Hambledon (10m-16km)** |
| HAMBLEDON | ▶ **Queen Elizabeth Country Park (7m-11km)** |
| QUEEN ELIZABETH COUNTRY PARK | ▶ **New Alresford (18m-29km)** |
| NEW ALRESFORD | ▶ **Winchester (8m-13km)** |

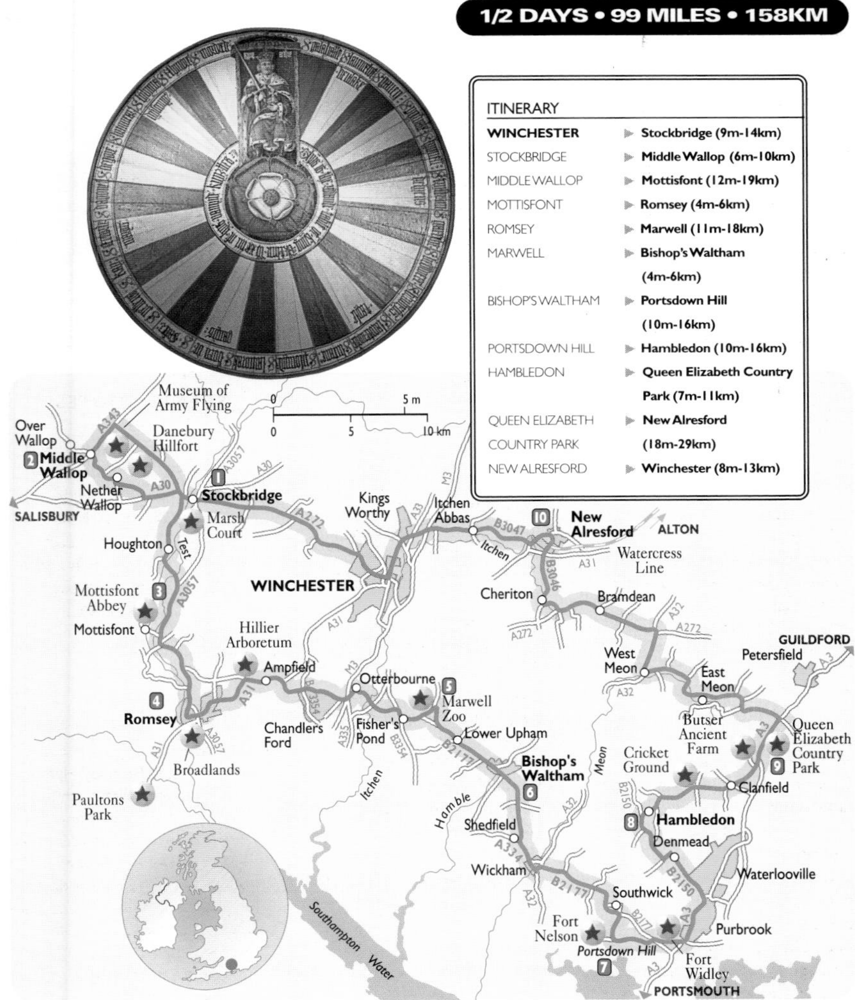

Statue of King Alfred, who made Winchester his capital

[i] *The Guildhall, The Broadway, Winchester*

▶ *Leave Winchester on the* ***A272*** *heading west for 9 miles (14km) to Stockbridge.*

**1 Stockbridge,** Hampshire
A curious 'one-horse' town unique in Hampshire, Stockbridge has a straight main street backed by water-meadows. Before the railways, Welsh cattlemen stopped here with their herds on the way to the great fairs at Farnham and Maidstone. On the north side of High Street, beyond the distinctive porch of the Grosvenor Hotel, is a charming Edwardian garage, a relic of the days of running boards and red flags. Stockbridge has several good antique shops, and exceptional crafts and fishing shops.

Outside the town to the east, Stockbridge Down, above your road of entry, is a downland nature reserve and is home to many rare flowers and butterflies, and Marsh Court, on the back road to King's Somborne, was designed by Lutyens and is partly built of chalk blocks.

RECOMMENDED WALKS

Houghton, on the route south of Stockbridge, is a pretty village on the Test, where the river is at its clearest and most beguiling. Two of Hampshire's major footpaths intersect here. The Clarendon Way, which runs between Salisbury and Winchester, meets rolling downland and lovely woods to east and west; and the Test Way, stretching 50 miles (80km) from the downs to Southampton Water, follows the old 'sprat-and-winkle' railway line along the valley between bursting hedgerows and rippling water.

▶ *Leave Stockbridge by the* ***A30****, then turn right signed Danebury Hillfort and in 2½ miles (4km) turn left on to the* ***A343*** *for Middle Wallop.*

**2 Middle Wallop,** Hampshire
The Wallops, Over, Middle and Nether, take their name from the brook which links these three pretty villages. Built as a wartime RAF base, where 'Cat's Eyes' Cunningham led his nightfighters into battle, the airfield is now the home of the Army Air Corps, and pilots train here in attack, reconnaissance and transport. Inside the modern Museum of Army Flying are many aircraft and ancient balloons, the world's first helicopter, a Tiger Moth and airworthy Sopwiths from World War I, as well as cockpits to clamber into, videos and displays.

FOR HISTORY BUFFS

Danebury Iron Age Hillfort, on the route between Stockbridge and Middle Wallop, is a fine example of a Celtic settlement. There is a small display to illustrate the historical background, and at Andover, a few miles away, the Museum of the Iron Age gives the history of the Celts at Danebury, using sound effects, replica excavations, models and dioramas.

▶ *From Middle Wallop take the road through Nether Wallop to join the* ***A30*** *heading back towards Stockbridge. Just before Stockbridge turn right and follow the unclassified road through Houghton to Mottisfont, a total distance of 12 miles (19km).*

**3 Mottisfont Abbey,** Hampshire
You will find no abbey here, but there is an elegant National Trust property in tree-lined grounds by the River Test; the original priory was converted after the Dissolution. Of special note is Rex Whistler's blue drawing room, with its visual tricks. Gardeners will appreciate the fine old roses here, and it is worth seeking out the 'font', a tamed spring of clear water. If this gives you a thirst, have lunch or tea at the village post office, where you can sit outside under the spreading walnut tree.

This is the heartland of the trout fishing for which the Test is world-famous, and the area is

The 12th-century church is all that remains of Romsey Abbey

jealously guarded, with barbed-wire fences protecting anglers' huts and benches by private manicured paths.

▶ *Return to the* ***A3057*** *and drive for 3 miles (5km) to Romsey.*

**4 Romsey,** Hampshire
A few years ago, travellers here were greeted at every turn by notices reading 'You're in the Strong Country'. Strong's brewery is no more: the waft of hops last drifted here in 1981, and the malthouse you see ahead awaits other uses, but lots of good things survive in this lively little place.

Its greatest treasure is the 12th-century abbey, a fine unspoiled Norman church, which only escaped the ravages of the Dissolution when the townspeople bought it for £100. Buried within is Earl Mountbatten of Burma, who lived at Broadlands. This imposing 18th-century mansion gives on to Capability Brown lawns sweeping down to the Test. Another former owner, Lord Palmerston, still keeps an eye on Romsey from his perch in Market Square. Traffic is poorly managed here, so it is worth parking at Broadlands and walking into town. Children should enjoy the Rapids leisure pool, with its giant flume and swirling water; and if you visit in November, go to Saddler's Mill, where Test Valley salmon perform gymnastic feats to reach their spawning grounds upstream.

*i Bus Station Car Park, Broadwater Road*

BACK TO NATURE

The Hillier Gardens and Arboretum. set in 160 acres (65 hectares), is a unique array of hardy plants, trees and shrubs from all over the world, situated just off the A31 between Ampfield and Braishfield near Romsey. The famous nursery firm, founded by Sir Harold Hillier in 1953, is based at Ampfield House near by, and for a small charge members of the public can enjoy a quiet and gentle stroll in beautiful surroundings. The rhododendrons and azaleas are particularly spectacular in season.

The Museum of Army Flying, Middle Wallop

▶ *Leave Romsey on the **A31** heading east. Shortly after Ampfield, turn right at the Potters Heron signed Chandlers Ford. Cross the **B3043** and drive along Hocombe Road. At a T-junction turn left over the flyover towards Otterbourne. On entering the village turn right on to an unclassified road, cross the River Itchen and the **A335** (dogleg right and left) and proceed along Church Lane, turning at its end on to the **B3354**. Turn right on to the **B2177**, then left for Marwell.*

### FOR CHILDREN

Paultons Park, off the A31 at Ower near Romsey, is a family leisure park offering a wealth of entertainment and activity for children. Opened just a few years ago and set in 140 acres (56 hectares) of beautiful parkland, Paultons grows every year as features are added; it is now the second-largest attraction in the South. A giant adventure playground, an astra glide, bumper boats, train rides and a pets' corner are just a few of the experiences to be had, along with a trip to Captain Blood's cavern.

## 5 Marwell Zoo, Hampshire

Set in the 100-acre (40-hectare) park of a Tudor hall, this is one of the biggest zoos in Britain. The approach here is modern, and the animals enjoy considerable freedom. Marwell's biggest claim to fame is the work done here for animal conservation – rescuing threatened species, breeding from them and returning them to the wild. You might bump into a scimitar-horned oryx or perhaps a Przewalski's horse, both snatched from imminent extinction. Children will particularly enjoy patting pot-bellied pigs in their own farmyard! Also recommended are Marwell's Wonderful Railway and the licensed Treetops restaurant.

*[i] Marwell Zoo Park, Colden Common*

▶ *Return to the **B2177** and continue to Bishop's Waltham.*

## 6 Bishop's Waltham, Hampshire

As you approach, tall flint ruins on the right give a clue as to how the town got its name. For 400 years, Bishops of Winchester lived here in a splendid palace, built in 1135, and all but destroyed by Cromwell's troops. Little remains but the walls of the great hall, but the site is open to the public. In the town centre, shops and houses span eight centuries of architecture, many hiding salvaged palace beams. Look out for the Bishop's Mitre in the Square, last remnant of the Market Hall. The town's history is charted in the small museum in Brook Street.

Four miles (6km) to the south of Bishop's Waltham, on the A334, is the elegant Georgian town of Wickham, birthplace of William of Wykeham, founder of Winchester College and Chancellor of England. As you leave on Bridge Street, watch for the Chesapeake Mill, built in 1820 from the timbers of a captured American Man o' War, the *Chesapeake*.

Peaceful Southwick, further on, is where Eisenhower made his 1944 headquarters at Southwick House. In the village he and Montgomery met world leaders and planned the world's greatest seaborne invasion.

▶ *From Southwick take the Porchester road to Portsdown Hill.*

### 7 Portsdown Hill, Hampshire

The view from Portsdown's chalk heights is one of the finest in Britain. Ahead is Portsmouth and its spreading harbour, home of the Royal Navy, and beyond is the Isle of Wight. In between lies Spithead, where naval fleet reviews take place and, further west, the Solent, now a yachtsman's paradise. Portchester's 3rd-century Roman castle, Nelson's flagship, Victoria's beloved Osborne House and the homes of Charles Dickens and Lord Tennyson are all within sight of Portsdown.

For a fascinating look at history, trek down the tunnels in one of 'Palmerston's follies'. These were giant forts built by the Prime Minister in the 1850s to guard the Solent against the French. Fort Nelson is open to the public.

▶ *From Portsdown Hill take the* ***A3*** *heading northwards, and at Waterlooville turn on to the* ***B2150*** *through Denmead to Hambledon.*

The Bat and Ball at Hambledon is full of cricketing memorabilia

### 8 Hambledon, Hampshire

The cause of Hambledon's worldwide fame lies 2 miles (3km) from its pretty Georgian centre on the Clanfield road. In front of the Bat and Ball pub, a granite monument stands near a thatched hut and beautifully mown sward of grass.

For sporting people the world over, this is a shrine, for it was here on Broadhalfpenny Down that Hambledon got its title 'the cradle of cricket'. It was in Sussex that shepherds first played the game, but here rules were established and skills honed. Nyren, landlord of the Bat and Ball in 1760, was the manager of the village team which, in its day, beat All England – and his victuals were equally good. Players, we are told, 'struck dismay into a round of beef' and his punch was 'such that would have made a cat speak'!

▶ *Leave Hambledon on an unclassified road, passing through Clanfield, then follow Petersfield signs to join the* ***A3****. In a mile (1.5km) turn off for Queen Elizabeth Country Park.*

### 9 Queen Elizabeth Country Park, Hampshire

Set in a deep valley, with steep downland on either side, this is the ideal place to leave the car and stretch your legs. On one side, dense woodland stretches upward; on the other, smooth grassland, speckled with sheep, climbs impressively to the viewpoint on Butser Hill.

Butser Ancient Farm is a reconstruction of real Iron Age farm remains. Here, visitors can walk freely round the huts and pens, finding out for themselves in a unique and graphic way what life was like in the prehistoric age. The Park Centre, with café and shop, organises a host of activities – pony trekking, grass skiing and guided walks are

The Iron Age reconstructed at Butser Ancient Farm
Right: Swan Green, Lyndhurst

daily occurrences, and there are annual 'specials', among them sheep events and in July, the Hampshire Country Fair.

*[i] Queen Elizabeth Country Park, Gravel Hill, Horndean*

▶ *Rejoin the **A3** towards Petersfield, shortly turning left via unclassified roads to East Meon and West Meon. Turn right on to the **A32**, then left at traffic lights on to the **A272** signposted Bramdean. In 4 miles (6km) go right (**B3046**) through Cheriton to New Alresford.*

**10 New Alresford,** Hampshire
Alresford (pronounced Orlsford) is a town rich in history. Built in the 13th century by the Bishops of Winchester as a wool centre, Alresford annually played host to 200,000 sheep, from medieval times to as recently as 1972. The best way to sample its charm is to descend picturesque Broad Street, turning left into Ladywell Lane to the ancient mill on the River Alre, where woollen cloth was fulled – that is, cleaned and thickened – returning to the town centre via The Dean.

Alresford's main attraction is its elegance, and everywhere there are small clues to the town's chequered history. For instance, the steep pitch of the tiled roofs hint at previous thatching. The town was ravaged by a series of fires between the early 15th century and 1689, which spread quickly along the thatch, but the practice continued despite an edict from Winchester banning it.

▶ *Leave Alresford on the **B3046** then turn left on to the **B3047**. In 6 miles (10km) cross the **A33** at Kings Worthy and return to Winchester.*

### SPECIAL TO...

Starting from Alresford and running 10 miles (16km) to Alton through peaceful agricultural scenery, the Watercress Line is a golden chance to enjoy steam-train travel. Volunteers do most of the restoration work, and West Country Pacific carries out most of the mechanical work on this line.

If you want to see how abandoned hulks from Welsh scrap yards are transformed into gleaming and steaming leviathans, stop off at Ropley, where the main restoration work is carried out.

### SCENIC ROUTES

Two stretches on the route epitomise the English village scene at its best. The Wallop brook idles past the thatched cottages of Middle and Nether Wallop between the A343 and the A30.

Cheriton, on the B3046 south of Alresford, is similarly lovely. Look out as you leave it for some really unusual cottages.

Hampshire's gentle valley scenery can be seen to advantage south of Stockbridge.

After threading your way from Houghton across the Test's many rippling carrier streams, there are delightful views from the A3057 across lush water meadows with cornfields and wooded ridges beyond.

**1/2 DAYS • 105 MILES • 168KM**

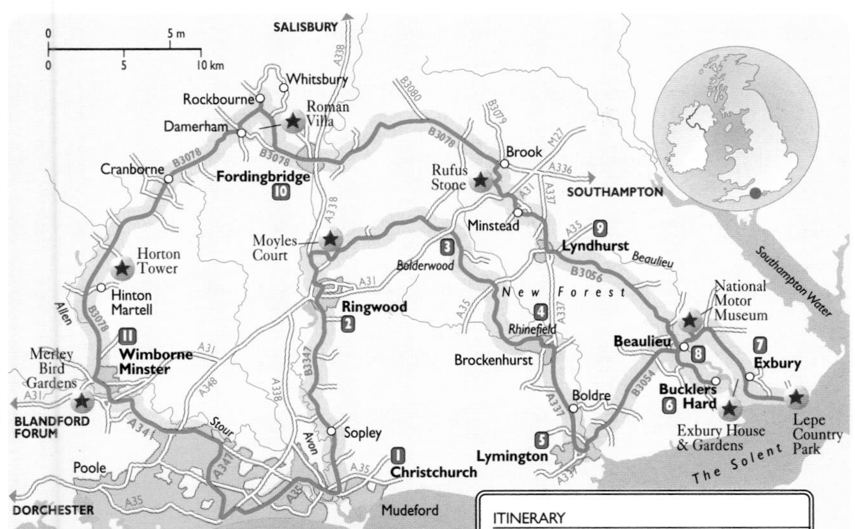

ITINERARY

| | |
|---|---|
| **BOURNEMOUTH** | ▶ **Christchurch (5m-8km)** |
| CHRISTCHURC H | ▶ **Ringwood (10m-16km)** |
| RINGWOOD | ▶ **Bolderwood (10m-16km)** |
| BOLDERWOOD | ▶ **Rhinefield (4m-6km)** |
| RHINEFIELD | ▶ **Lymington (8m-13km)** |
| LYMINGTON | ▶ **Bucklers Hard (8m-13km)** |
| BUCKLERS HARD | ▶ **Exbury (6m-10km)** |
| EXBURY | ▶ **Beaulieu (4m-6km)** |
| BEAULIEU | ▶ **Lyndhurst (7m-11km)** |
| LYNDHURST | ▶ **Fordingbridge (14m-23km)** |
| FORDINGBRIDGE | ▶ **Wimborne Minster (20m-32km)** |
| WIMBORNE MIINSTER | ▶ **Bournemouth (9m-14km)** |

# **Ancient** Hunting Ground of Kings

A combination of seashore, downland and forest should satisfy the appetite of those who like their terrain varied but not too rugged. On the way are picturesque towns and villages reflecting 1,500 years of history, peaceful trout streams flowing south to the sea and, at the heart of the tour, the New Forest, an ancient hunting ground of kings.

Native ponies in the New Forest

*i* *Westover Road, Bournemouth*

▶ *Leave Bournemouth on the **A35** and head east for 5 miles (8km) to Christchurch.*

**1 Christchurch,** Dorset
Formerly Twineham, this town was one of Alfred the Great's walled strongholds against the Danes, between the Rivers Avon and Stour. The walls have long gone, and dominating the busy centre now is the fine 12th-century priory church, the reason for the town's change of name. Legend has it that a beam, cut too short, was lengthened and positioned overnight by a mystery workman, thought to have been Christ. Within easy reach are the museum, art gallery and ancient Place Mill on the Quay.

*i* *23 High Street*

**FOR CHILDREN**

Try a spot of crab fishing at Mudeford, near Christchurch. You will need some simple equipment – a line or string – and a hook is optional: you can tie the bait on instead. The shops on the quayside should have all the necessities. Station yourself by the rails near the shops and have a go.

**RECOMMENDED WALKS**

One different option from the many forest walks on the tour is to sample the seaside breezes at Mudeford. Take the little ferry across the mouth of the harbour, and walk along the beach to Hengistbury, which rises steadily to over 120 feet (36m) – a gentle round trip of 2 to 3 miles (3 to 5km).

▶ *Take the **B3347** to Ringwood.*

**2 Ringwood,** Hampshire
Upstream on the Avon lies this unassuming bustling market town. The trout fishing is good

here, and the town has many attractive Georgian and Queen Anne houses, with a splendid Early English parish church near the bypass. Near by, on the A31, is the Avon Forest Park, with many acres of contrasting meadow, heath and moorland. From Ringwood you can take in the New Forest, which spreads east and north. A narrow road between old gravel pits, converted into reservoirs, brings your first taste of the Forest at Moyles Court. The manor house, now a school, was the home of Alice Lisle, who sheltered the rebellious Duke of Monmouth's men, and was sentenced to death by Judge Jeffreys. The route winds through open heaths and lovely woods to high parts of the Forest, past the spot where naturalist Eric Ashby makes his fascinating films of the badgers, foxes and other creatures that thrive here. If you want to walk you are spoiled for choice: forest tracks with shafting sunlight to your right, high sandy ridges with panoramic views and open heathland to your left.

*i* *The Furlong*

▶ *Leave Ringwood by the **A338** signed Salisbury, then turn right in 2 miles (3km) on to an unclassified road and continue east for about 5 miles (8km) before going under the **A31** for Bolderwood.*

**3 Bolderwood,** Hampshire
Here, in the heart of the New Forest, the Forestry Commission has created three waymarked walks of different lengths among the trees, which range from native oak and beech to foreign wellingtonia. A leaflet helps you identify them as you walk. There are many deer in the New Forest, but normally only the silent, the patient or the fortunate see them – except at the Bolderwood Deer Sanctuary, where a sighting is guaranteed; bring your binoculars. Near by is a memorial among the pines dedicated to Canadian fliers serving at Stony Cross who were killed in the war.

The ponies which wander in parts of the Forest are not wild, but belong to Commoners, people living in the Forest with rights to graze animals (and to an annual ration of free cordwood for their fires). Look out for the brand mark of the owner; every autumn the ponies are rounded up and rebranded, and surplus ponies are sold at the Beaulieu Road sales. Feeding the ponies is illegal.

You might like to stop at the Knightswood Oak, reputedly the oldest in the Forest (600 years old) and 21 feet (7m) round. In the snake pit at Holidays Hill (on the A35, just east of your crossing point), the less squeamish can get a close-up look at the native vipers and adders.

▶ *From Bolderwood follow an unclassified road southeast across the **A35** to Rhinefield.*

**4 Rhinefield,** Hampshire
Towering above you are some of the tallest conifers in Britain – Douglas firs, redwoods and spruces – planted in 1859 as an approach to Rhinefield hunting lodge, now demolished. Behind the drive, on either side, are attractive mixed woodlands of oaks, beeches and pines, through which runs the 1½-mile (2km) Tall Trees nature trail.

Rhinefield House, near by, is a hotel housed in a mad Victorian creation that is half-castle, half-house. You can have a meal or afternoon tea here.

Brockenhurst is a lively and prosperous village, popular as a centre for New Forest camping and touring. Within the shadow of the Norman/Early English church lie the bones of Brusher Mills, New Forest character and killer of snakes.

▶ *From Brockenhurst turn right on to the **A337** for Lymington.*

**5 Lymington,** Hampshire
Signs of Lymington's early prosperity as a salt town, spa and seaport can still be seen in the charming houses which line the quay and the wide High Street climbing the hill. The town enjoys a different sort of maritime wealth these days: it has become a popular yachting centre. The Isle of Wight car ferry snakes down the Lymington River through serried masts of luxury yachts. Two buildings of particular note here are Pressgang Cottage, by the quay; and Georgian St Thomas's Church at the top of High street, unusual for its cupola.

*i* *St Thomas Street Car Park*

▶ *Leave Lymington by the **B3054** signed Beaulieu and*

*in 6 miles (10km), just before Beaulieu, turn right for Bucklers Hard.*

**BACK TO NATURE**

Pennington and Keyhaven Marshes are reached by walking along the sea wall from the car park at Keyhaven, a few miles southwest of Lymington. There are good views across the saltmarsh at low tide and over the pools and marshes inland from the wall. Waders and wildfowl are abundant during the winter and, in summer, several species of terns as well as black-headed gulls grace the area.

**6 Bucklers Hard,** Hampshire
When you leave your car on the edge of Bucklers Hard, prepare to step back in time. Little has changed here since 1800, when this was one of Britain's shipbuilding centres. Three of the ships which fought under Nelson at Trafalgar were built here. Twin rows of shipbuilders' cottages, carefully preserved, slope down to the water, where the slipways were. Some are open for the public to view, and a Maritime Museum tells the story of this unique place.

▶ *From Bucklers Hard turn right for Exbury.*

**7 Exbury,** Hampshire
The name of de Rothschild is synonymous with wealth, and at Exbury House, home of the banking family, no expense was spared to create the magnificent 200-acre (81-hectare) woodland garden, which is open to the public. Crowning glories here are the displays of rhododendrons and azaleas, best seen in late spring.

Exbury Gardens are famous for their rhododendrons and azaleas

Beside the waters of the Solent, Lepe Country Park offers a chance to picnic or walk the shore, with lovely views across to the Isle of Wight. To the east is the Spithead shore near Portsmouth; ahead, Cowes and Osborne, Queen Victoria's final home; and to the west, Yarmouth, Hurst Castle and the open sea. Half a mile (1km) of crumbling concrete marks the point where D-Day's Mulberry Harbour was made. Evenings can be particularly lovely here, and big ships describe wide arcs as they follow the deep water out to sea.

▶ *Return to Beaulieu.*

### 8 Beaulieu, Hampshire

Charming Beaulieu, with its pond and river, is the setting for a world-famous museum. The National Motor Museum stands in the grounds of 13th-century Beaulieu Abbey, home of the Montagus, which retains much beauty despite the destruction wrought after the Dissolution. A monorail winds through the 3rd Baron Montagu's modern show-case for over 250 vintage cars and motorcycles. The collection includes record breakers *Bluebird* and *Thrust 2*, and there are many other attractions in the grounds.

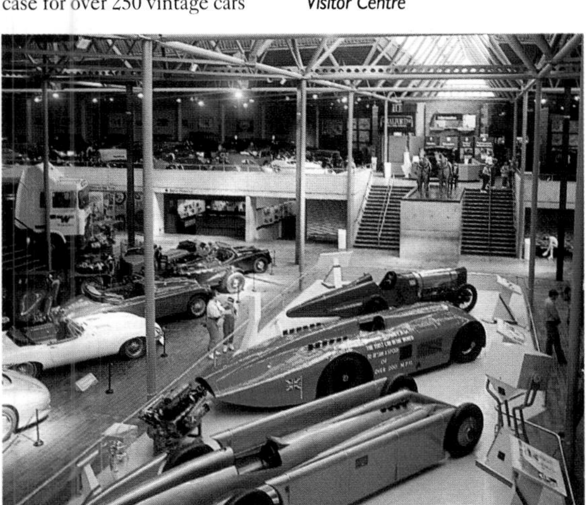

Beaulieu – home of Lord Montagu and his National Motor Museum

*i* *John Montagu Building*

▶ *Take the **B3056** to Lyndhurst.*

### 9 Lyndhurst, Hampshire

Open roads through rolling gorse heathlands bring you to Lyndhurst, the 'capital' of the New Forest, a busy tourist town in the summer. Alice Hargreaves (née Liddell), the original Alice of Lewis Carroll's *Alice in Wonderland*, is buried in Lyndhurst churchyard. At Queen's House the Verderers, guardians since Norman times of Commoners' rights, hold their bi-monthly ancient court on Mondays. They employ agisters to patrol the forest daily, often on horseback, to supervise and control animals grazing on the 90,000 acres (36,423 hectares). Forest ponies have their tails cut specially to indicate their own agister. The New Forest Museum offers an insight into the fascinating history and traditions of the popular area.

*i* *New Forest Museum and Visitor Centre*

▶ *Leave Lyndhurst on the **A337** signposted Cadnam. In 2 miles (3km) turn left through Minstead, then left, immediately left and immediately right to cross the **A31** to Brook, then keep left on the **B3078** for Fordingbridge.*

### 10 Fordingbridge, Hampshire

The comfortable little town of Fordingbridge, on the River Avon, had a quiet time in the 1970s and '80s, but is now coming to life again, with new shops opening and industries arriving. Stand on the old bridge and look for trout or pike. On this spot, during the time of William the Conqueror, a guard was posted to arrest New Forest deer poachers on their only escape route to the west. The fine medieval parish church stands on the Alderholt road.

▶ *Take the **B3078** signed Damerham and follow unclassified roads through Rockbourne, rejoining the **B3078** to Cranborne, and on to Wimborne Minster.*

### 11 Wimborne Minster, Dorset

On the way to Wimborne Minster, you pass through Rockbourne, with its pretty Tudor and Georgian cottages by a stream. To the south of the village is the excavated site of a Roman villa, open to the public. Wimborne Minster itself, though medieval in its street pattern, is no sorry relic of a bygone age. It has a Town Trail which explores its rich heritage of fine medieval and Georgian buildings – details obtainable from the Information Bureau. Central to it all is the Minster, of Saxon origin and curiously chequered in grey and brown stone. After all the history, you might want to browse through the hundreds of stalls at Wimborne's huge week-end market, or visit the model town on King Street.

*i* *29 High Street*

▶ *Leave by the **B3078** crossing the **A31** and immediately bear left via Canford Magna to join the **A341** and the **A347** to Bournemouth.*

#### FOR HISTORY BUFFS

King William II (Rufus or red-haired), son of the Conqueror, fully deserved the fate which met him while out hunting in the New Forest in August 1100. An arrow, supposedly fired by a companion, missed the stag and mortally wounded him. But questions remain. Was it an accident? Was it Sir Walter Tirel who fired the arrow, and then fled to France? Or was it the mysterious Purkes, who took the body to Winchester? You can visit the site of the king's death, marked by the Rufus Stone in a glade just off the A31 near Minstead.

# WALES & THE MARCHES

Caernarfon Castle, begun during Edward I's conquest of Wales

Wales is a small country of great beauty. Few parts of the world can contain as much varied scenery in such a restricted area. North Wales has the nation's highest peaks, in the Snowdon area, but there are dramatic mountain ranges in central and southern Wales, too. The Brecon Beacons, which are a dividing line between the south and the rural midlands, form one of the Welsh National Parks, the others being Snowdonia and the old county of Pembrokeshire. Here, in the narrow strip of land around the coastline, is the Pembroke Coastal National Park, which winds its way round inlets and coves, cliffs and beaches, and is marked by a long-distance footpath. Even in the industrial parts of Wales, especially in the south where the coal valleys are world famous, there is fine hill scenery just a few miles from the old mining towns. Wales is also a land of railways and castles. There are a few main line railways along the north and south coasts and a scenic cross-country route to Aberystwyth, but there are several small, privately or voluntarily operated lines, such as at Ffestiniog, Bala or Llanberis.

Wales has a long history of rebellion and conflict, and centuries of struggle against English rule have left a legacy of imposing fortresses. Caernarfon is probably the outstanding example, built to mark Edward I's conquest of the north. Penrhyn, near Bangor, is really a stately home, providing an ornate illustration of the wealth generated by the North Wales slate industries – for a few, at least.

The Welsh coastline has several popular resorts with sandy beaches, but for quieter attractions venture inland, where the wild landscape is sparsely populated. Wales is a walkers' paradise, and wherever you are you will find walks of all distances to suit all tastes. You should leave the car whenever possible, to enable you to appreciate the landscape to the full.

**Chepstow**
This is a border town which has grown up at a crossing point of the River Wye and is now located conveniently close to the M4. There was an Iron Age as well as a Roman settlement near here, but the town was really created by the Normans. They began to build the castle in 1067, and it still dominates the town from its site over the River Wye. The museum opposite the castle describes the history of the town throughout the ages, and St Mary's parish church is worth a visit.

**Tenby**
Described as 'the Jewel in the Crown of the Welsh Riviera', Tenby's narrow streets and tiny shops are huddled within medieval town walls. This is one of Britain's finest historic towns, containing over 300 buildings of special architectural or historic interest. The picturesque harbour has long been a hub of activity, and there are regular sailings to Caldy Island. Fine sandy beaches and excellent walking provide an abundance of holiday entertainment for young and old.

**Aberystwyth**
Aberystwyth, the largest town and principal shopping centre of mid Wales, is set in the middle of glorious Cardigan Bay, into which flow the rivers Ystwyth and Rheidol. The ruined castle, built by Edward I, overlooks the small harbour in the Rheidol Estuary, and on a hill above the town is the modern campus of the University College of Wales, which includes the National Library of Wales, housing early Welsh manuscripts. The narrow-gauge Vale of Rheidol Railway line runs to the deep gorge of Devil's Bridge, and at the northern end of the beach and promenade the longest electric cliff railway in Britain climbs to the top of Constitution Hill.

Beddgelert is a beautiful wooded village set deep in the heart of the Snowdonia National Park

**Barmouth**
Situated where the mountains meet the sea, this is one of the most picturesque resorts on Cardigan Bay. It has a fine golden beach and a small harbour busy with pleasure craft and fishing boats. Visit the Royal National Life-boat Institution Museum and two other buildings which recreate the history of this area: Tŷ Gwyn, the old lock-up for drunken seamen, and Tŷ Gwyn y Bermo, a restored 15th-century building. After exploring the town you could take a walk alongside the estuary to take in the lovely coastal scenery all around.

**Bangor**
This ancient town, surrounded by water and high mountains in an area of great natural beauty, is a long-established religious centre: the present cathedral was built on the site of a monastery founded in AD525 – earlier than the cathedral in Canterbury. The northern college of the University of Wales is based here, on a high ridge overlooking the city. Bangor sits on the Menai Strait, and you can see the island of Anglesey from its restored pier, or cross the Strait on Telford's Menai Bridge or the later Britannia Bridge. The Museum of Welsh Antiquities traces life in Wales from prehistoric times; and on the outskirts of town is the magnificent Penrhyn Castle.

**2/3 DAYS • 172 MILES • 277KM**

# Castles on the Welsh Marches

This route passes through the Wye and Usk Valleys. The castles built along the Welsh borders are testaments to a turbulent age, when this was an area of constant fighting between the Normans and the Welsh.

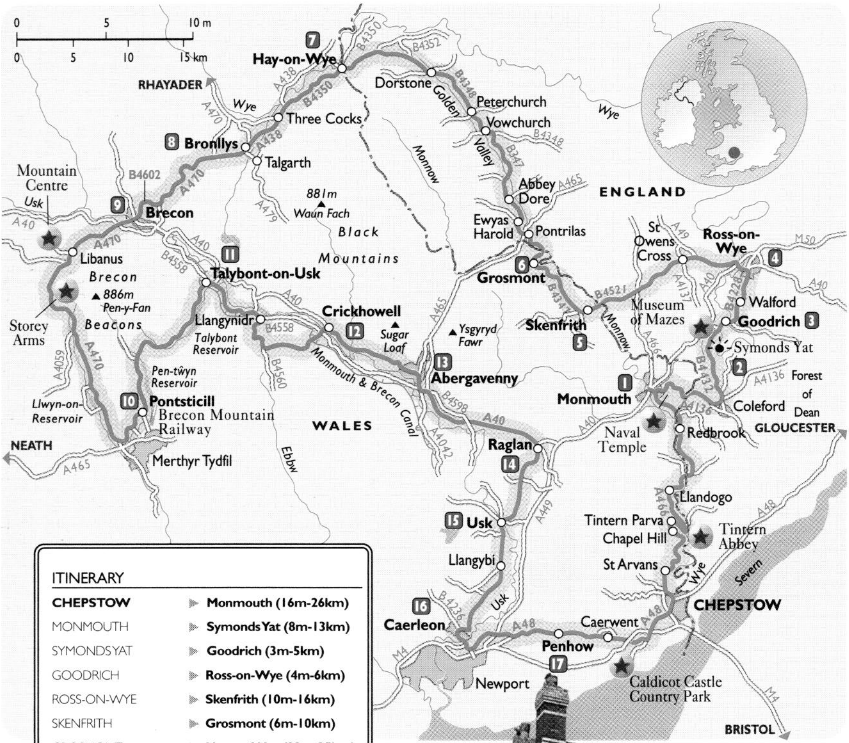

ITINERARY

| | |
|---|---|
| **CHEPSTOW** | ► **Monmouth (16m-26km)** |
| MONMOUTH | ► **Symonds Yat (8m-13km)** |
| SYMONDS YAT | ► **Goodrich (3m-5km)** |
| GOODRICH | ► **Ross-on-Wye (4m-6km)** |
| ROSS-ON-WYE | ► **Skenfrith (10m-16km)** |
| SKENFRITH | ► **Grosmont (6m-10km)** |
| GROSMONT | ► **Hay-on-Wye (22m-35km)** |
| HAY-ON-WYE | ► **Bronllys (8m-13km)** |
| BRONLLYS | ► **Brecon (8m-13km)** |
| BRECON | ► **Pontsticill (20m-32km)** |
| PONTSTICILL | ► **Talybont-on-Usk (11m-18km)** |
| TALYBONT-ON-USK | ► **Crickhowell (11m-18km)** |
| CRICKHOWELL | ► **Abergavenny (7m-11km)** |
| ABERGAVENNY | ► **Raglan (10m-16km)** |
| RAGLAN | ► **Usk (5m-8km)** |
| USK | ► **Caerleon (8m-13km)** |
| CAERLEON | ► **Penhow (7m-11km)** |
| PENHOW | ► **Chepstow (8m-13km)** |

*The Castle Car Park, Chepstow*

▶ *Drive north for 16 miles (26km) on the **A466** to Monmouth.*

**1 Monmouth,** Gwent
Monmouth was an old Roman settlement, but its main growth came after 1066, and in 1673 the 1st Duke of Beaufort built Great Castle House on the site of the old Norman castle. Near Agincourt Square, dominated by the 18th-century Shire Hall, is a statue of C S Rolls, of Rolls Royce fame, whose family lived near here. East of town is Kymin Hill, where the Naval Temple commemorates British admirals. The walk up to it from town follows the line of Offa's Dyke Long Distance Footpath.

*Shire Hall*

**FOR HISTORY BUFFS**

Tintern Abbey, just off the road to Monmouth in the Wye Valley, was a Cistercian foundation in 1131 which survived until the Dissolution of the Monasteries under Henry VIII. The abbey church has survived almost intact, and the ruins of many monastic buildings can still be seen.

▶ *Take the **A4136**, then turn left on to the **B4228** just past Staunton. Bear left on to the **B4332** after a further ½ mile (1km) to Symonds Yat.*

The River Wye, from Symonds Yat
Left: Hay Cinema bookshop

**2 Symonds Yat,** Hereford and Worcester
The scenery of the Wye Valley is among the finest in Britain and Symonds Yat is a particularly impressive beauty spot, above the deep gorge. The river flows for 4 miles (6km) in a large meander before returning to within 400 yards (365m) of the same point. An AA viewpoint on the summit at 473 feet (144m) affords magnificent views.

▶ *Continue north via an unclassified road, turning right on to the **B4227** to Goodrich.*

**3 Goodrich,** Hereford and Worcester
Imposing Goodrich Castle is a red sandstone ruin which

**FOR CHILDREN**

As you enter the Jubilee Maze at the Museum of Mazes in Symonds Yat, you will be met by a maze man, wearing Victorian boating costume. There are 12 routes to the centre, where the Temple of Diana awaits you. Evening illuminations create a labyrinth of eerie shadows. The museum tells the history of mazes, and of magic spells and witchcraft.

Cromwell lost to the Royalists during the Civil War, but then battered with a mortar which fired 200lb (90kg) shots. This dramatically situated castle had a moat which was excavated from solid rock, and you can still look down the 168-foot (51km) well in the courtyard.

▶ *Cross the River Wye and take the **B4228** to Ross-on-Wye.*

**4 Ross-on-Wye,** Hereford and Worcester
The splendid 208-foot (63m) spire of St Mary's Church rises high above the roofs of this attractive town. Interesting old streets spread out from the market place, with its 17th-century red sandstone Market Hall. Notable features include several ancient alms houses and 16th-century Wilton Bridge.

[i] *20 Broad Street*

▶ *Leave on the **A49**, then the **B4521** Abergavenny road to Skenfrith.*

**5 Skenfrith,** Gwent
Skenfrith Castle was built as one of a group of three castles, along with Grosmont and White, to guard the Marches against Welsh uprisings. Its remains include a central keep enclosed by a four-sided curtain wall and a moat. A small stone village clusters round the castle, with a quaint little 13th-century church and a mill with a working water wheel.

▶ *Continue along the **B4521**, then turn north on to the **B4347** to Grosmont.*

**6 Grosmont,** Gwent
Set on a hillside by the River Monnow, Grosmont is the site of another Norman fortress, taken and re-taken several times during the Welsh uprisings of the 13th to 15th centuries. The castle ruins can be reached by footpath from the town. Grosmont's 13th-century parish church is noted for its huge but crude effigy of an armoured knight. At Abbey Dore, further along the road, the abbey remains include a vast, atmospheric church, tucked away in the Golden Valley.

▶ *Follow the **B4347**, then the **B4348** through the Golden Valley and on to Hay-on-Wye.*

**7 Hay-on-Wye,** Powys
Hay stands high above the southern bank of the River Wye.

Hay Castle was built by the Marcher Lord William de Braose

Folk hero Owain Glyndŵr destroyed its castle during the 15th century, but the keep, parts of the walls and a gateway remain. The town's cinema has become the biggest second-hand book shop in the world; in fact the whole town seems to be taken up with second-hand books.

[i] *The Car Park*

▶ *Head southwest for 8 miles (13km) along the **B4350** and **A438** to Bronllys.*

**8 Bronllys,** Powys
From Bronllys there are clear views of the Brecon Beacons ahead and the Black Mountains, which dominate the scenery to the left. The 12th-century church, now rebuilt, has a very odd detached tower, and a stone-built Malt House is still in excellent condition and contains its original equipment. Bronllys Castle is half a mile (1km) along the A479.

▶ *From Bronllys take the **A438**, the **A470** and the **B4602** to Brecon.*

### 9 Brecon, Powys

Brecon is a pure delight, encircled by hills at the meeting point of the Rivers Usk and Honddu. The cathedral, originally the church of a Benedictine priory, dates mainly from the 13th and 14th centuries, and Brecon Castle is now in the grounds of the Castle Hotel. The County Hall houses the Brecknock Museum, with its wealth of local history, and the South Wales Borderers Army Museum has relics ranging from the Zulu War in 1879 to World War II and later. East of town is the terminus of the Monmouth and Brecon Canal, and to the south is the Brecon Beacons National Park. The Mountain Centre, off the A470, west of the little village of Libanus, is an ideal starting point for exploring the Park.

*i Cattle Market Car Park; The Mountain Centre, Libanus*

**SPECIAL TO...**

Brecon's Brecknock Museum has a superb display of Welsh lovespoons, traditional gifts of betrothal which were carved out of single pieces of wood. From the 17th to the 19th centuries the lovespoon developed into complex and intricate works of art, with keys, bells and other motifs worked into the design.

▶ *Continue southwards along the* ***A470*** *then take unclassified roads northwards to Pontsticill.*

**RECOMMENDED WALKS**

A good starting point for walking on the Brecon Beacons is at Storey Arms on the A470, which is at 1,425 feet (427m) above sea-level and gives the shortest route to Pen y Fan, the highest point in the Beacons. Be sure to take an OS map, food supplies and weatherproof clothes, even in fine weather.

### 10 Pontsticill, Mid Glamorgan

Walking and boating are major attractions in this area; or you could have a journey on the steam train of the Brecon Mountain Railway, which runs for 4 miles (6km) down the valley, through splendid scenery.

▶ *Take unclassified roads to Talybont-on-Usk.*

### 11 Talybont-on-Usk, Powys

This delightful little village is now a tourist centre, especially for walkers and outdoor activities; there is an Outdoor Pursuits Centre in the old railway station. The 18th-century Monmouth and Brecon Canal, which passes through the village, was built to carry coal and iron ore. It eventually closed in 1962, but was reopened by volunteers in 1970 for use by pleasure craft.

▶ *Follow the* ***B4558*** *to Llangynidr, then the* ***B4560*** *and an unclassified road to Crickhowell.*

### 12 Crickhowell, Powys

The name of this little market town is derived from the Iron Age fort Crug Hywel (Howell's Cairn). The town grew up around Alisby's Castle, which was captured and destroyed in 1403 by Owain Glyndŵr, and is now a picturesque ruin. The River Usk is crossed by an old bridge, dating from the 17th century, which appears to have 13 arches on one side but only 12 on the other – the result of 19th-century alterations.

▶ *Take the* ***A40*** *to Abergavenny.*

### 13 Abergavenny, Gwent

At the edge of the Brecon Beacons National Park Abergavenny, the 'Gateway to the Vale of Usk', is overlooked by the Sugar Loaf mountain, 1,955 feet (596m) high, and Ysgyryd (Skirrid) Fawr, 1,595 feet (486m). Its ruined castle was founded in 1090. Impressive buildings in the town include the stone tythe barn, and the red sandstone Lloyds Bank. St Mary's Church is built on the site of a former Benedictine priory.

Working a lock on the Brecon and Monmouth Canal

*i Swan Meadow, Cross Street*

▶ *Continue along the* ***A40*** *to Raglan.*

### 14 Raglan, Gwent

One of Britain's finest ruins is 15th-century Raglan Castle which was actually built as a fortified manor. The keep is outside the main castle and Parliamentary troops overcame the Royalists here during the Civil War, by approaching from the opposite side. The castle houses an exhibition on the history of Raglan.

▶ *Follow an unclassified road south to Usk.*

### 15 Usk, Gwent

Usk is a small market town on the site of an ancient Roman settlement, *Burrium*. Visit the church to see the remarkable restored Tudor rood screen; and, at the other end of the town, the Gwent Rural Life Museum, in an old stone malt barn, which is

Raglan Castle was the last to fall to Cromwell in the Civil War
Right: Dylan Thomas's writing shed, Laugharne

crammed with exhibits about life in the area. Usk Castle is privately owned but you can visit the ruins of the Priory next to the church.

▶ *Cross the river and continue along unclassified roads for 8 miles (13km) to Caerleon.*

**16 Caerleon,** Gwent
One of the four permanent Roman legions in Britain was based here, and parts of the Roman city of *Isca* are displayed in an excellent new exhibition room. The major find has been the amphitheatre outside the city walls. This oval earth mound seated 5,000 people, and is the only fully excavated amphitheatre in Britain. The Legionary Museum has more information and relics from the barracks.

▶ *Take the* ***B4236****, then an unclassified road to join the* ***A48*** *for Penhow.*

**17 Penhow,** Gwent
The oldest inhabited castle in Wales is Penhow Castle, which is perched on a hillside above the main road. Now privately owned, it is open to the public and is an excellent example of the smaller type of fortified manor house.

Three miles (5km) further is Caerwent, on the site of *Venta Silurium*, the only walled Roman civilian town in Wales. Remnants of the wall and mosaic pavements can still be seen. Caldicot Castle Country Park, 2 miles (3km) away, surrounds the 12th-century castle.

▶ *Continue straight along the* ***A48*** *to Chepstow.*

BACK TO NATURE

The Forest of Dean is an excellent area for the birdwatcher. Woodpeckers, tits and nuthatches can be see, and pied flycatchers are often spotted at the RSPB's Nagshead reserve, where nest boxes encourage the species.

# The Pembroke Coast National Park

**2 DAYS • 137 MILES • 219KM**

The old county of Pembrokeshire has a magnificent coastline. The inland scenery, though less dramatic, is enhanced by pretty villages and several fine castles.

ITINERARY

| | |
|---|---|
| **TENBY** | ▶ **Manorbier (6m-10km)** |
| MANORBIER | ▶ **Lamphey (5m-8km)** |
| LAMPHEY | ▶ **Pembroke (2m-3km)** |
| PEMBROKE | ▶ **Haverfordwest (11m-18km)** |
| HAVERFORDWEST | ▶ **Solva (13m-21km)** |
| SOLVA | ▶ **St David's (3m-5km)** |
| ST DAVID'S | ▶ **Mathry (9m-14km)** |
| MATHRY | ▶ **Fishguard (7m-11km)** |
| FISHGUARD | ▶ **Newport ( 8m-13km)** |
| NEWPORT | ▶ **Cardigan (11m-18km)** |
| CARDIGAN | ▶ **Drefach Felindre (15m-24km)** |
| DREFACH FELINDRE | ▶ **Carmarthen (15m-24km)** |
| CARMARTHEN | ▶ **Laugharne (13m-21km)** |
| LAUGHARNE | ▶ **Pendine (6m-9km)** |
| PENDINE | ▶ **Saundersfoot (9m-14km)** |
| SAUNDERSFOOT | ▶ **Tenby (4m-6km)** |

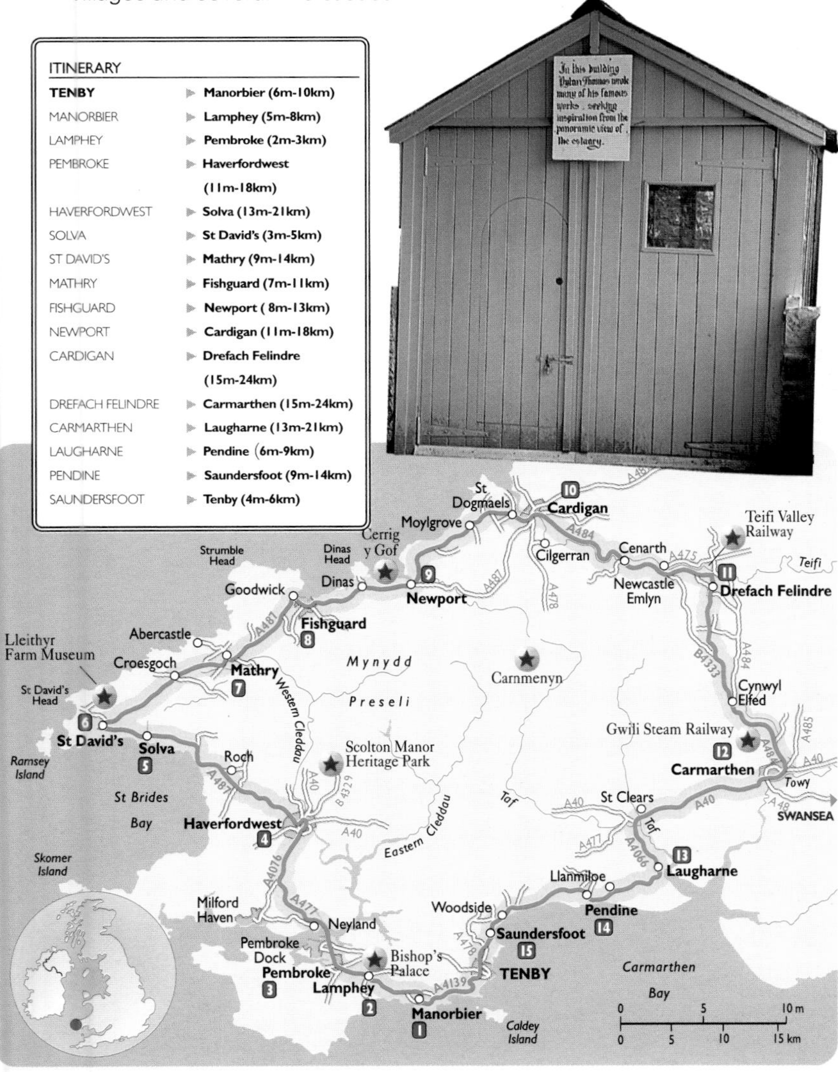

# TOUR 11 **The Pembroke** Coast National Park

[i] *The Croft, Tenby*

▶ *Leave Tenby on the **A4139** and then turn left on to the **B4585** to Manorbier.*

**1 Manorbier,** Dyfed
The medieval traveller and scholar, Gerald of Wales (Giraldus Cambrensis), was born here in 1147 and described it as the 'pleasantest spot in Wales'. There is a castle dating from Gerald's time, which gives an impressive view out to sea from the ramparts. The sandy beach has rocky pools, and is a perfect playground for the children.

▶ *Return to the **A4139** for 5 miles (8km) to Lamphey.*

**2 Lamphey,** Dyfed
The romantic ruins of a 13th-century Bishop's Palace lie to the northeast of Lamphey. The Palace, with its ornate parapets, fishponds and notable 16th-century chapel, was built as a country retreat for the Bishops of St David's. At Herberts Moor Open Farm you can wander round the nature trail, as well as seeing the farmyard animals and pets.

▶ *Continue for another 2 miles (3km) along the **A4139** to Pembroke.*

**3 Pembroke,** Dyfed
This ancient town was built around the great fortress of Pembroke Castle, the largest castle in the area, and the birthplace of Henry Tudor. It still has its fine round keep, and beneath the castle is a huge natural cavern known as The Wogan. A more modern building is the Power Station, which runs guided tours throughout the summer months. Pembroke still retains some of its original town wall, and has an interesting Museum of the Home.

[i] *The Commons Road*

▶ *Take the **A477**, then join the **A4076** to Haverfordwest – 11 miles (18km).*

**4 Haverfordwest,** Dyfed
The castle here now houses the museum and art gallery. St Mary's Church has exquisite Early English-style lancet windows and the mutilated effigy of a pilgrim with scallops on his satchel. The town is cut in two by the River Cleddau.

[i] *Old Bridge*

**FOR CHILDREN**

Scolton Manor, 4 miles (6km) northeast of Haverfordwest, is set in magnificent grounds where there is plenty to keep children occupied: nature trails, guided walks, an adventure playground and play area, exhibitions and, in the summer months, a vintage car rally and model aircraft show.

Tenby Harbour overlooks two bays

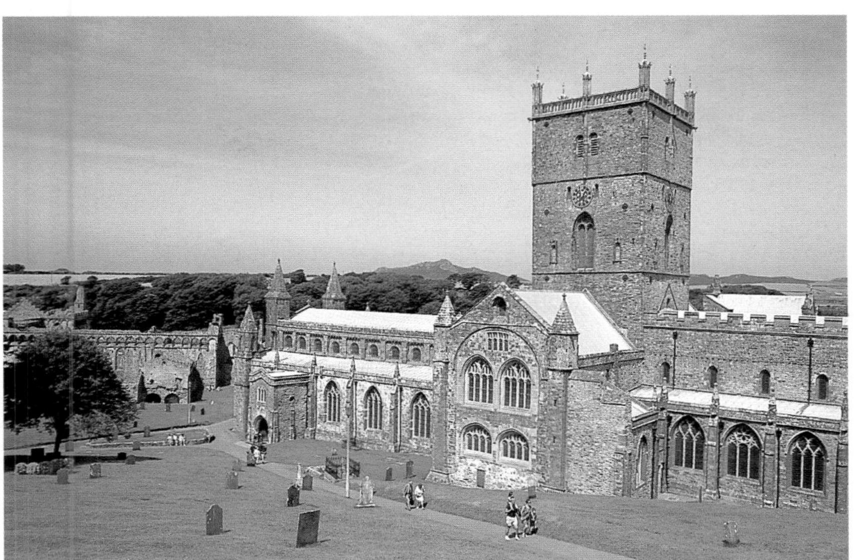

St David lies buried in the town which bears his name

▶ *Head northwest along the **A487** to Solva.*

**5 Solva,** Dyfed
Solva's old port still has warehouses and a restored lime kiln, and is a favourite sailing spot. The tiny, beautiful bay set on a coastline of cliffs is now also noted for the tropical butterfly farm or Nectarium, where you can see butterflies close up, as well as caterpillars, locusts and spiders.

▶ *Keep on along the **A487** for 3 miles (5km) to St David's.*

**6 St David's,** Dyfed
The city of St David's – the smallest in Britain – was founded on the site of an early Christian community, and is dominated by the cathedral and the graceful, walled Bishop's Palace. Also in the city is the Oceanarium, a purpose-built sea aquarium, and the Marine Life Centre, where over 70 species of local marine creatures can be seen. The outdoor rural life of the past can be seen in the Lleithyr Farm Museum, which has one of the largest Welsh collections of agricultural implements.

*i* *City Hall*

**BACK TO NATURE**

St David's Head has some superb coastal scenery and a wonderful display of coastal heathland flowers. Look for ling, bell heather and dwarf gorse growing alongside thrift and sea campion. For the best views of seabirds, visit Stackpole, or better still Skomer Island, a few miles off the coast and reached by ferry from Martin's Haven. Puffins, razorbills, kittiwakes, lesser black-backed gulls and choughs all put on a fine display.

**SPECIAL TO...**

A boat trip around Pembrokeshire's offshore islands with the Thousand Islands Company at St David's takes you on a 50-mile (80km) voyage past the highest sea cliffs in Wales, the longest sea caves and the largest grey seal colony, on Ramsey Island. The boat speeds over strong tidal currents in the narrows between the islands, including the notorious Bitches of Ramsey Sound, with its 20mph tidal current.

**RECOMMENDED WALKS**

Walk from St David's cathedral to the coast at Whitesand Bay. If you wish to add 2 miles (3km) and double the length of this walk, go north and do a round tour of St David's Head.

▶ *Turn northeastwards, still on the **A487** to Mathry.*

**7 Mathry,** Dyfed
This little village overlooks the Western Cleddau source stream. Mountain bikes can be hired for rides into the Preseli Hills, from where 33 dolerite stones were transported to Stonehenge. Northwest of Mathry is Abercastle, where there is a burial chamber with a 16-foot (5m) capstone resting on three of its original seven supports.

▶ *Continue along the **A487** to Fishguard.*

**8 Fishguard,** Dyfed
Fishguard has two parts. Upper Fishguard stands back from the sea, and from it the road falls

steeply to Lower Fishguard, a quaint and largely unspoilt town. There are many ancient links with boating here, and also with textiles. Tregwynt Mill draws on centuries of skill and craftsmanship to produce quality woollen goods. The July Fishguard Music Festival is another attraction. For a windblown and bracing day, take a return trip on the ferry to Rosslare, across the Irish Sea.

*[i] 4 Hamilton Street*

▶ *Head east to Newport, still travelling on the **A487**.*

**9 Newport,** Dyfed
Just outside the town is the Cilgwyn Candle Workshop, where you can see handmade candles being produced, and the Mini Museum, next door, has displays on the history of candle making. The remains of Newport's 12th-century castle can still be seen and the owners, the Baronry of Cemaes, still have the power to appoint the Mayor.

One and a half miles (2.5km) west of town is Cerrig y Gof, a group of burial chambers forming a circle, an arrangement unique to Wales.

▶ *Turn left along unclassified roads through Moylgrove and St Dogmael's, then take the **B4546** to Cardigan.*

The Ship Inn, Fishguard

**10 Cardigan,** Dyfed
St Dogmael's Abbey, just outside Cardigan, was founded in 1115, and the ruins include large fragments of the north and west walls standing almost to their original height. One of Cardigan's most striking architectural features is the ancient bridge, which spans the River Teifi, but little now remains of Cardigan Castle, where the first National Eisteddfod took place in 1176.

The magnificent towers of Cilgerran Castle, best reached from along the A484, overlook the gorge of the Teifi just upstream from the town. Watch out for the coracle demonstrations in the Cardigan Wildlife Park, and there is a coracle centre and mill at Cenarth, a few miles along the A484.

*[i] Theatr Mwldan, Bath House Road*

▶ *Follow the **A484**, then turn right along an unclassified road to Drefach Felindre.*

**11 Drefach Felindre,** Dyfed
Just before the turning to Drefach Felindre, a left turn leads to the Teifi Valley Railway at Henllan, where tiny engines pull the trains along a narrow-gauge railway. The Teifi valley has long been a woollen producing area, and the Museum of the Welsh Woollen Industry is in the town near a large leisure centre.

There are still a few small mills in the area where you can see the cloth being made. The original mill building houses an exhibition showing the processes involved in making the cloth, and there are demonstrations of spinning and weaving.

▶ *Continue south along unclassified roads to join the **B4333**, then the **A484** to Carmarthen.*

**12 Carmarthen,** Dyfed
Carmarthen is believed to be the oldest town in Wales, and the birthplace of Merlin. Remains of Roman occupation include an amphitheatre site. The Gwili Steam Railway, opened in 1860, but closed in 1973 when the milk traffic was transferred to road tankers, was reopened by volunteers in 1978 and now operates for 1.6 miles (2.5km) from Bronwydd Arms to Llwyfan Cerrig, following the course of the River Gwili. A nature trail has been developed

Gwili Steam Railway, Bronwydd Arms Station

at Llwyfan Cerrig and there is also a children's activity area.

[i] *Lammas Street*

► *Go west along the **A40**, turning left at St Clears to join the **A4066** for Laugharne.*

**13 Laugharne,** Dyfed
Laugharne had a strong influence on Dylan Thomas, and the town hall, clock tower and many of the people became part of *Under Milk Wood*. Thomas moved into the Boathouse with his family in 1949 and along the path to it is 'The Shack', which became his workshop. The Boathouse is now a museum, Dylan Thomas is buried in the local churchyard and there is a festival of his work every third year in July. The castle by the sea was built in the 12th century, but the present building is mainly Tudor.

► *Continue along the **A4066** to Pendine.*

**14 Pendine,** Dyfed
Pendine is best noted for its golden sand, on which Sir Malcolm Campbell and others made land speed record attempts. Amy Johnson took off from here in 1933 for the start of her epic transatlantic flight. Nowadays the beach is used for bathing and some fishing, and there are beautiful cliff walks near by.

► *Take the **B4314**, then unclassified roads following the coast to Saundersfoot.*

**15 Saundersfoot,** Dyfed
This 19th-century fishing port and coal port has become a family holiday centre with three sandy beaches, rock pools and a sheltered harbour. Boats are available for fishing and pleasure trips. The village is in a sheltered valley, and there are good walks along the coast.

[i] *The Harbour*

► *Drive south along the **B4316**, then the **A478** back to Tenby.*

**SCENIC ROUTES**

There are superb views of the coastline on the route from Pendine to Saundersfoot.

**FOR HISTORY BUFFS**

Ancient settlements were numerous in the Preseli Hills and elsewhere in southwest Wales; among the important Bronze Age relics are those at Carnmenyn. An ancient route known as the Great West Road passes a pile of rocks called Mynachlog Ddu; the bluestone which is also found at Stonehenge.

TOUR
12

# Land of Rivers & Mountains

From the sandy beach of Borth and the muddy estuary of the Dyfi, this drive takes you through the man-made scenery of Llyn Clywedog – a striking contrast with the wild hills all around. There are rivers and waterfalls, wooded valleys and wide rolling hills.

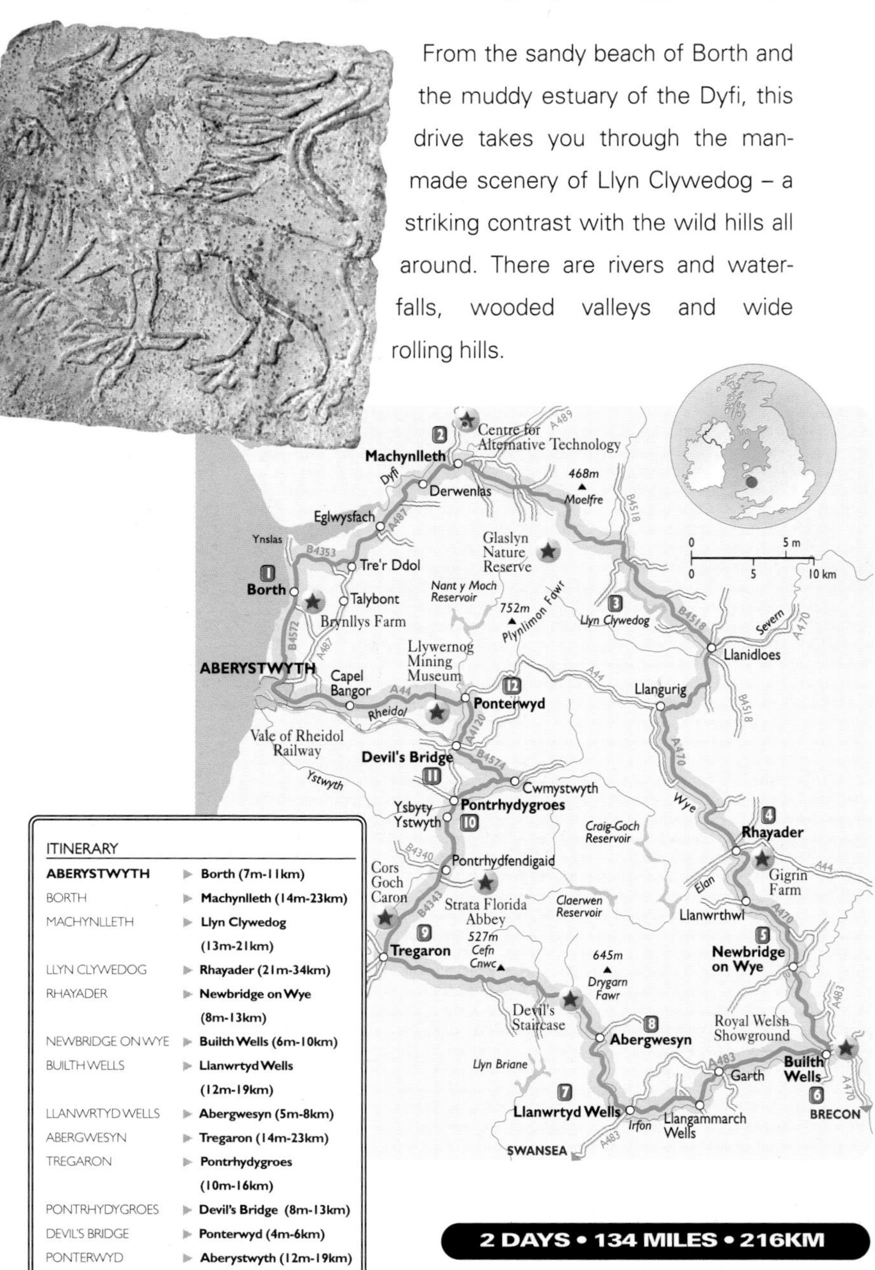


ITINERARY

| | |
|---|---|
| **ABERYSTWYTH** | ▶ **Borth (7m-11km)** |
| BORTH | ▶ **Machynlleth (14m-23km)** |
| MACHYNLLETH | ▶ **Llyn Clywedog (13m-21km)** |
| LLYN CLYWEDOG | ▶ **Rhayader (21m-34km)** |
| RHAYADER | ▶ **Newbridge on Wye (8m-13km)** |
| NEWBRIDGE ON WYE | ▶ **Builth Wells (6m-10km)** |
| BUILTH WELLS | ▶ **Llanwrtyd Wells (12m-19km)** |
| LLANWRTYD WELLS | ▶ **Abergwesyn (5m-8km)** |
| ABERGWESYN | ▶ **Tregaron (14m-23km)** |
| TREGARON | ▶ **Pontrhydygroes (10m-16km)** |
| PONTRHYDYGROES | ▶ **Devil's Bridge (8m-13km)** |
| DEVIL'S BRIDGE | ▶ **Ponterwyd (4m-6km)** |
| PONTERWYD | ▶ **Aberystwyth (12m-19km)** |

**2 DAYS • 134 MILES • 216KM**

Rock-hopping at Aberystwyth
Left: carving, Strata Florida Abbey

[i] *Terrace Road, Aberystwyth*

► *Follow the coast northwards for 6 miles (10km) along the* ***A487*** *and the* ***B4572*** *to Borth.*

**1 Borth,** Dyfed
Three miles (5km) of sand can be found just to the north of this small village, which consists mainly of one street of cottages. Brynllys Farm near by demonstrates organic farming methods; there are nature walks here, and an information centre explains the farm's policies. Strong boots or wellingtons are advisable.

► *Head inland along the* ***B4353****, then turn left on to the* ***A487*** *at Tre'r Ddol and follow it through to Machynlleth.*

**SPECIAL TO...**

Ynyslas is the area of sand dunes to the north of Borth which block off much of the Dyfi estuary from the sea. Behind the dune is an expanse of reclaimed marsh; this area is now a major nature reserve. Ferries used to run across the estuary to Aberdyfi, and remains of a refuge tower can still be seen, where passengers could wait if they became stranded by the incoming tide.

**2 Machynlleth,** Powys
On the journey to Machynlleth, pause to visit the old Wesleyan chapel at Tre'r Ddol which is now a museum of religious life in Wales; further along the road, Eglwysfach has a recently restored waterwheel near the old Dyfi furnace. Machynlleth itself is the chief market town of the Dyfi Valley and gained fame in the 15th century as the seat of Owain Glyndŵr's short-lived Welsh parliament. The Owain Glyndŵr Centre houses an exhibition of his campaigns. The Centre for Alternative Technology, to the north of the town, is a fascinating place to visit. Here you can see a whole Green Community at work, using windmills, solar panels and water-driven machinery. There is an ecological maze to explore, a restaurant and children's play area. You can see a traditional form of energy at Felin Crewi, just outside the town, one of Wales' last working water mills.

[i] *Canolfan Owain Glyndŵr*

**BACK TO NATURE**

The Glaslyn Nature Reserve, off the road between Machynlleth and Llanidloes, contains heather moorland and blanket bog, together with small areas of scree, crag, rough grass and narrow river valley. Breeding birds include pipits, wheatears, ring ouzel and red grouse, and red kites, peregrines and merlins are sometimes seen.

► *Leave on the* ***A489****, then take the unclassified road south-eastwards to join the* ***B4518*** *and on to Llyn Clywedog.*

**3 Llyn Clywedog,** Powys
This reservoir, built between 1964 and 1968, has the highest concrete dam of its kind in Britain – 237 feet (72m) high – and holds up to 11,000 million gallons (50,000 million litres) of water behind it. There are excellent views of the surrounding hill country from the dam and Glyndŵr's Way and other waymarked walks follow the Clywedog valley.

Four miles (6km) further is Llanidloes, the first town on the River Severn, and there are several interesting buildings along its tree-lined streets. The most famous is the 16th-century half-timbered Market Hall, with its open ground floor – one of the last of its kind in Wales; the upper floor now houses a museum.

*Longbridge Street*

► *Drive southwards along the* ***A470*** *from Llanidloes for 21 miles (34km) to Rhayader.*

**RECOMMENDED WALKS**

Llanidloes is a marvellous centre for walking with Owain Glyndŵr's Way and the Cross Wales Walk both passing through the town. Shorter walks include Allt Goch, which takes less than an hour and gives excellent views over the town and the Severn valley.

### 4 Rhayader, Powys

This small market town on the River Wye is an ideal centre for visiting the 'Lakeland of Wales'. The lakes are the reservoirs of the Elan valley, which provide Birmingham with its water supply. Pony trekking and angling are particularly popular here. Although Rhayader is now a peaceful little town, it has had its share of excitment in the past. The 19th-century Rebecca riots, protesting against toll gate impositions, centred around the town, and the castle was destroyed during the Civil War. At the Welsh Royal Crystal Glass Factory you can watch the art of glass-blowing, and there are numerous craft shops and a pottery. Gigrin Farm, ½ mile (1km) to the south, offers a farm trail of nearly 2 miles (3km) in beautiful surroundings, and there are pets and a children's playground.

*Leisure Centre, North Street*

**BACK TO NATURE**

The Elan Visitor Centre, near Rhayader, organises guided walks for bird watchers. Golden plover, ring ouzel and dunlin nest near by, and there are red grouse and a few merlins up on the moors. Dippers, grey wagtails and a flashing blue kingfisher may be seen on the streams, and the rare kite floats around overhead.

► *Follow the* ***A470*** *to Newbridge on Wye.*

### 5 Newbridge on Wye, Powys

The 'new' bridge of the town's name was built in 1910 to replace an old wooden structure. The church was founded in the late 19th century by the Venables-Llewellyn family, who own Llysdinam Hall. There is a Field Study Centre in the Hall's grounds belonging to the University of Wales' Institute of Science and Technology.

► *Continue southwards on the* ***A470*** *to Builth Wells.*

### 6 Builth Wells, Powys

Builth Wells was one of a string of Welsh spa towns which drew crowds of health-seeking Victorians, but it was an important centre long before that. The castle was built in Norman times by James de San George, who was also responsible for Harlech, Caernarfon, Beaumaris and Conwy castles. The Wyeside Arts Centre provides a fine selection of entertainment throughout the summer with films, exhibitions and theatre. Just outside town, in the village of Llanelwedd, is the Royal

Newbridge on Wye

Welsh Showground, which hosts the Royal Welsh Agricultural Show in July.

[i] *Groe Car Park*

▶ *Take the **A483**, then turn left along unclassified roads at Garth to Llanwrtyd Wells.*

**7 Llanwrtyd Wells,** Powys
The smallest town in Britain, Llanwrtyd Wells is situated on the River Irfon. There are still traces of Victorian grandeur recalling the town's heyday, when travellers flocked here to sample its sulphur water – which can still be smelt along the river. The Abergwesyn Pass, which leads over the mountain from Llanwrtyd, has some Wales' finest scenery. On the A483 is the Cambrian Factory, where you can see traditional Welsh tweed being spun and woven.

▶ *Drive northwards into the hills along an unclassified road to Abergwesyn, 5 miles (8km).*

**8 Abergwesyn,** Powys
The mountain road from Abergwesyn to Tregaron is one of Britain's most spectacular roads. It was originally a drovers' route, used to take cattle to the Midlands and London in the 18th and 19th centuries, and there are amazing views near the Devil's Staircase, a steep and tortuous zig-zag section of the road.

▶ *Take the mountain road to Tregaron.*

**9 Tregaron,** Dyfed
At the foot of steep hills, and at the southern end of a great expanse of bog, Tregaron is a popular pony trekking centre.

Cors Goch Caron, the Red Bog

The often bleak and misty marshland, Cors Goch Caron, was formerly a lake fed by the River Teifi, and is now a National Nature Reserve, with restricted public access. Tregaron is a small, Welsh-speaking community, famous as the birthplace of outlaw Twm Sion Catti, and of Henry Richard, the 'Apostle of Peace' who founded the Peace Union, forerunner of the League of Nations.

▶ *Follow the **B4343** for 10 miles (16km) to Pontrhydygroes and the **B4574** to Cwmystwyth, 4 miles (6km) further*

**10 Pontrhydygroes,** Dyfed
The village of Pontrhydygroes grew around the lead-mining industry and is now a quiet

Devil's Bridge straddles the lovely Mynach Gorge

community set among wooded hills. The surrounding area was part of the Hafod estate in the 18th century, where Thomas Johnes began the task of afforesting the land. Further along, Cwmystwyth is another old mining settlement; the mines here were once worked by the Romans and the monks of Strata Florida Abbey.

> *Head northwest along the **B4574** for another 4 miles (6km) to Devil's Bridge.*

### 11 **Devil's Bridge,** Dyfed

The River Mynach meets the River Rheidol here to create spectacular falls over 300 feet (91m) high. Three bridges were built across the chasm, one above the other, and Devil's Bridge is the earliest one, probably the 12th-century work of the monks from nearby Strata Florida Abbey. The higher bridges date from 1753 and the early 20th century. Ninety-one steep steps, called Jacob's Ladder, lead down to the river. The narrow-gauge Vale of Rheidol Railway climbs 680 feet (207m) in the 12 miles (19km) from Aberystwyth along a breathtakingly scenic route to terminate at Devil's Bridge Station.

> *Take the **A4120** northwards to Ponterwyd.*

### 13 **Ponterwyd,** Dyfed

This small cluster of houses round a craggy gorge featured in the writings of 19th-century traveller George Borrow, whose book *Wild Wales* relates his stay at the village inn, now the Borrow Arms. A mile west of the village is the Llwernog Silver-Lead Mine and there are fine views stretching to Cardigan Bay from Bwlch Nant-yr-Arian Visitor Centre, further along the road.

> *Head east along the **A44** back to Aberystwyth.*

#### FOR HISTORY BUFFS

On the road from Tregaron to Pontrhydygroes you will pass the ruins of the Cistercian Strata Florida Abbey, founded in 1164. It was here, in 1238, that Llywelyn the Great gathered all the Welsh princes to swear allegiance to his son Dafydd. The abbey fell into disrepair after the Dissolution, but the magnificent Norman arch still remains.

#### FOR CHILDREN

Gold, silver, lead and copper were mined from the rocks of the Cambrian Mountains in former centuries, and many of the relics of these days can still be seen.
The Llywernog Silver-Lead Mine near Ponterwyd has many old machines, some of which have been restored to make a fascinating working museum. You can try your hand at panning for gold and working the hand pumps, and visit the underground drift mine, with its floodlit cavern.

#### SCENIC ROUTES

Just before descending into Borth there are fine views of the sandy coast with the estuary and hills beyond. There are magnificent hill views all around Clywedog; as well as on the minor roads near Abergwesyn and the B4574 near Cwmystwyth.

# Water, Water Everywhere

Follow the magnificent coastline with glorious sandy beaches before turning inland and heading into the hills. Tumbling rivers and large lakes are constant companions from Trawsfynydd as far as Corris, and man-made features include dams and a huge nuclear power station.

**2 DAYS • 150 MILES • 244KM**

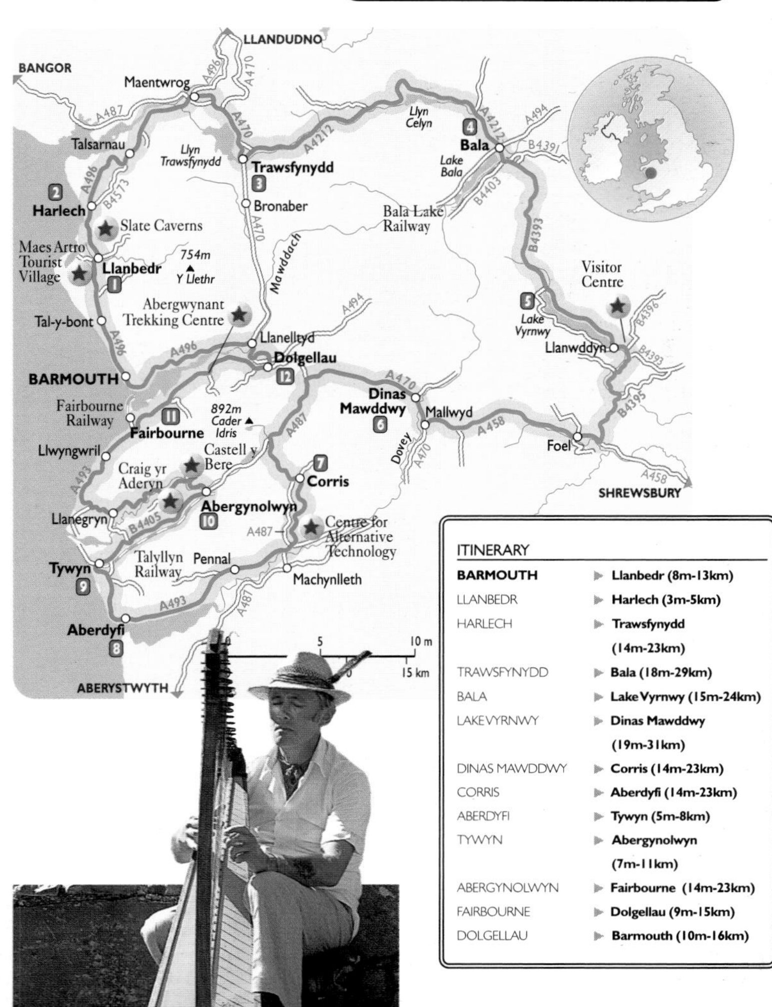


| ITINERARY | |
|---|---|
| **BARMOUTH** | ► **Llanbedr (8m-13km)** |
| LLANBEDR | ► **Harlech (3m-5km)** |
| HARLECH | ► **Trawsfynydd (14m-23km)** |
| TRAWSFYNYDD | ► **Bala (18m-29km)** |
| BALA | ► **Lake Vyrnwy (15m-24km)** |
| LAKE VYRNWY | ► **Dinas Mawddwy (19m-31km)** |
| DINAS MAWDDWY | ► **Corris (14m-23km)** |
| CORRIS | ► **Aberdyfi (14m-23km)** |
| ABERDYFI | ► **Tywyn (5m-8km)** |
| TYWYN | ► **Abergynolwyn (7m-11km)** |
| ABERGYNOLWYN | ► **Fairbourne (14m-23km)** |
| FAIRBOURNE | ► **Dolgellau (9m-15km)** |
| DOLGELLAU | ► **Barmouth (10m-16km)** |

Magnificent Harlech Castle

*i* *The Old Library, Barmouth*

▶ *From Barmouth follow the **A496** north to Llanbedr.*

**1 Llanbedr,** Gwynedd
At Llanfair, just to the north of Llanbedr on the A496, are the exciting old slate caverns, where you can walk through the old workings and see the enormous Cathedral cavern, but be sure to wear warm clothing, as the temperature inside is normally 10°C (50°F) or below.

▶ *Continue along the **A496** to Harlech.*

**2 Harlech,** Gwynedd
Harlech Castle is one of the most magnificently sited of Welsh castles, looking out over Cardigan Bay. It was built in the 13th century by Edward I to subdue the Welsh but was captured by Owain Glyndŵr in 1404. Harlech's theatre presents a varied programme throughout the year and there are plenty of interesting craft shops in town.

### BACK TO NATURE

Shell Island, also known as Mochras, near Llanbedr is not really an island but a peninsula with sand dunes and sandy beaches covered with shells – more than 200 varieties are believed to have been found. It is a great place for birds, including terns and shelduck, and waders such as sandpipers, dunlin, oystercatchers and gulls, and there is a great selection of flowers – over 170 species have been seen in the summer, including a few orchids.

### FOR CHILDREN

Maes Artro Village, an old wartime RAF camp, has been converted and now offers a range of exhibitions, displays and activities, with museums, an aquarium, a Log Fort playground. old farm implements, a 'Village of Yesteryear' and an air raid shelter, with light and sound effects.

### RECOMMENDED WALKS

Stroll through Llanbedr village from Maes Artro Craft Village and then follow the north side of the Artro estuary to the coast at Llandanwg, where there is a small medieval church which is often half covered with wind-blown sand.

*i* *High Street*

▶ *Keep on along the **A496**, then turn off right on to the **A487** for 2 miles (3km) before joining the **A470** for Trawsfynydd.*

**3 Trawsfynydd,** Gwynedd
The lake here is a man-made reservoir providing cooling water for the nuclear power station which dominates the scenery. Nature trails have been created around the lake, and there is excellent fishing. To the south along the A470 is the Rhiw Goch Ski Centre at Bronaber, where all-year skiing is possible.

▶ *Drive into the hills along the **A4212** to Bala.*

**4 Bala,** Gwynedd
Situated at the top of Bala Lake (Llyn Tegid in Welsh), the largest natural lake in Wales, Bala has become a great water sports centre. Sailing, windsurfing, fishing and canoeing all take place on the River Tryweryn. The other big lake near by is Llyn Celyn, a man-made reservoir, which supplies Liverpool

with some of its water and is a popular trout-fishing lake. The Bala Lake Narrow Gauge Scenic Railway runs 4½ miles (7km) to Llanuwchllyn through splendid scenery. Bala was the home of the Methodist cause and has retained much of its Welsh character and culture.

[i] *High Street*

▶ *Leave Bala on the **B4391**, then follow the unclassified road southwards over the hills and on to the **B4393** for 15 miles (24km) to Lake Vyrnwy.*

**5 Lake Vyrnwy,** Gwynedd
This vast reservoir was created in the late 19th century to supply Liverpool with water; the village of Llanwddyn was levelled to make way for it and rebuilt on higher ground. The lake and the surrounding woodlands are now a reserve of the RSPB. There is a small visitor centre, and nature trails and hides are provided to enable you to view the wildlife in the area, which includes red squirrels, polecats and badgers.

▶ *Continue along the **B4393**, then turn right on to a minor road to join the **B4395**. Turn right again on to the **A458** through Mallwyd, then head north on the **A470** to Dinas Mawddwy.*

**6 Dinas Mawddwy,** Gwynedd
This little village is an ideal base for outdoor holidays in the area. At the old railway station is Meirion Mill, a large working woollen mill open to visitors in the summer. Pottery and slate goods are available as well as woollens, and the old railway line is a good place for a stroll.

▶ *Continue along the **A470** and then left on the **A487** for 14 miles (23km) to Corris.*

**7 Corris,** Gwynedd
Corris is an old mining village with a new centre for traditional industries, where tourists can watch craftsmen at work. There is also a Railway Museum and, to the south, at the disused Llwyngwern Quarry, is the Centre for Alternative Technology (see page 69).

[i] *Craft Centre*

▶ *Drive southwards along the unclassified road on the eastern side of the river through Esgairgeiliog. Turn right on to the **B4404**, join the **A487** for a short distance, then turn right on the **A493** to Aberdyfi.*

**8 Aberdyfi,** Gwynedd
Sailing boats have now replaced the cargo ships that once traded at this harbour on the sheltered Dyfi Estuary. There is a fine sandy beach along the coast, and you can take a ferry trip across to Ynyslas, with its vast expanse of sand dunes and marshland. The town achieved fame in the song *The Bells of Aberdyfi*; ghostly church bells are said to ring from an ancient town which was completely flooded by the sea.

Dinas Mawddwy is an ideal base for exploring the area

[i] *The Wharf*

▶ *Drive north along the **A493** for 5 miles (8km) to Tywyn.*

**9 Tywyn,** Gwynedd
There are miles of golden sandy beaches at this popular seaside resort which is excellent for surfing and sailing. St Cadfan's Church dates back to Norman times and houses St Cadfan's Stone, a 7-foot (2m) monument some 1300 years old. The inscriptions on it are thought to be the oldest known writing in Welsh. Tywyn is famous for the

Dolgellau is situated in an area of outstanding scenery
Right: the Ffestiniog Railway

Talyllyn Railway, which runs inland for 7 miles (11km).

[i] *High Street*

> **SPECIAL TO...**
>
> **The Talyllyn Railway, which runs inland from Tywyn to Nant Gwernol, was built in 1865 to handle slate traffic. This was the first railway in the world to be taken over by a voluntary preservation society, and it is now operated as a tourist attraction.**

▶ *Leave Tywyn on the **A493**, but turn inland along the **B4405** to Abergynolwyn.*

**10 Abergynolwyn,** Gwynedd
Two miles (3km) west of Abergynolwyn, along an unclassified road, is the romantic ruin of Castell y Bere, built by Llywelyn the Great in the 13th century. Further still is Craig yr Aderyn (Bird Rock), thought to be the only inland nesting place of cormorants in Britain, but also the home for choughs, kestrels and feral goats.

▶ *Take an unclassified road heading westwards through Llanegryn back to the coast, then the **A493** to Fairbourne.*

**11 Fairbourne,** Gwynedd
Fairbourne is a popular holiday base with a sandy beach and miles of safe swimming, where windsurfing is a great attraction. So, too, is the narrow-gauge Fairbourne Railway which was built in the 1890s as a horse-drawn tramway. It was later converted to steam and now runs 1½ miles from Fairbourne to the end of the peninsula. The main line Cambrian coast railway also runs through here.

▶ *Rejoin and continue along the **A493** to Dolgellau.*

**12 Dolgellau,** Gwynedd
Dolgellau has always been a major route centre and is still an important regional capital and market centre. Tourism has replaced its main industry, flannel-weaving, and all that remains of this former occupation are the ruins of the fulling mills on the banks of the River Aran. Pony trekking is popular, and ponies can be hired at the Abergwynant Trekking Centre, west of town. Walking is also popular, and there are strenuous walks up to the summit of Cader Idris, as well as gentle strolls. A delightful route near by is the Torrent Walk, from Brithdir to the falls of the Afon Clywedog.

[i] *Ty Meirion, Eldon Square*

▶ *Join the **A470** to Llanilltyd, then turn left on to the **A496** back to Barmouth.*

> **FOR HISTORY BUFFS**
>
> **Dolgellau is built on the site of an ancient settlement among green hills. Three Roman roads met here, and it remained an important centre for the Welsh people throughout the Middle Ages. The Welsh leader Owain Glyndŵr signed his alliance with Charles VI, the King of France, here.**

# **Quarries,** Castles & Railways

From Bangor make a brief visit to the island of Anglesey before heading down the coast to Caernarfon and then inland to Snowdonia. The hills are scarred with quarries in places, but still create an overpoweringly beautiful backdrop.

**2 DAYS • 113 MILES • 180KM**

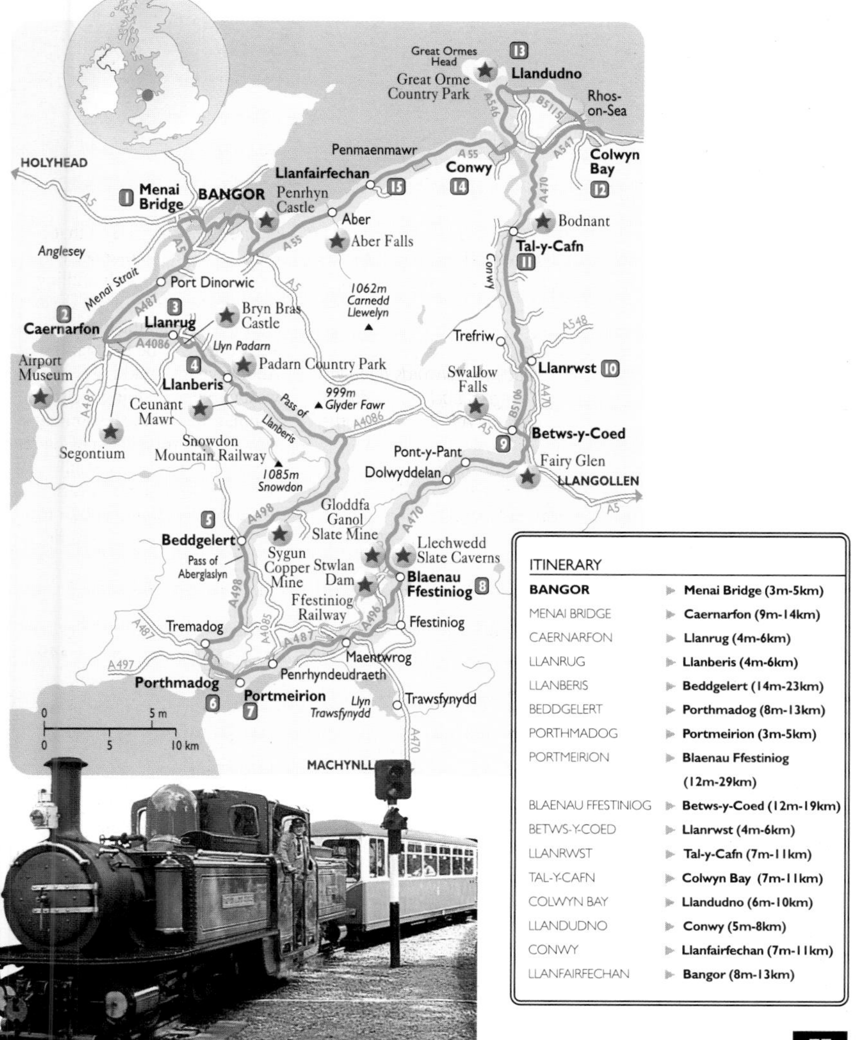


| ITINERARY | |
|---|---|
| **BANGOR** | ► **Menai Bridge (3m-5km)** |
| MENAI BRIDGE | ► **Caernarfon (9m-14km)** |
| CAERNARFON | ► **Llanrug (4m-6km)** |
| LLANRUG | ► **Llanberis (4m-6km)** |
| LLANBERIS | ► **Beddgelert (14m-23km)** |
| BEDDGELERT | ► **Porthmadog (8m-13km)** |
| PORTHMADOG | ► **Portmeirion (3m-5km)** |
| PORTMEIRION | ► **Blaenau Ffestiniog (12m-29km)** |
| BLAENAU FFESTINIOG | ► **Betws-y-Coed (12m-19km)** |
| BETWS-Y-COED | ► **Llanrwst (4m-6km)** |
| LLANRWST | ► **Tal-y-Cafn (7m-11km)** |
| TAL-Y-CAFN | ► **Colwyn Bay (7m-11km)** |
| COLWYN BAY | ► **Llandudno (6m-10km)** |
| LLANDUDNO | ► **Conwy (5m-8km)** |
| CONWY | ► **Llanfairfechan (7m-11km)** |
| LLANFAIRFECHAN | ► **Bangor (8m-13km)** |

## **Quarries,** Castles & Railways

*i* *Theatr Qwynedd, Bangor*

▶ *Drive along the **A5122** for 3 miles (5km) to Menai Bridge.*

### 1 Menai Bridge, Gwynedd

Menai Bridge takes its name from the suspension bridge built by Telford between 1819 and 1826 high above the Menai Strait. Nowadays, traffic on the busy A5 uses Stephenson's Britannia Bridge, whose original tubular structure was rebuilt after a fire in 1970, with a road deck above the railway.

From a lay-by on the A545 beyond Menai Bridge, there are superb views of both bridges, with the mountains of Snowdonia beyond. In Menai Bridge itself is the Tegfryn Art Gallery, which features the work of contemporary Welsh artists.

▶ *Follow the **A4080** to the **A5**, recross the Menai Strait on the Britannia Bridge, then on to the **A487** to Caernarfon.*

### 2 Caernarfon, Gwynedd

The airport south of Caenarfon is a great all-weather attraction. It used to be an RAF camp during World War II, and is now a hands-on museum, where you can climb into exhibits, touch the controls and use a flight simulator. You can also have a flight over Caernarfon Castle or round Snowdon. In 1969, Prince Charles was invested in the castle, following a tradition set by Edward I, whose first-born son was presented to the people as the Prince of Wales. Inside the castle you can see the investiture robes, and an explanation of the history of the castle and surrounding area, as well as the Museum of the Royal Welch Fusiliers.

Just outside the town, at Segontium, are the remains of a fine Roman fort which served as an important outpost of the Empire for three centuries.

*i* *Oriel Pendeitsh*

▶ *Take the **A4086** eastwards and turn on to an unclassified road to Llanrug.*

### 3 Llanrug, Gwynedd

The lived-in castle at Bryn Bras, to the south of Llanrug, has spacious lawns, tranquil woodland walks and excellent mountain views. This neo-Norman building on the fringe of Snowdonia was built in the 1830s on the site of an earlier castle, and the majestic gardens are worth visiting in their own right.

▶ *Return to and continue along the **A4086** to Llanberis.*

### 4 Llanberis, Gwynedd

At Llanberis you can take a 40-minute trip in a narrow-gauge train along the shores of Llyn Padarn, in the Padarn Country Park. The famed modern pump storage hydro scheme is close by at Dinorwic. Dolbadarn Castle is in the town, and less than a mile (1.6km) from the High Street is Ceunant Mawr, one of the most impressive waterfalls in Wales. The most popular footpath up Snowdon starts here, as does the Snowdon Mountain Railway, the only public rack-and-pinion railway, which climbs 3,000 feet (915m) to the summit in less than 5 miles (8km). Each train can take a maximum of 59 passengers and will normally not run with fewer than 25. Services depend on demand and weather conditions, which can be very harsh at the top of Snowdon, even when Llanberis is pleasant and sunny. The views can be superb.

*i* *Amgueddfa'r Gogledd Museum of the North*

▶ *Leave on the **A4086**, then turn right on to the **A498** for 14 miles (23km) to Beddgelert.*

Thomas Telford's graceful suspension bridge over the Menai Strait

## RECOMMENDED WALKS

From Llanberis, walk around the eastern end of Llyn Padarn at the foot of the Dinorwic quarries and then along the northern side of the lake. Visit the Slate Museum and pass through the woods and via the tramway bridge, before going round the western end of the lake and back into Llanberis.

**5 Beddgelert,** Gwynedd
The grave of Gelert is one of the saddest memorials you are likely to see. According to legend, which may actually be a 19th-century invention, Gelert was a faithful wolfhound killed by Prince Llywelyn, who thought it had killed his son, when in fact the dog had saved him from a wolf. Just outside this small town is the award-winning Sygun Copper mine, where you can explore the tunnels of a 19th-century mine which was once one of the world's major copper producers. A guided tour will take you past veins of ore containing gold, silver and other metals. From Beddgelert the drive takes you through the picturesque Pass of Aberglaslyn.

[i] *Llewelyn Cottage*

▶ *Follow the **A498** southwards to Porthmadog.*

**6 Porthmadog,** Gwynedd
Porthmadog was the creation of William Alexander Madocks, who hoped to benefit from the tourist traffic to Ireland; in fact, the town made its money from slate. The Ffestiniog Railway, which runs through magnificent scenery to Blaenau Ffestiniog, once carried the slate here to be shipped abroad, and is now a major tourist attraction. It uses horseshoe bends and a complete spiral at one point to gain height. Porthmadog also has the little Welsh Highland Railway, and a Motor Museum next to the Porthmadog Pottery.

[i] *High Street*

▶ *Drive along the **A487** before turning right on to an unclassified road to Portmeirion.*

**7 Portmeirion,** Gwynedd
This Italianate garden village, surrounded by woods and beaches, was created by the Welsh architect Sir Clough Williams-Ellis. Portmeirion was used as the setting for the 1960s cult television series *The Prisoner*, and now produces a distinctive range of colourful pottery.

## FOR CHILDREN

Padarn Country Park is open all year round and has picnic spots, boats for hire, a slate museum and a deserted village. You can ride on the narrow-gauge railway running along the shore of Llyn Padarn and walk along the nature trail or the archaeological trail, by the lakeside or in the woodlands.

Italian-style Portmeirion

▶ *Return to and take the **A487** eastwards, turning left on to the **A496** at Maentwrog. Shortly turn right on to the **B4391** which joins the **A470** at Ffestiniog. Turn left on to the **A470** and continue to Blaenau Ffestiniog.*

**8 Blaenau Ffestiniog,** Gwynedd
Blaenau Ffestiniog depended for its livelihood on the slate quarries, until demand for slate fell away. Now visitors can get first-hand experience of the slate miners' working conditions at the Llechwedd Slate Caverns, where the Deep Mine tour will take you down on Britain's steepest passenger incline. Just above the town is the world's largest slate mine at Gloddfa Ganol, where you can walk into the mine and see craftsmen at work. A modern industry is established at Tanygrisiau, where hydro electricity is produced in a pumped storage

Set on a rock above the town, Conwy Castle is an imposing sight

scheme. Drive up the mountain road to the Stwlan Dam for the remarkable view along the Vale of Ffestiniog. The Ffestiniog Railway runs through 13½ (22km) scenic miles to Porthmadog, and the more energetic can visit the Rhiwgoch dry ski slope at Trawsfynydd Holiday Village.

*i* *High Street*

▶ *Continue along the* ***A470*** *to Betws-y-Coed.*

**9 Betws-y-Coed,** Gwynedd
Betws-y-Coed is a popular inland resort set among forested land and magnificent mountains. The River Conwy is met by three tributaries here, and there are numerous bridges, waterfalls, and river pools with walks and play areas for children. Upstream are the Swallow Falls, one of the most famous of all tourist attractions in North Wales, and downstream is Fairy Glen, a much photographed and painted beauty spot. Back in the centre of the small town, there are many interesting shops and a craft centre. The 14th-century Church of St Mary has a Norman font and an effigy of the great-nephew of Llywelyn the Great. There is also a Motor Museum here.

*i* *Royal Oak Stables*

▶ *Leave Betws-y-Coed on the* ***A5****, shortly turning right on to the* ***B5106*** *and follow it north for 4 miles (6km) to Llanrwst.*

**10 Llanrwst,** Gwynedd
This historic market town is set in a delightful landscape of hills, forests, rivers and lakes. The bridge was designed by Inigo Jones in 1636, and the Gwydir Chapel contains the coffin of Llywelyn, Prince of Wales. Take a tour around the Trefriw Wells Roman Spa, where the water has been used as an aid to healthy living since Roman times, and is said to ease rheumatism and nervous tension. At the Trefriw Woollen Mills, you can see bedspreads and tweeds being manufactured, using electricity generated from the River Crafnant.

**FOR HISTORY BUFFS**

Trefriw has been known for its spa water since the 1st century, when Roman soldiers tunnelled into the Allt Coch mountains to reach the source. The water is rich in chalybeate, an iron solution; at the Victorian Pump House you can enjoy a sample of the water, which is said to help eliminate fatigue, nervous tension, stress, lumbago and anaemia.

▶ *Continue along the* ***A470*** *to Tal-y-Cafn.*

**11 Tal-y-Cafn,** Gwynedd
The 80-acre (32-hectare) garden at Bodnant is claimed to be one of the finest gardens in the world. Now owned by the National Trust, it is located in the beautiful Conwy Valley, with views out to the Snowdon mountains. Throughout the year visitors can find much of interest, with native and exotic trees and flowers, and there is a nursery where plants are propagated.

▶ *Keep going along the* ***A470*** *and then the* ***A547*** *to Colwyn Bay.*

**12 Colwyn Bay,** Clwyd
Colwyn Bay is a lively seaside town, which grew in the late 19th century as a result of the arrival of the railway, and the pier, promenade and many hotels and shops date from this period. The town is famous for its parks and gardens. The

The impressive Aber Falls

Welsh Mountain Zoo has chimpanzees, free-flying eagles, a sealion display and jungle adventure land. Other wild animals, though less lively, can be seen in the Dinosaur World in Eirias Park, which contains the largest collection of model dinosaurs in the British Isles.

*i Station Road*

▶ *Follow the **B5115** coast road for 6 miles (10km) to Llandudno.*

**13 Llandudno,** Gwynedd
St Tudno gave his name to the town in the 5th century, and a church still stands on the site of his cell. The town is the largest holiday resort in Wales, with two excellent sandy beaches situated between the headlands of Great and Little Orme. The Great Orme Country Park can be reached on the Great Orme Tramway, which has been taking passengers up to the top of the 679-foot (207m) summit since 1902. The energetic can enjoy the artificial ski slope and the 2,300-foot (700m) toboggan run, and there are fun rides for the children. Llandudno retains some of its Victorian elegance while catering for modern visitors. Lewis Carroll was a visitor and Alice Liddell for whom he wrote *Alice in Wonderland*, stayed here. A White Rabbit statue recalls Carroll's connections with the town, and there is an Alice exhibition in The Rabbit Hole, on Trinity Square.

*i Chapel Street*

▶ *Drive south along the **A546** for 5 miles (8km) to Conwy.*

**14 Conwy,** Gwynedd
Conwy's castle dominates the town, and inside it is a model of the castle and town as they were in the 14th century. This ancient city still has its complete medieval walls, and you can take a pleasant stroll along the ramparts. There are three remarkable bridges crossing the river, including the Conwy Suspension Bridge, designed and built by Thomas Telford in 1826 and renovated in 1990. The smallest house in Britain, a mere 6 feet (2m) wide and 10 feet (3m) high, stands on the quay. There is a Butterfly House in Bodlodeb Park, where exotic varieties fly freely around in a natural environment.

*i Conwy Castle Visitor Centre*

▶ *Head west along the **A55** to Penmaenmawr and further along to Llanfairfechan.*

**15 Llanfairfechan,** Gwynedd
Penmaenmawr has one of the finest beaches in North Wales, stretching between two granite headlands, and this is a fun holiday centre for the children. Further along, at Llanfairfechan, there is a sandy beach and beautiful inland scenery. There are excellent walks near by, notably up to the Aber Falls, 3 miles (5km) west of the town. The village of Aber was once the location of the palace of the Welsh king, Llywelyn the Great.

▶ *Keep on along the **A55** before turning right on to the **A5122** passing Penrhyn Castle on the return to Bangor.*

### BACK TO NATURE

The shores of the Menai Strait harbour a rich variety of marine creatures, best looked for at low tide among the seaweeds. This abundance of life supports thousands of birds; waders such as redshanks, dunlins and curlews can be seen feeding alongside gulls and wigeon, and you can scan the open water for divers, grebes and cormorants.

### SPECIAL TO...

Contained in the 840 square miles (2,175sq km) of the Snowdonia National Park are mountain peaks over 3,000 feet (915m) high, as well as miles of coastline and sandy beaches, and old mines and quarries, museums, castles and railways add further interest to this remarkable area.

# CENTRAL ENGLAND & EAST ANGLIA

This large area of England stretches from the Welsh Borders to the North Sea, and covers a great variety of scenery: volcanic peaks in Shropshire; the steep scarp of the Cotswolds; the lowlands of East Anglia, and the flat Fens near King's Lynn.

The Fens and East Anglia are rich agricultural lands, growing potatoes, sugar beet and flowers and large expanses of prairie-like wheat fields. Further west, in the cattle country of Shropshire and Gloucestershire, the climate is wetter and the countryside takes on a patchwork appearance – in marked contrast to the open landscapes of Norfolk, Suffolk and Lincolnshire. On the higher lands of the Cotswolds, a golden, mellow stone is used to build walls and houses, giving a gentle beauty to farmland, villages and towns. Grand mansions such as Blenheim Palace and imposing churches have been built out of the Cotswold limestone, as have some of the Oxford colleges. Fine churches are characteristic of this area and are generally the result of wealth earned from the sale of wool.

Timber-framed house, Saffron Walden

The Cambridge colleges include some of the most impressive buildings in England, but perhaps the most dramatic sight on this flat landscape is Ely cathedral, which can be seen from many miles away. Other striking landmarks on the fenlands are the windmills, which were once vitally important means of pumping away surplus water.

From Lincoln the landscape changes as the tour moves into Robin Hood country, where a considerable expanse of forest has survived. There are also areas of forest to be seen on the Shrewsbury tour which follows the trail of industrial development, visiting Ironbridge, the birthplace of the 'industrial revolution'. After tracing the achievements of industry you can celebrate a literary genius at Stratford, on the Gloucester tour, where visitors from all over the world make their pilgrimage to the birthplace of William Shakespeare.

## Lincoln

Lincoln's triple-towered cathedral dominates the city and the surrounding countryside, from its site on a limestone ridge overlooking the River Witham. A fascinating collection of old buildings can be seen in the cathedral close, including the old tithe barn and the Bishop's Palace and the 11th-century castle sits high on the city's steep hill. Other attractions include the Museum of Lincolnshire Life and the City and County Museum.

## King's Lynn

This historic port and market town grew up in the 'Lin', a marshy area alongside the River Ouse along which ships travelled, bringing wealth into the town. Warehouses and merchants' houses can be seen today, but particularly notable features include the amalgam of buildings forming the Guildhall; the 1683 Custom House, standing alone alongside the quay; and the 12th-century St Margaret's Church.

## Ipswich

There has been a settlement here since the Stone Age, but the port's real development started with Anglo-Saxon settlers in the 7th century. Cardinal Wolsey was born here in 1475. Industry has contributed much to the growth of this important regional and shopping centre, and there are some fine old buildings, such as the 16th-century Ancient House and the Custom House. The Ipswich Museum and the Wolsey Art Gallery are both worth a visit.

## Oxford

Oxford is a captivating place. Its ancient university buildings in their mellow stone have a tranquil dignity, despite being within walking distance of the busy shopping centre. Magdalene, built in the 15th century, is a particularly beautiful college. The 17th-century Ashmolean is Britain's oldest museum and the Bodleian Library, begun in 1598, contains over 5 million books. There are countless other collections and museums and a walk through the streets or along the Cherwell or Thames will convey the city's unique charm.

## Gloucester

The Romans built the fortified port of Glevum here to aid their attack on Wales; a small part of the wall survives, and there are many more relics to be seen in the City Museum. Gloucester's cathedral is one of the finest in the world, with a massive nave and 14th- to early 15th-century cloisters. The port has declined in recent years, but be sure to visit the National Waterways Museum in the Llanthony Warehouse.

King's College Chapel, Cambridge

## Shrewsbury

Shrewsbury, on the River Severn is bordered by parkland and crossed by many bridges. The red sandstone castle guards a narrow strip of land leading into the original town, where there are many fascinating buildings including Rawley's Mansion and the Lion Coaching Inn, as well as a good selection of modern shops. The famous Shrewsbury School, where Charles Darwin was a pupil, looks down on the town and the river.

TOUR
**15**

# Through Fen, Forest & Farmland

**2 DAYS • 122 MILES • 196KM**

This is a tour through history and legend, visiting the land of Robin Hood, one of England's most famous folk heroes. It crosses the edge of the fenland region of Britain, taking in the great ducal estates of Nottinghamshire – Clumber Park, Thoresby Hall and Welbeck Abbey – as well as the ancient woodlands of Sherwood Forest.

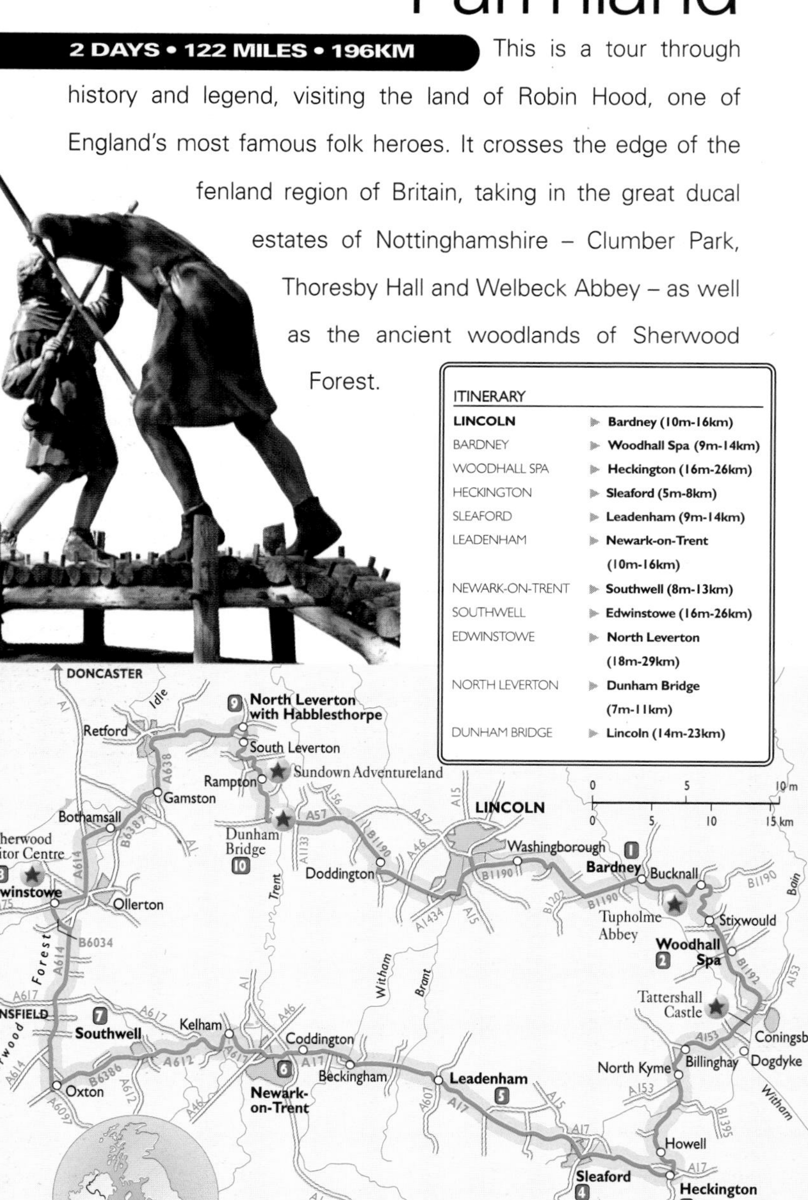


| ITINERARY | |
|---|---|
| **LINCOLN** | ▶ **Bardney (10m-16km)** |
| BARDNEY | ▶ **Woodhall Spa (9m-14km)** |
| WOODHALL SPA | ▶ **Heckington (16m-26km)** |
| HECKINGTON | ▶ **Sleaford (5m-8km)** |
| SLEAFORD | ▶ **Leadenham (9m-14km)** |
| LEADENHAM | ▶ **Newark-on-Trent (10m-16km)** |
| NEWARK-ON-TRENT | ▶ **Southwell (8m-13km)** |
| SOUTHWELL | ▶ **Edwinstowe (16m-26km)** |
| EDWINSTOWE | ▶ **North Leverton (18m-29km)** |
| NORTH LEVERTON | ▶ **Dunham Bridge (7m-11km)** |
| DUNHAM BRIDGE | ▶ **Lincoln (14m-23km)** |

One of the Spitfires housed in the old RAF station at Coningsby

*i* *9 Castle Hill; 21 Cornhill, Lincoln*

▶ *From Lincoln take the* ***B1190*** *east to Bardney.*

**1 Bardney,** Lincolnshire
A small fen town on the River Witham, Bardney is dominated by its sugar beet factory, which was opened in 1927. The town's appearance is more practical than beautiful, but some fine examples of Georgian buildings can be seen among the Victorian houses. Bardney Abbey, dating from the 7th century, was destroyed by Vikings and refounded in 1087. Ethelred the Unready built Tupholme Abbey, 2 miles (3km) beyond the river bridge, and restoration work is being carried out here.

BACK TO NATURE

Chamber's Wood, near Bardney, is a Forestry Commission oak woodland which is particularly good for the birdwatcher, especially in the spring when everything is singing. Look for several species of tits as well as chaffinches, woodpeckers, nuthatches and treecreepers. Interesting flowers include giant bellflower and lily of the valley.

▶ *Continue along the* ***B1190,*** *then just after Bucknall turn south on to unclassified roads to Woodhall Spa.*

**2 Woodhall Spa,** Lincolnshire
This inland watering place was once famous for its natural springs and has a pump room built in the 19th century after the discovery of medicinal waters. Today it is best known for its championship golf course. The 60-foot (18m) Tower on the Moor is thought to have been erected by the builders of Tattershall Castle, further south, whose fine keep is a relic of the castle built in 1440 by Ralph Cromwell, one of the richest men in the kingdom. He also built a magnificent collegiate church, in which perpetual prayers for his soul were to be said. There are excellent views from the castle looking across the low countryside as far as Lincoln and Boston. The only working fen steam engine in the country is at near by Dogdyke Pumping Station, worth a visit.

▶ *From Tattershall take the* ***A153****, the* ***B1395*** *at North Kyme, and in a short distance turn right on to an unclassified road, crossing the* ***A17*** *into Heckington.*

**3 Heckington,** Lincolnshire
The flat, exposed landscape round Heckington is an ideal location for a windmill, and there has been one on the same site since 1830. The Friends of Heckington Windmill have fully restored the present mill, which is the only eight-sailed windmill still working in the country, and was used for drainage as well as grinding corn. The Information Centre next door to it is in the Pea Room, which until the 1960s was used for sorting pea seeds. One of the pubs in the village, the Nag's Head, claims that Dick Turpin, the infamous highwayman, once stayed there. The magnificent decorated cruciform church dates from the 14th century.

*i* *The Pearoom Craft Centre, Station Yard*

▶ *Follow the* ***B1394****, then the* ***A17*** *to Sleaford, entering the town on the* ***B1394****.*

**4 Sleaford,** Lincolnshire
Sleaford is a small town set on the River Slea and the partly navigable Sleaford Canal. St Denys' Church, which dominates the town, has a 144-foot

The keep of Tattershall Castle
Opposite: Robin Hood and Little John, Sherwood Visitor Centre

(44m) solid stone spire, one of the oldest in the country, and its window tracery is exceptionally fine. The Black Bull Inn's sign dates from 1689 and illustrates the old sport of bull-baiting, which continued in these parts until 1807. The mounds beside Castle Causeway are all that remains of the 12th-century castle, where King John was taken ill with a fatal fever on the night after losing his crown jewels while crossing the Wash.

*i Money's Yard, Carre Street*

> **RECOMMENDED WALKS**
>
> Pleasant walks in the Sleaford area include the Culverthorpe Walk, starting from a lakeside picnic site southwest of Sleaford, and the Blankney Walk to the north of Sleaford, near the B1188.

▶ *Take the* ***A15*** *north to rejoin the* ***A17*** *and continue to Leadenham.*

### 5 Leadenham, Lincolnshire

This little village grew up along the line of limestone hills called Lincoln Cliff, which stretches from near Humberside as far south as Grantham. It is worth visiting just for the lovely church spire, but there are many attractive stone houses and the Old Hall is built entirely of golden-coloured stone.

▶ *Follow the* ***A17*** *to Newark-on-Trent.*

### 6 Newark-on-Trent, Nottinghamshire

The sign on the edge of the town reads 'Historic Newark-on-Trent', and this is certainly a treasure house of history. The ruined 12th-century castle is where King John died in 1216, and stands opposite the Ossington Coffee Tavern, a Victorian flight of fancy. Travellers have been passing through the town for centuries: the Roman Fosse Way and the Great North Road intersect near by, and the River Trent has been canalised here. The cobble-stoned market place, the scene of Prime Minister William Gladstone's first major political speech, still survives, and you cannot miss the massive 252-foot (77m) spire of St Mary Magdalen, which is 30 feet (9m) higher than the total length of the church.

*i The Gilstrap Centre, Castlegate*

> **FOR HISTORY BUFFS**
>
> Lady Godiva of Coventry fame and wife of Earl Leofric of Mercia, was the first official owner of the town of Newark, and presented it to the monastery of Stow, further down the River Trent. In the next century Newark was owned by the Bishop of Lincoln, who used the stone to rebuild the wooden castle. The new version was destroyed by Oliver Cromwell's troops.

▶ *Take the* ***A617*** *and the* ***A612*** *west to Southwell.*

### 7 Southwell, Nottinghamshire

Visitors to this market town are taken by surprise as the spires of the magnificent Minster suddenly come into view above the rolling countryside. This 12th- and 13th-century building, with a Romanesque nave and transept, is the mother church of Nottinghamshire and replaced an earlier Saxon church. Charles I spent his last few hours of freedom at the Saracen's Head Inn, just along the road, and another famous visitor, the poet Lord Byron, often stayed at Burgage Manor near by – Byron wrote the well-known epitaph for the local carrier, John Adams, who died of drunkenness:

*John Adams lies here, of the parish of Southwell,*
*A carrier who carried his can to his mouth well.*
*He carried too much, and he carried so fast,*
*He could carry no more – and so was carried at last.*

> **SPECIAL TO...**
>
> The spires of Southwell's Norman Minster are visible for miles around. It was built during the 12th century and contains early English Gothic as well as Norman architecture, which has survived turbulent times: during the Civil War, Cromwell's soldiers stabled their horses in the nave. The octagonal Chapter House is a unique feature, dating from the 13th century, with twin Norman towers.

▶ *Take the* ***B6386*** *to Oxton, then the* ***A6097*** *north which becomes the* ***A614***, *and finally turn left on to the* ***B6034*** *to Edwinstowe.*

## 8 Edwinstowe,

Nottinghamshire

Edwinstowe is an old colliery village, and it was at St Mary's Church that Maid Marian is said to have married Robin Hood. The massive and ancient Major Oak, named after Major Rooke, a local 18th-century antiquary, is claimed to be the oldest tree in the forest. Near by is the Sherwood Visitor Centre, where there are walks, nature trails, exhibitions and amusements. Sherwood Forest Village, just down the road, is a holiday complex with indoor facilities.

*i* *Sherwood Information Centre, Church Street*

▶ *Return via the* ***A6075*** *to the* ***A614*** *heading north then turn right on to unclassified roads passing Bothamsall, then along the* ***B6387*** *crossing the* ***A1*** *to the* ***A638*** *to Retford. Take unclassified roads east from Retford to North Leverton.*

## 9 North Leverton,

Nottinghamshire

Dutch-style houses give this village a flavour of Holland, which fits in well with the flat, fenland landscape. A windmill, three storeys high and still in working order, stands above the plain, but is dwarfed by the vast cooling towers of the power station to the north along the Trent valley. Further south is the village of Rampton, surrounded by rich farmland criss-crossed with drainage ditches, used to reclaim the area from marshland.

### FOR CHILDREN

Sundown Adventureland is a children's theme park on the road from North Leverton to Rampton. Its many attractions include a pirate ship, Noah's ark, a miniature farm with pets and farm animals, and there are secret passages to explore in a Tudor village.

Lincoln's majestic cathedral soars above the rooftops of the town

▶ *Continue south along unclassified roads then join the* ***A57*** *to Dunham Bridge.*

## 10 Dunham Bridge,

Nottinghamshire

Prepare to pay when you cross the River Trent, as a toll is levied here – a rare occurrence on British roads. The A57 out of Dunham runs alongside a major drainage ditch which dates from Roman times. Further along, Doddington brings you back into Lincolnshire. The landscape round here has been drained and cultivated for hundreds of years, and this delightful village has a fine Elizabethan hall as its focal point, with impressive ceramics and a medieval scold's bridle is among many other curiosities.

▶ *Return to Lincoln on the* ***B1190****.*

TOUR
16

# Fen, Farm & Coast

**2 DAYS • 151 MILES • 242KM**

Through flat fields and across the fenland, you are drawn to the magnificence of Ely's cathedral, then on to the undulating ground of rural Norfolk. The farming landscape continues to the coast, before ending with lavender and a royal residence.

BURNHAM

| ITINERARY | |
|---|---|
| **KING'S LYNN** | ▶ **Wisbech (14m-22km)** |
| WISBECH | ▶ **Downham Market (13m-21km)** |
| DOWNHAM MARKET | ▶ **Ely (14m-22km)** |
| ELY | ▶ **Weeting (23m-37km)** |
| WEETING | ▶ **Thetford (8m-13km)** |
| THETFORD | ▶ **East Dereham (22m-36km)** |
| EAST DEREHAM | ▶ **Fakenham (13m-21km)** |
| FAKENHAM | ▶ **Houghton St Giles (4m-6km)** |
| HOUGHTON ST GILES | ▶ **Wells-next-the-Sea (6m-10km)** |
| WELLS-NEXT-THE-SEA | ▶ **Holkham (2m-3km)** |
| HOLKHAM | ▶ **Burnham Market (4m-6km)** |
| BURNHAM MARKET | ▶ **Hunstanton (12m-19km)** |
| HUNSTANTON | ▶ **Sandringham (8m-13km)** |
| SANDRINGHAM | ▶ **King's Lynn (8m-13km)** |

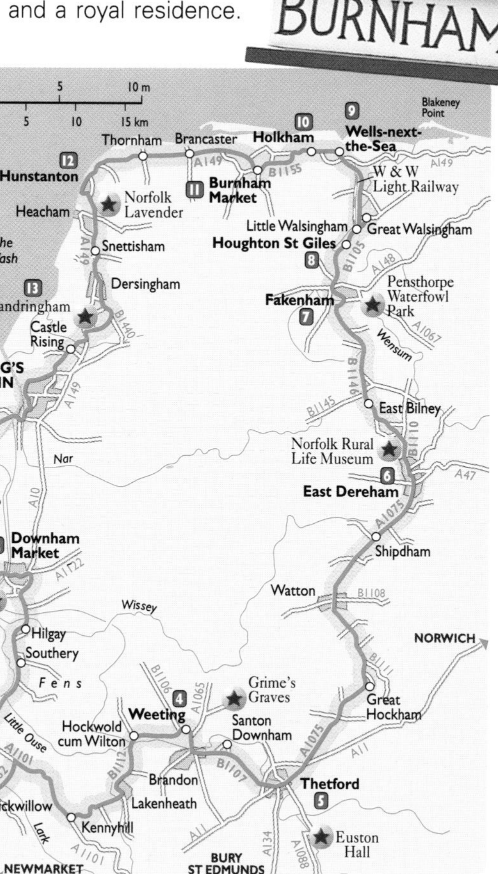

Above: Thetford Forest gives way to natural woodland

*i The Old Gaol House, Saturday Market Place, King's Lynn*

▶ *Take the **A47** to Wisbech, entering via the **B198**.*

**1 Wisbech,** Cambridgeshire
Wisbech is at the centre of a rich flower- and fruit-growing area. It was once only 4 miles (6km) from the sea, but due to land reclamation is now 11 miles (17km) inland. The Wisbech and Fenland Museum illustrates local history. Near by is the Aviation Museum, containing an interesting but rather morbid exhibition of aircraft equipment recovered from crashes in the area. The church has two naves, and a Braille Plan for blind visitors in the garden. The Brinks, two rows of houses along the River Neme, are among the finest examples of Georgian architecture in England, and Peckover House contains fine panelling and furniture; in its garden is the ginkgo, or maidenhair tree – the tallest in the land until a storm took away the top.

*i District Library, Ely Place*

▶ *Follow the **A1101**, then the **A1122** to Downham Market.*

**2 Downham Market,** Norfolk
There has been a settlement in this area since Roman times. Denver Sluice, 2 miles (3km) away, is where the River Great Ouse and the Old and New Bedford Rivers are regulated in order to prevent flooding. The most interesting building in the town is the Church of St Edmund, with its Early English tower.

▶ *Leave Downham Market eastwards to join the **A10** then turn south and follow to Ely.*

**3 Ely,** Cambridgeshire
Ely ('Eel Island') refers to the staple diet of the Saxons who once lived here. The Fens cathedral city is still a small market centre with ancient buildings and medieval gateways but has a busy quayside. It was founded as a religious community in the 7th century, and during the Norman Invasion was the centre of Anglo-Saxon resistance under Hereward the Wake. Ely also has a parish church, St Mary's, and the vicarage was the home of Oliver Cromwell for 11 years. Nine hundred-year-old Ely Cathedral's greatest glory is its unique octagon, designed by Alan de Walsingham after the earlier tower collapsed in 1322.

*i Oliver Cromwell's House, 29 St Mary's Street*

▶ *Leave Ely on the **B1382** through Prickwillow, then take the **A1101** to Kennyhill, turning left on to an unclassified road to Lakenheath. Pick up the **B1112** as far as Hockwold cum Wilton, and finally another unclassified road to Weeting.*

**4 Weeting,** Norfolk
Weeting is a good centre for exploring Breckland, a region of heathland that straddles the Suffolk and Norfolk border. Grime's Graves are and Thetford Forest Park is at Santon Downham. There are deer and red squirrels in the forest, and a rich variety of trees. Weeting Heath is the place to see the classic Breckland bird, the stone curlew.

**FOR HISTORY BUFFS**

Grime's Graves, named after the Anglo-Saxon god Grim, are situated on a patch of common land in Breckland. These grassy hollows are about 4,000 years old, and this is the largest known group of flint mines in Britain. You can climb down one on an iron ladder to see where the miners worked with wooden tools or deer antlers.

▶ *Follow the **B1106** and **A1065** to Brandon, then the **B1107** to Thetford.*

**5 Thetford,** Norfolk
Formerly the capital of the region, Thetford is a cathedral city and contained as many as five monasteries. Some of the oldest fragments are the remains

A lone windmill stands sentinel in the Fens

of the 12th-century Cluniac priory, Castle Hill, the site of Iron Age earthworks, and a Norman castle mound. You should find time to visit Euston Hall, the 18th-century home of the Duke and Duchess of Grafton, which has fine paintings by Stubbs, Van Dyck and Lely. The 15th-century timber-framed Ancient House Museum has beautifully carved beam ceilings and exhibits on local history.

▶ *Leave Thetford on the **A1075** heading northwards to East Dereham.*

### 6 East Dereham, Norfolk

St Withburga founded a nunnery here in the 7th century, and St Withburga's Well is in the churchyard of St Nicholas's Church. The town has some fine Georgian buildings, and Bishop Bonner's Cottage has attractive pargeting. At Gressenhall, on the road north to Fakenham, is the Norfolk Rural Life Museum and Union Farm, which has rare breeds of sheep, cattle, pigs and poultry, and a museum on farming.

▶ *Continue north on the **B1110**, then the **B1146** to Fakenham.*

### 7 Fakenham, Norfolk

Fakenham is a delightful small market town which dates from Saxon times. Its parish church has a commanding 15th-century tower, and the two old coaching inns in the Market Place have traces of earlier architecture behind their Georgian façades. The fascinating Gas Museum, which is open on occasional days throughout the summer, explains how gas was made and contains the only complete gasworks in England. Just a mile away is the Pensthorpe Waterfowl Park, which houses a large selection of birds, and aims to protect waterfowl and wetland habitats.

*i* *Red Lion House, 37 Market Place*

▶ *Cross the **A148** and follow the **B1105** to Houghton St Giles.*

### 8 Houghton St Giles, Norfolk

The attractive village of Houghton St Giles has old links with Walsingham, including a

small chapel on the old Walsingham Way, known as the Slipper Chapel because pilgrims would remove their shoes before completing their journey barefoot to Little Walsingham, which has been a Christian shrine since 1061. The Anglican Shrine and the Roman Catholic Shrine are at either end of the Holy Mile, and a ruined abbey stands in pleasant gardens. Great Walsingham, just a few minutes along the B1388 from Little Walsingham, is noted for its textile centre, where you can watch the screen-printing process.

*i Shire Hall Museum, Common Place, Little Walsingham*

▶ *Return to the **B1105** from Great Walsingham and follow to Wells-next-the-Sea.*

### 9 Wells-next-the-Sea, Norfolk

The Wells and Walsingham Light Railway runs through 4 miles (6km) of countryside to the famous pilgrimage villages of Walsingham, and is the longest 10¼-inch (26cm) narrow-gauge steam railway in the world.

The town of Wells still has many of its 18th- and 19th-century houses, set in a network of alleys and yards near the small quay, which first started trading in wool over 600 years ago.

*i Staithe Street*

**BACK TO NATURE**

East of Wells-next-the-Sea, much of the coastline is owned by the National Trust, and there are several miles of nature reserves.

The sand and shingle spit of Blakeney Point can be reached by foot from Cley, or by boat from Blakeney or Morston Quay. Common and sandwich terns nest on the spit, together with waders such as ringed plover and oystercatcher, and several species of duck.

The Norfolk Naturalists' Trust reserve at Cley has hides overlooking pools and reedbeds. Bitterns, spoonbills, bearded tits and grey herons are regularly seen and a wide range of waders can be found during migration times.

▶ *Follow the **A149**, west for 2 miles (3km) to Holkham.*

### 10 Holkham, Norfolk

In a beautiful deer park with a lake landscaped by Capability Brown, is the 18th-century mansion of Holkham Hall, just south of the village of Holkham. Its art collection includes work by Rubens, Van Dyck and Gainsborough and there is an amazing marble hall. In the Bygones Collection, over 4,000 items have been assembled from kitchens, dairies and cars.

▶ *Continue further along the **A149** then left on to the **B1155** to Burnham Market.*

### 11 Burnham Market, Norfolk

Burnham Market is the main village in a group of seven Burnhams, clustered closely together, and has a handsome, wide village green surrounded by elegant 18th-century houses. The Burnhams were made famous by Horatio Nelson, who probably learned to sail on the muddy creeks of the coast before being sent away to sea at the age of 12. He was born in 1758 at Burnham Thorpe, where his father was the rector, and the lectern in the church is made from timbers from his ship, the *Victory*.

▶ *Return to the **A149** for 12 miles (19km) to Hunstanton.*

### 12 Hunstanton, Norfolk

Hunstanton developed as a seaside resort in the 19th century, and is famous for its red-and-white striped chalk cliffs and excellent beaches. At the Sea Life Centre fish, seals

Bishop Bonner's Cottage at East Dereham

The seaside resort of Hunstanton
Opposite: fine house in Lavenham

and crabs are all around as you walk through varied marine settings. England's only lavender farm, Norfolk Lavender, is just south of town, at Heacham. A national collection of lavender plants is being assembled here, and there is a herb garden with over 50 varieties of culinary and decorative plants.

*i* *The Green*

▶ *Head south on the **A149**, then the **B1440** from Dersingham to Sandringham, and further south to Castle Rising.*

**13 Sandringham,** Norfolk
The royal estate of Sandringham covers 20,000 acres (8,094 hectares) and was bought by Queen Victoria for the Prince of Wales in 1862. The extensive grounds contain the parish Church of St Mary Magdalene, a museum, nature trails and an adventure playground.

A former royal residence can be seen at Castle Rising, where the splendid Norman castle was built in the 12 century for the Earls of Sussex but subsequently belonged to the Earls of Norfolk. Set within huge earthworks, the shell of the Great Hall is still impressive.

▶ *Take the **B1439** back to rejoin the **A149**, then an unclassified road back to King's Lynn.*

### RECOMMENDED WALKS

Both the Norfolk Coastal Path and the Peddar's Way can be walked from Hunstanton, the one along the coast and the other through the heart of rural west Norfolk. Wherever you are on this tour of west Norfolk you will find a selection of gentle walks along rivers, across heathland, in the forests or along the coast.

### FOR CHILDREN

Hunstanton is an ideal place for children, with its sandy beach, rock pools and endless entertainment; and the Oasis all-weather leisure centre offers swirl pools, a toddlers' pool and a variety of indoor sports.

### SPECIAL TO...

Hunstanton cliffs were laid down on the bed of the sea between 135 and 70 million years ago, in the Cretaceous period. Different colours mark the layers of rock. The carstone is reddish or brown, and is often used locally as a building stone; and most of the chalk is white. It is in the chalk that fossils are found: bivalves similar to those found on the beach today, as well as brachiopods, belemnites and ammonites.

### SCENIC ROUTES

Driving anywhere near Ely, the tower of the cathedral will draw you towards it like a magnet.
Near Thetford, dark forests dominate the scene, but there are still a few patches of open heathland.

# **East Anglia's** Churches & Colleges

Thatch, stone and brick are major features of the villages in this rural area, but dominating the countryside are the churches and their spires. This gentle landscape, covered with colourful fields of rape in spring and wheat in summer, provided the inspiration for Constable's paintings and Brooke's poetry.

**2 DAYS • 143 MILES • 229KM**

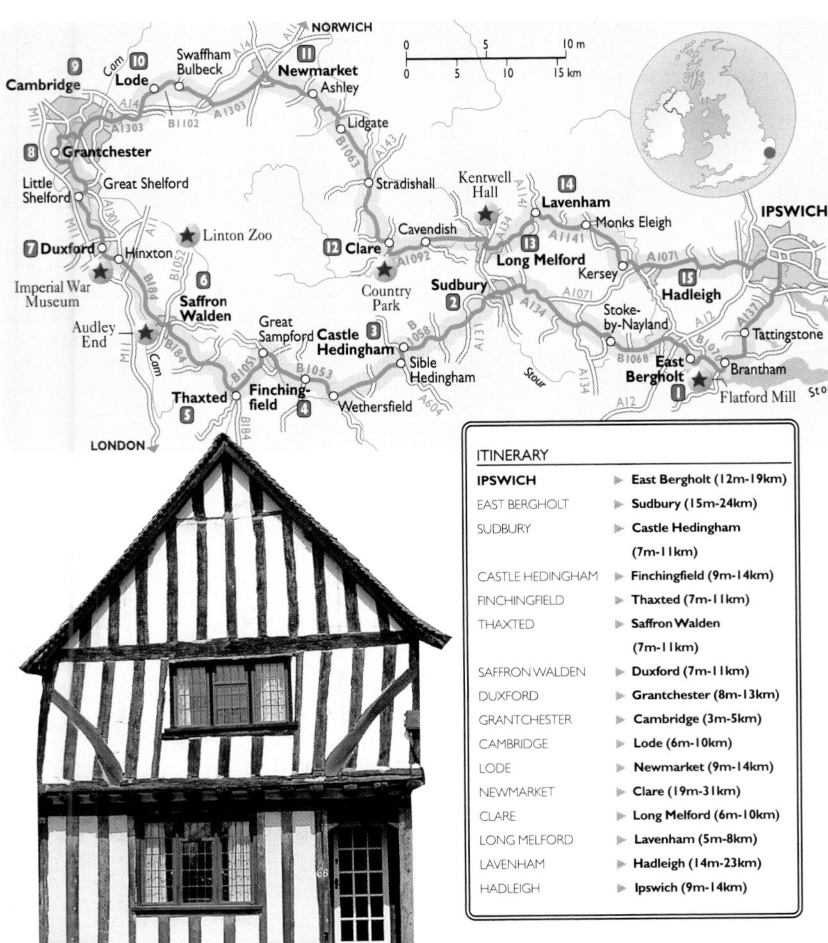


| ITINERARY | |
|---|---|
| **IPSWICH** | ▶ **East Bergholt (12m-19km)** |
| EAST BERGHOLT | ▶ **Sudbury (15m-24km)** |
| SUDBURY | ▶ **Castle Hedingham (7m-11km)** |
| CASTLE HEDINGHAM | ▶ **Finchingfield (9m-14km)** |
| FINCHINGFIELD | ▶ **Thaxted (7m-11km)** |
| THAXTED | ▶ **Saffron Walden (7m-11km)** |
| SAFFRON WALDEN | ▶ **Duxford (7m-11km)** |
| DUXFORD | ▶ **Grantchester (8m-13km)** |
| GRANTCHESTER | ▶ **Cambridge (3m-5km)** |
| CAMBRIDGE | ▶ **Lode (6m-10km)** |
| LODE | ▶ **Newmarket (9m-14km)** |
| NEWMARKET | ▶ **Clare (19m-31km)** |
| CLARE | ▶ **Long Melford (6m-10km)** |
| LONG MELFORD | ▶ **Lavenham (5m-8km)** |
| LAVENHAM | ▶ **Hadleigh (14m-23km)** |
| HADLEIGH | ▶ **Ipswich (9m-14km)** |

# East Anglia's Churches & Colleges

*i St Stephen's Church, St Stephen's Lane, Ipswich*

▶ *Take the **A137** from Ipswich, then right on to the **B1070** shortly after Brantham and finally an unclassified road via Flatford to East Bergholt.*

**1 East Bergholt,** Suffolk
The artist John Constable was born here in 1776 and said of the area: 'These scenes made me a painter'. Clustered round the 15th-century Church of St Mary, with its unfinished tower and remarkable bell house, are Elizabethan cottages set in beautiful gardens. Flatford Mill now used as a Field Study Centre. Willy Lott's Cottage, an early 18th-century mill-house which appears in Constable's *The Hay Wain*, still stands beside the mill stream.

SPECIAL TO...

Dedham, near East Bergholt, is proud of its connections with the artist John Constable. As a boy he went to school here and the beautiful scenery of Dedham Vale is now the area referred to as Constable Country. The Art and Craft Centre is on three floors of a converted congregational church, and prints, paintings and various crafts are on display and for sale. There is also a working pottery and a toy museum.

RECOMMENDED WALKS

From Flatford Mill there are several beautiful walks in Constable Country. Try the walk to Dedham Mill, a well-known scene to Constable enthusiasts, and only requiring 2 miles (3km) of easy walking.

▶ *Leave on an unclassified road, and cross the **A12** on to the **B1068** and **A134** to Sudbury.*

Thaxted's 15th-century timbered guild house

**2 Sudbury,** Suffolk
Charles Dickens used this ancient cloth and market town on the River Stour as the model for 'Eatanswill' in *The Pickwick Papers*. There is a bronze statue to Thomas Gainsborough, the artist, who was born here in 1727, in an elegant Georgian town house now containing many of his paintings. The town was formerly a river port, and one of the old warehouses has been turned into the Quay Theatre. St Peter's Church has fine painted screen panels and a splendid piece of 15th-century embroidery on velvet, the 'Alderman's Pall'.

*i Sudbury Town Hall, Market Hill*

▶ *Leave Sudbury on the **A131**, turning right on to the **B1058** to Castle Hedingham.*

**3 Castle Hedingham,** Essex
The De Vere family, Earls of Oxford, built Hedingham Castle on the hilltop in about 1140, and the banqueting hall with its minstrel gallery still survives. The keep overlooks medieval houses, which cluster round the Norman Church of St Nicholas. There are many reminders of the town's prosperous days in the 15th-century Moot Hall and the elegant Georgian houses of the wealthy wool merchants. Just outside the village is the Colne Valley Railway, where there are restored steam engines and carriages.

▶ *Join the **A604** south for a short distance, then take unclassified roads on the right via Wethersfield, then right on to the **B1053** to Finchingfield.*

**4 Finchingfield,** Essex
Finchingfield's charm has survived in spite of its great popularity. One of its many fine buildings is the gabled and barge-boarded Hill House, set opposite a row of 16th-century cottages and Georgian houses. The Church of St John the Baptist has a Norman tower and Georgian-style bell-cote.

▶ *Continue on the **B1053** to Great Sampford, then turn left on to the **B1051** to Thaxted.*

**5 Thaxted,** Essex
Thaxted's 14th-century, cathedral-like flint church is one of the largest in Essex, with a thin, graceful spire rising 181 feet (55m). Another tall building, the

tower windmill, was built in 1804, and now houses a small rural museum; and the 15th-century Guildhall is built of local wood and plaster, on a foundation of flint. Composer Gustav Holst once lived in Thaxted, and Sir John Betjeman wrote of it: 'There are few places in England to equal the beauty, compactness and juxtaposition of medieval and Georgian architecture'.

▶ *Head northwest on the **B184** to Saffron Walden.*

**6 Saffron Walden,** Essex
Saffron Walden's flint church rivals that of Thaxted in magnificence and size; 200 feet (61m) long and nearly as high. Its spire was added in 1831. Wool was a major industry here, but the town also prospered from growing saffron for medicine and dyes. There are delightful old narrow streets to explore, and the museum has exhibitions of furniture, ceramics and toys. Jacobean Audley End House, near by, is in grounds landscaped by Capability Brown. Elizabeth I stayed here with the poet, Sir Philip Sidney, in 1578, and the rooms have been laid out to give a 'lived in' feeling.

i *1 Market Place*

FOR CHILDREN

Linton Zoo, north of Saffron Walden on the B1052, was created by the Simmons family and opened in 1972. This is the Cambridgeshire Wildlife Breeding Centre, which focuses on conservation and education. Set in beautiful gardens, the centre has lions, pumas, snakes, owls, spiders and many others, as well as a children's play area.

▶ *Continue on the **B184** taking the **A1301** at **M11** junction and, in a short distance, turn left on to an unclassified road through Hinxton to Duxford.*

**7 Duxford,** Cambridgeshire
Duxford is a small village with a low, squat church and attractive thatched pub, the John Barley Corn. It is famous for the Imperial War Museum at Duxford Airfield, a former Battle of Britain fighter station.

▶ *Continue along unclassified roads through Little Shelford to Great Shelford, then left on to the **A1301** and finally left on to unclassified roads again to Grantchester.*

**8 Grantchester,** Cambridgeshire
Grantchester was immortalised in a poem written by Rupert Brooke in 1912 about the Old Vicarage, where he lived. The village has a characteristic low church, with a small spire protruding.

▶ *Head north to Cambridge.*

**9 Cambridge,** Cambridgeshire
Cambridge became famous as a seat of learning when the University was established early in the 13th century, and its elegant colleges and chapels of mellow stone give this beautiful city a stately air. But this is an important market centre and a

Duxford Imperial War Museum

Punting along the River Cam under the Bridge of Sighs

leader in high technology industries, as well as a university city, and there are many fine buildings and riverside parklands. King's College Chapel and the Bridge of Sighs are musts for all visitors, and in summer you can punt along the River Cam that flows around the city. No visit would be complete without seeing the Fitzwilliam Museum, with its priceless collections of porcelain, antiquities, paintings and armour.

BACK TO NATURE

The Fowlmere RSPB Reserve lies just off the Royston to Cambridge road (A10) near the village of Fowlmere. It comprises an area of reed-bed with open water, and attracts breeding birds including sedge and reed warblers. In the winter, look for water rails, kingfishers and bearded tits.

*i* *Wheeler Street*

▶ *Take the **A1303** east, then turn north on to the **B1102** to Lode.*

**10 Lode,** Cambridgeshire
Lode is famous for the Augustinian priory known as Anglesey Abbey, founded in the 12th century and converted into a house in about 1600. The estate was bought by Huttleston Broughton, who created 100 acres (40 hectares) of gardens. A vast collection of paintings, sculpture and *objets d'art* has been assembled inside amid sumptuous furnishings. Lode Watermill, across the lode, or canal, that skirts the gardens, has been restored and grinds corn on the first Sunday of each month.

▶ *From Lode follow the **B1102** to Swaffham Bulbeck, then follow an unclassified road to the **A1303** to Newmarket.*

**11 Newmarket,** Suffolk
Newmarket has been the headquarters of horse racing in Britain since the 17th century, and the National Stud and many training stables are located on the surrounding heath. Guided tours of the Stud, where you can see some of racing's superstars, are possible by appointment. The National Horse Racing Museum takes you back to the origins of racing.

The famous Rowley Mile is named after a horse owned by Charles II, and a former coaching inn called the Rutland Arms, parts of which date back to his day, has kept some of its rooms in the style of the 1850s.

▶ *Follow the **B1063** for 17 miles (27km) to Clare, then eastwards to Cavendish along the **A1092**.*

**12 Clare,** Suffolk
This ancient little market town has excellent examples of pargeting – fine plasterwork – such as those seen on the 15th-century Priest's House or Ancient House, now the local museum. The church, which has a most unusual design, is well

Newmarket: the headquarters of horse racing in Britain

worth visiting. Norman Clare Castle was built in 1090 and stands high on a 100-foot (30m) mound.

At Clare Castle Country Park there is a butterfly garden, and you can take a pleasant walk along the old railway track. Three miles (5km) east is Cavendish, the ancestral village of the Dukes of Devonshire, and its attractions include a 16th-century farmhouse near the church, and philanthropist Sue Ryder's 16th-century rectory, which contains memorabilia and photographs explaining the origins and aims of her work.

▶ *Continue east on the **A1092**, then turn south on to the **A134** to Long Melford.*

## 13 Long Melford, Suffolk

Long Melford is another of Suffolk's lovely villages, with fine wool merchants' houses. At the end of the mile-long main street is the Church of the Holy Trinity, one of the finest in the country, exhibiting a superb display of flushwork – ornate decoration in flint. The village green is overlooked by Elizabethan Long Melford Hall, a turreted Tudor mansion with tall chimneys.

One mile (1.6km) north of the village is Kentwell Hall (National Trust), a moated Elizabethan mansion with a brickpaved mosaic maze in the shape of a Tudor rose.

▶ *Follow unclassified roads northeast for 5 miles (8km) to Lavenham.*

## 14 Lavenham, Suffolk

Lavenham's remarkable church, the Church of St Peter and St Paul, has a flint tower 140 feet (43m) high, and the Guildhall, an early 16th-century timber-framed building, contains a display of local history. The Swan Inn is a famous hostelry which has been carefully preserved. Some of the black-and-white buildings have been painted pink to add to the colour of this pretty village.

*i* *Lady Street*

### RECOMMENDED WALKS

The route from Lavenham to Long Melford, along a disused railway line, gives a gentle 3-mile (5km) walk between two of Suffolk's most appealing small towns.

### FOR HISTORY BUFFS

Many of the local towns and villages were important for wool, but the most famous was probably Lavenham. In the time of Henry VIII it was one of the wealthiest towns in England, and the main source of this wealth was wool, yarn and various kinds of cloth.

The town has not changed much since then: there are still half-timbered houses which lean over the narrow streets. Over 300 of the buildings are listed for architectural or archaeological interest.

▶ *Follow the **A1141**, turning right to pass through Kersey, then on to Hadleigh.*

## 15 Hadleigh, Suffolk

Before reaching Hadleigh, enjoy the rural charm of Kersey, with its old priory, ducks paddling in the ford and thatched cottages. In Hadleigh itself, the Guildhall and Deanery tower are listed buildings dating from the 15th century. Interesting marks on the side of the 1813 Corn Exchange show where the brick-work was used by schoolchildren for sharpening their slate pencils as they went to school.

*i* *Toppesfield Hall*

▶ *Return to Ipswich on the **A1071**.*

### SCENIC ROUTES

The Dick Turpin Heritage Route passes through Saffron Walden and Thaxted, as well as other attractive villages, historic sites and open countryside. On the approach to Thaxted on the B1051, the church and the windmill add variety to the rural charm of the rich farmland.

# Cotswold Wool & Stone

This is mainly a circuit of Cotswold countryside – a landscape of stone walls surrounding fertile fields and distinctive village architecture. The villages contain many fine churches, but the best known structure is the cross in the centre of Banbury. The family homes of two great men can be seen; one Englishman in Blenheim and one American in Sulgrave.

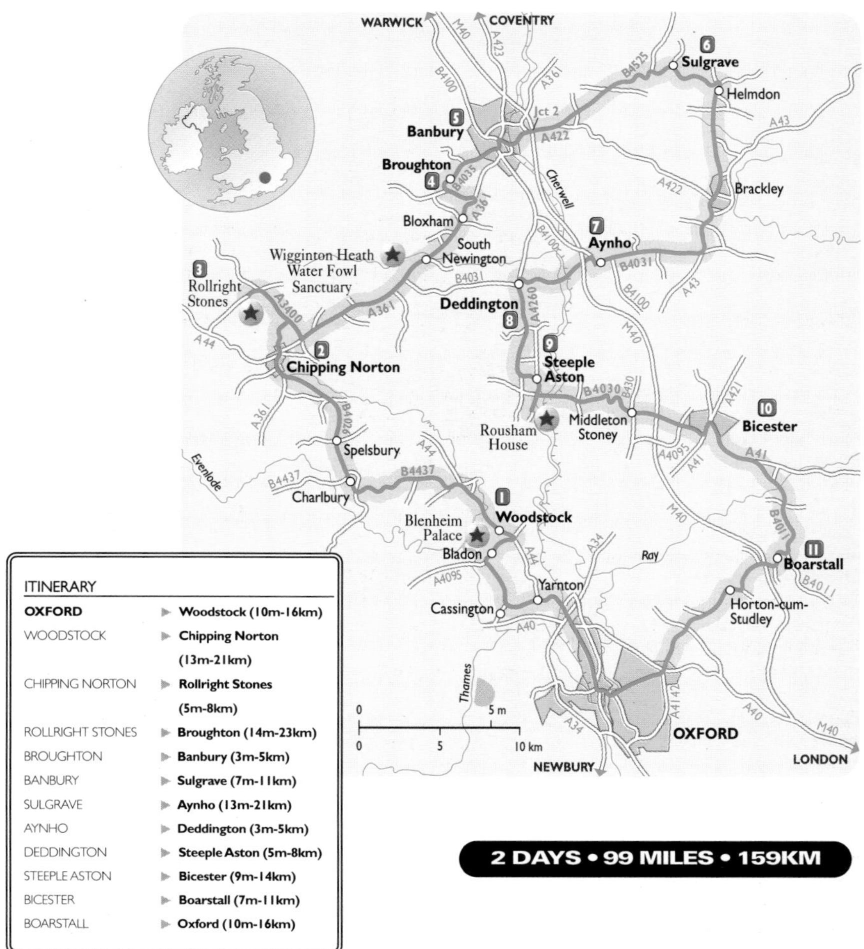


| ITINERARY | |
|---|---|
| **OXFORD** | ▶ **Woodstock (10m-16km)** |
| WOODSTOCK | ▶ **Chipping Norton (13m-21km)** |
| CHIPPING NORTON | ▶ **Rollright Stones (5m-8km)** |
| ROLLRIGHT STONES | ▶ **Broughton (14m-23km)** |
| BROUGHTON | ▶ **Banbury (3m-5km)** |
| BANBURY | ▶ **Sulgrave (7m-11km)** |
| SULGRAVE | ▶ **Aynho (13m-21km)** |
| AYNHO | ▶ **Deddington (3m-5km)** |
| DEDDINGTON | ▶ **Steeple Aston (5m-8km)** |
| STEEPLE ASTON | ▶ **Bicester (9m-14km)** |
| BICESTER | ▶ **Boarstall (7m-11km)** |
| BOARSTALL | ▶ **Oxford (10m-16km)** |

**2 DAYS • 99 MILES • 159KM**

Bliss Tweed Mill, now flats, near the old wool town of Chipping Norton

*i* *St Aldates, Oxford*

▶ *Leave Oxford on the **A44** and turn left along an unclassified road towards Cassington. Turn right to Bladon on the **A4095** then left on the **A44** to Woodstock.*

**1 Woodstock,** Oxfordshire
You can stop off in Bladon, to visit the churchyard where Sir Winston Churchill and his wife and parents are buried, before continuing along the road to Blenheim, where he was born. Blenheim Palace was given to the Marlborough family by Queen Anne as a reward for a major victory by the 1st Duke of Marlborough over the French at Blenheim in 1704. Just outside the park is the old town of Woodstock, with its mellow stone buildings. Kings of England used to come here for the excellent hunting in the Forest of Wychwood, but modern visitors have gentler interests. A quiet hour can be spent in the Oxfordshire County Museum, in the town centre, where the history of the people and the changing landscape is conveyed in exhibitions which range from the Stone Age to the present time.

BACK TO NATURE

**The grounds of Blenheim Palace, at Woodstock, were landscaped by Capability Brown and comprise rolling, formal parkland and an attractive lake. This harbours breeding dragonflies and is home to Canada geese, mute swans, great crested grebes and kingfishers. In the winter months, look for roaming flocks of siskins, redpolls and long tailed tits in the birch trees.**

*i* *Hensington Road*

▶ *From Woodstock take the **A44** turning left on to the **B4437** to Charlbury and then the **B4026** to Chipping Norton.*

**2 Chipping Norton,** Oxfordshire
Gateway to the Cotswolds and historic market town, this was the market for the sheep farmers of the area, and the wide main street is a relic of those days (the name 'chipping' means market). There are many fine old stone buildings, including the church, market hall, pubs and big houses, but it is the fine wool church which dominates the town, one of over 40 in the Cotswolds. Paid for by the proceeds from sheep farming, it is mainly 14th- and 15th-century, but much of its stonework has been restored. Another of the town's landmarks is the chimney of Bliss Tweed Mill which is an important reminder of local history.

*i* *5 Middle Row*

▶ *Take the **B4026**, then go north along the **A3400** for just over a mile (1.6km) and turn left along an unclassified road signed Little Rollright.*

**3 Rollright Stones,** Oxfordshire
This Bronze Age circle, which dates from earlier than 1000BC, was nearly as important as Stonehenge in the Neolithic period. Nicknamed the 'King's Men', it measures a full 100 feet (30m) across. Over the road is the King Stone, a monolith, and near by, just along the road, is the group of stones called the Whispering Knights, at the site of a prehistoric burial chamber. The surrounding countryside is

Broughton Castle is a fine example of a gracious Elizabethan Manor

patterned with stone walls of weathered limestone.

▶ *Return to the **A3400** and turn south before branching left on to the **A361**, then turn left in Bloxham along unclassified roads to Broughton.*

> **FOR CHILDREN**
>
> Just before reaching Bloxham, on the road from Rollright to Broughton, you will pass the Wigginton Heath Water Fowl Sanctuary. Conservation is the main aim, with flowers, goats, sheep, lambs and other animals, as well as a bewildering assortment of birds. Various ducks, geese, black swans, owls, doves and peacocks can all be seen at very close quarters. There is also a nature trail and an adventure playground.

### 4 Broughton, Oxfordshire

Broughton Castle is a fortified manor rather than a castle, turned into an Elizabethan house of style by the Fiennes family in about 1600. Surrounded by a great moat lake, it is set in gorgeous parkland, and has a stone church near by. The present owners, Lord and Lady Saye and Sele, are descendants of the family that has lived here for centuries. Celia Fiennes, the 17th-century traveller and diarist, was a member of this family. William de Wykeham, founder of Winchester School and New College, Oxford, acquired the manor and converted the manor house into a castle. The medieval Great Hall is the most impressive room, and suits of armour from the Civil War are on show.

▶ *Drive 3 miles (5km) east along the **B4035** to Banbury.*

### 5 Banbury, Oxfordshire

Banbury is a town of charm and character, with its interesting buildings and narrow medieval streets. Famous for the nursery rhyme 'Ride a cock horse to Banbury Cross', the town is also known for its spice cakes, which have been made here since the 16th century. The unusual church with its round tower replaced an older one demolished in the 18th century. There is still a weekly street market, which has been held regularly for over 800 years, and there used to be a livestock market, too, but nowadays the animals are taken to a permanent site on the edge of town, Europe's largest cattle market.

*i* *Banbury Museum, 8 Horsefair*

> **FOR HISTORY BUFFS**
>
> Banbury's wool industry was helped by the opening of the Oxford Canal in 1790, connecting Banbury with the Midland coalfields and markets in London. The narrow boats on the canals used to be pulled by horses which walked along the towpath, and a family would live permanently on the boat.

> **RECOMMENDED WALKS**
>
> Along the Oxford Canal, near Banbury, is the delightful 9-mile (14km) Banbury circuit, which takes in the villages of Wroxton with its duckpond, Horley, Hornton, Alkerton, an old Saxon village with ironstone houses, Shennington and Balscott.

**SPECIAL TO...**

Banbury's cross, in Horsefair, was built in 1859 to commemorate the marriage of Victoria, Princess Royal, and the Crown Prince of Prussia. Its design is based on the Eleanor Crosses, built in the 13th century to mark the resting stages of Queen Eleanor's funeral cortège *en route* to London for burial.

▶ *Head eastwards along the* ***A422****, turning left after 2 miles (3km) on to the* ***B4525*** *to Sulgrave.*

**6 Sulgrave,** Northamptonshire

The old manor in this attractive stone village was the home of ancestors of George Washington from 1539 to 1659, having been bought by Lawrence Washington, wool merchant and twice Mayor of Northampton. Not to be missed is the family coat of arms with its stars and stripes carved above the entrance porch, and the most treasured possession inside is an original oil painting of George Washington.

▶ *Take the unclassified road through Helmdon, heading south to Brackley to join the* ***A43, then shortly*** *right on to the* ***B4031*** *to Aynho.*

**7 Aynho,** Northamptonshire

This limestone village contains apricot trees from which, legend has it, fruit was paid as a toll to the Cartwrights, Lords of the Manor. They lived in the mansion in Aynhoe Park, and there are several memorials to them, including a Victorian marble cross in the church.

▶ *From Aynho go west along the* ***B4031*** *to Deddington.*

**8 Deddington,** Oxfordshire

Dominating this village, which is built out of the honey-coloured local stone, is the church, with each of its eight pinnacles topped with gilded vanes. Adjacent Castle House was formerly the rectory, and parts of the building date from the 14th century. The area has many links with the days of the Civil War, and Charles I is believed to have slept at the 16th-century Castle Farm near by.

▶ *Drive southwards for 5 miles (8km) along the* ***A4260*** *and then left on to an unclassified road to Steeple Aston.*

**9 Steeple Aston,** Oxfordshire

Steeple Aston was winner of the Oxfordshire Best Kept Village Award in 1981 and 1983, and is still an eye-catching village. The village inn, Hopcroft's Holt, had associations with Claude Duval, a French highwayman who worked in these parts. Just beyond Steeple Aston is the Jacobean mansion of Rousham House, built by Sir Robert Dormer in 1635 and still owned by the same family. William Kent improved the house in the 18th century by adding the wings and stable block. In the magnificent garden, the complete Kent layout has survived. There is a fine herd of rare Long Horn cattle in the park, and you should be sure not to miss the walled garden.

▶ *Another unclassified road leads south on to the* ***B4030*** *in turn leading to the* ***A4095*** *for the 9 miles (14km) to Bicester.*

**10 Bicester,** Oxfordshire

Little can be seen of the Roman town at Alchester, to the south of Bicester, but excavations show that people lived here from about the middle of the 1st century AD until the late Roman period. Bicester itself is a market town with many old streets. Its church contains elements of a 13th-century building, and there was once a 12th-century priory near by.

▶ *Take the* ***A41*** *following the line of an old Roman road and then the* ***B4011*** *towards Thame before turning sharp right to Boarstall.*

**11 Boarstall,** Buckinghamshire

This tiny hamlet is the location of Boarstall Tower, an amazing stone gatehouse which was originally part of a massive fortified house. It dates from the 14th century and is now looked after by the National Trust, who also own Boarstall Duck Decoy. This 18th-century decoy is in 13 acres (5 hectares) of natural old woodland. Attractions include a small exhibition hall, nature trail and bird hide.

▶ *Take unclassified roads via Horton-cum-Studley along the edge of Otmoor for the return to Oxford.*

**SCENIC ROUTES**

The A44 from Woodstock to Chipping Norton gives excellent views across rolling countryside. Bloxham and the village of South Newington show Cotswold settlements at their best, especially in the summer, and the skyline of Oxford, with its impressive array of dreaming spires, is unique.

TOUR 19

# **The Rural** Heart of England

Across the Severn plain, through **2 DAYS • 128 MILES • 207KM** a gap in the Malvern Hills and into the Avon valley, this route eventually climbs up on to the hills of the Cotswolds, where stone-built villages have become part of the countryside.

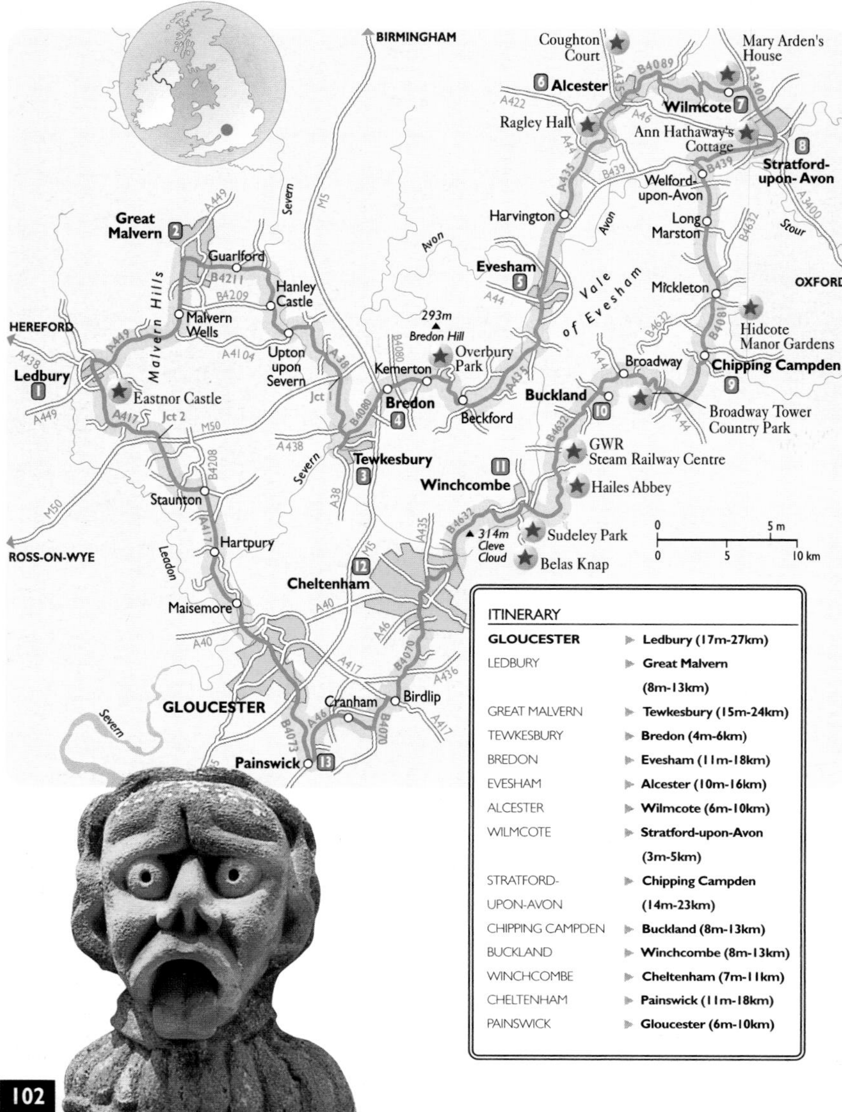


ITINERARY

| | |
|---|---|
| **GLOUCESTER** | ▶ **Ledbury (17m-27km)** |
| LEDBURY | ▶ **Great Malvern (8m-13km)** |
| GREAT MALVERN | ▶ **Tewkesbury (15m-24km)** |
| TEWKESBURY | ▶ **Bredon (4m-6km)** |
| BREDON | ▶ **Evesham (11m-18km)** |
| EVESHAM | ▶ **Alcester (10m-16km)** |
| ALCESTER | ▶ **Wilmcote (6m-10km)** |
| WILMCOTE | ▶ **Stratford-upon-Avon (3m-5km)** |
| STRATFORD-UPON-AVON | ▶ **Chipping Campden (14m-23km)** |
| CHIPPING CAMPDEN | ▶ **Buckland (8m-13km)** |
| BUCKLAND | ▶ **Winchcombe (8m-13km)** |
| WINCHCOMBE | ▶ **Cheltenham (7m-11km)** |
| CHELTENHAM | ▶ **Painswick (11m-18km)** |
| PAINSWICK | ▶ **Gloucester (6m-10km)** |

Bredon's medieval tithe barn

[i] *St Michael's Tower, The Cross, Gloucester*

**BACK TO NATURE**

The Wildfowl Trust reserve at Slimbridge, southwest of Gloucester off the A38, is known the world over for its impressive collection of wildfowl, at their most spectacular in late winter and early spring when the males are in full breeding plumage.

▶ *Take the **A417** for 17 miles (27km) to Ledbury.*

### 1 Ledbury, Hereford and Worcester

The unspoilt market town of Ledbury, with its half-timbered buildings, has many literary links: Robert Browning and William Wordsworth used to visit, and John Masefield was born here. Elizabeth Barrett Browning spent her childhood at Hope End, just out of town, and her father lies buried in the north aisle of St Michael's Church. One of the most attractive buildings is the 16th-century Feathers Inn, and Ledbury Park is the house Prince Rupert used as his headquarters during the Civil War. Nineteenth-century Eastnor Castle, with its impressive interior is surrounded by a beautiful park.

[i] *1 Church Lane*

▶ *Follow the **A449** through Wynds Gap and Malvern Wells to Great Malvern, 8 miles (13km).*

### 2 Great Malvern, Hereford and Worcester

Pure spring water from the Malvern Hills made this a popular spa town in Victorian days. A steep flight of steps by the Mount Pleasant Hotel leads up to St Anne's Well, the source of this water. The town is centred round its greatest treasure, the Priory Church of St Mary and St Michael, which contains exquisite 15th- and 16th-century stained glass and beautiful tiles. Malvern Museum portrays the town through the ages, and there is an elegant Victorian bandstand where bands play on Sunday afternoons in summer.

[i] *Winter Gardens, Grange Road*

▶ *Take the **B4211** to Upton upon Severn, turning left on to the **A4104**, and in 1 mile (1.6km) on to the **A38** to Tewkesbury.*

### 3 Tewkesbury, Gloucestershire

Almost all Tewkesbury's buildings are old timber-framed structures, notably the Bell Inn, and the Royal Hop Pole Inn is mentioned in *The Pickwick Papers* by Charles Dickens. Tewkesbury Abbey is one of the finest Norman abbeys in the country and contains several medieval stained-glass windows.

[i] *The Museum, 64 Barton Street*

▶ *Return on the **A38** for a short distance, then take the **B4080** to Bredon.*

### 4 Bredon, Hereford and Worcester

Bredon, alongside the River Avon, at the foot of Bredon Hill, is a picturebook village. Its impressive Norman church has a graceful spire which soars 160 feet (48m) high, and the tithe barn dates from the 14th century. A mile (1.6km) east is the village of Kemerton, with its fine church. Overbury Park, just outside the village, leads to Bredon Hill, which rises to 961 feet (293m). It has a fine Gothic folly on its slopes and the remains of prehistoric and Roman earthworks on its summit.

► *Continue along an unclassified road through Kemerton and Beckford, then take the* ***A435*** *to Evesham.*

### 5 Evesham, Hereford and Worcester

Evesham is a market town in the heart of the Vale of Evesham, noted for its fruit blossom in spring. A 15th-century half-timbered gateway in the market place is one of the few remains of Evesham Abbey.

At the centre of town is the 110-foot (33m) high Bell Tower, which was built in 1539. There are two fine churches: 12th-century All Saints' Church and the Church of St Lawrence. A plaque near the river marks the burial spot of Simon de Montfort, the 'father of the English parliament', who led barons in revolt against Henry III and was killed at the Battle of Evesham in 1265.

*i The Almonry Museum, Abbey Gate*

► *Take the* ***A435*** *for another 10 miles (16km) to Alcester.*

### 6 Alcester, Warwickshire

Pronounced 'Olster', this former Roman town contains many old streets and houses, notably Malt Mill Lane, which is lined with ancient houses. Coughton Court, 2 miles (3km) to the north, is the family home of the Throckmortons, who were implicated in the Gunpowder Plot to blow up Parliament in 1605. The house contains the 'Throckmorton coat', which was made in 1811 to prove that it was possible to take the wool off a sheep and produce a coat from it in one day! Southwest of town is Ragley Hall, a Jacobean mansion whose great hall is decorated with exquisite rococo plaster-work.

► *Follow the* ***B4089****, then unclassified roads east to Wilmcote.*

### 7 Wilmcote, Warwickshire

This sprawling village is best known for the lovely timbered farmhouse which was the home of Mary Arden, Shakespeare's mother. It is now a museum of furniture and the farm buildings contain exhibitions of agricultural implements and country bygones, including man traps which were used to catch poachers.

The unpretentious simplicity of Mary Arden's home, Wilmcote

► *Continue along the unclassified road, then the* ***A3400*** *for 3 miles (5km) to Stratford-upon-Avon.*

### 8 Stratford-upon-Avon, Warwickshire

Stratford has retained its role as a market town despite being one of the world's most famous tourist centres. Shakespeare's Birthplace in Henley Street is now a museum and contains exhibits about the poet's life. Stratford is full of interesting places to visit, including the Royal Shakespeare Company Gallery and the World of Shakespeare. One of the most ornate timbered houses is Harvard House, the former home of the mother of John Harvard, who founded Harvard University in the US. In a house in Greenhill Street, dating from Shakespeares' days, is the National Teddy Bear Museum which will appeal to all ages.

*i Bridgefoot*

**SPECIAL TO...**

**With the exception of London, Shakespeare's Stratford is probably the best known town in England. A tour of selected locations can take you through his life, starting with his birth-place in Henley Street, then on to the 15th-century half-timbered Grammar School in Church Street, which he attended. Most famous of all is Anne Hathaway's cottage, home of the woman he was to marry. New Place, on Chapel Street, was the site of his last home.**

► *Leave Stratford, going west along the* ***B439*** *for 4 miles (6km) before turning south along unclassified roads through Welford-on-Avon and Long Marston to the* ***B4632****. Turn right and soon left on to the* ***B4081*** *to Chipping Campden.*

### 9 Chipping Campden, Gloucestershire

Wool made this town rich, and it retains a wealth of beautiful architecture. The Jacobean Market Hall in the High Street

Anne Hathaway's House, Shottery, where she lived before her marriage to William Shakespeare

was built in 1627, and the Woolstaplers' Hall is now the town museum. The Church of St James is one of the most splendid Cotswold churches. Hidcote Manor Gardens, to the northeast have six gardens with winter borders, camellia corners, terraces and walks.

[i] *Woolstaplers Museum, High Street*

► *Take the **B4081** and the **A44** through Broadway, then the **B4632** and a minor road to Buckland.*

**10 Buckland,** Gloucestershire

Buckland is a quiet village nestling at the foot of the Cotswolds, whose rectory is England's oldest and most complete medieval parsonage. Further along the B4632 is the GWR Steam Railway Centre at Toddington, where you can make a 6-mile (9km) round trip.

Leave the B4632 to visit Hailes Abbey, where the old Cistercian ruins stand alongside the 12th-century parish church. In 1270 a small jar of blood, supposedly that of Christ, was given to the abbey, and brought it much fame as a centre of pilgrimage.

**FOR CHILDREN**

Broadway Tower Country Park, to the east of Buckland, is an ideal place to spend the day with the family. The late 18th-century mock castle has an observation room and telescope giving views over 12 counties. Other attractions include an educational display of local geology, an adventure playground, and a collection of rare animals.

► *Follow the unclassified road to Winchcombe, a distance of 8 miles (13km).*

**11 Winchcombe,** Gloucestershire

This attractive town was once the capital of the Kingdom of Mercia. Its abbey, founded 797, was destroyed during the Dissolution, but the site has been excavated. The Railway Museum has many relics of the steam age, and the town hall houses the Folk Museum and a Police Museum.

Sudeley Park, reached through the village, was once the house of Catherine Parr, the last of Henry VIII's wives. The magnificent gardens have been developed and renovated.

Just east of town on the B4632, at the top of the hill at Cleeve Hill, are the remnants of a settlement and earthworks, and much good walking, including the Cotswold Way, a long distance footpath. Cleeve Cloud,

1031 feet (314m), is one of the highest points in the Cotswolds, and the views from its summit are quite spectacular.

> FOR HISTORY BUFFS
>
> From Winchcombe you can drive to within ¾ mile (1km) of the Bronze Age ancient long barrow at Belas Knap on its hilltop site, probably the finest example of a false-entrance longbarrow in the Cotswolds. When it was excavated 36 skeletons were found in 10 separate chambers.

*i* *Town Hall, High Street*

▶ *Continue along the **B4632** to Cheltenham.*

### 12 Cheltenham, Gloucestershire

Cheltenham started life as a typical Cotswold village, but the discovery of a mineral spring in 1718 turned it into a fashionable spa. The Promenade, a wide street with Regency houses, has been described as the most beautiful thoroughfare in Britain. The famous Pittville Pump Room, with its colonnade and dome, is a masterpiece of 19th-century Greek revival. There are many other old buildings and museums worth visiting, such as the Gustav Holst Museum housed in the composer's birthplace and containing rooms with period furnishing. The town is famous for its two schools, the College for Boys and Cheltenham Ladies' College.

*i* *77 Promenade*

▶ *Take the **B4070** south to Birdlip and follow the Stroud road until an unclassified road leads through Cranham and on to the **A46** to Painswick.*

### 13 Painswick, Gloucestershire

Painswick is an old wool town with many buildings of note, but is dominated by 15th-century St Mary's Church and its collection of '99' yew trees. Tradition says that only 99 will grow at any one time – the Devil always kills off the 100th. Among the town's many old houses are Court House, with its tall chimneys, and 18th-century Painswick House. South of town a few old cloth mills have survived on Painswick stream.

*i* *Painswick Library, Stroud Road*

▶ *Return to Gloucester on the **B4073**.*

> SCENIC ROUTES
>
> Cotswold villages and towns are all attractive but the view over Cranham from the unclassified road to Painswick is one of the most exciting. The Malvern Hills and the dramatic silhouette of the Herefordshire Beacon (the British Camp) are best seen along the A449 from Ledbury.

> RECOMMENDED WALKS
>
> Footpaths on this tour range from very easy gentle strolls to much longer and arduous walks. A climb to the top of the Worcestershire Beacons in the Malverns will give one of the finest views in England, with the green undulations of Hereford to the west and the flatter Severn valley to the east.

Below: Hailes Abbey, Winchcombe
Right: Bridgnorth open-air market

# Old Volcanoes & Bridges in Shropshire

**1/2 DAYS • 102 MILES • 164KM**

The Welsh border counties are among the greenest parts of Britain. Gentle hills and steep-sided volcanic cones add variety to the scenery. The Severn Valley is the birthplace of the industrial revolution.

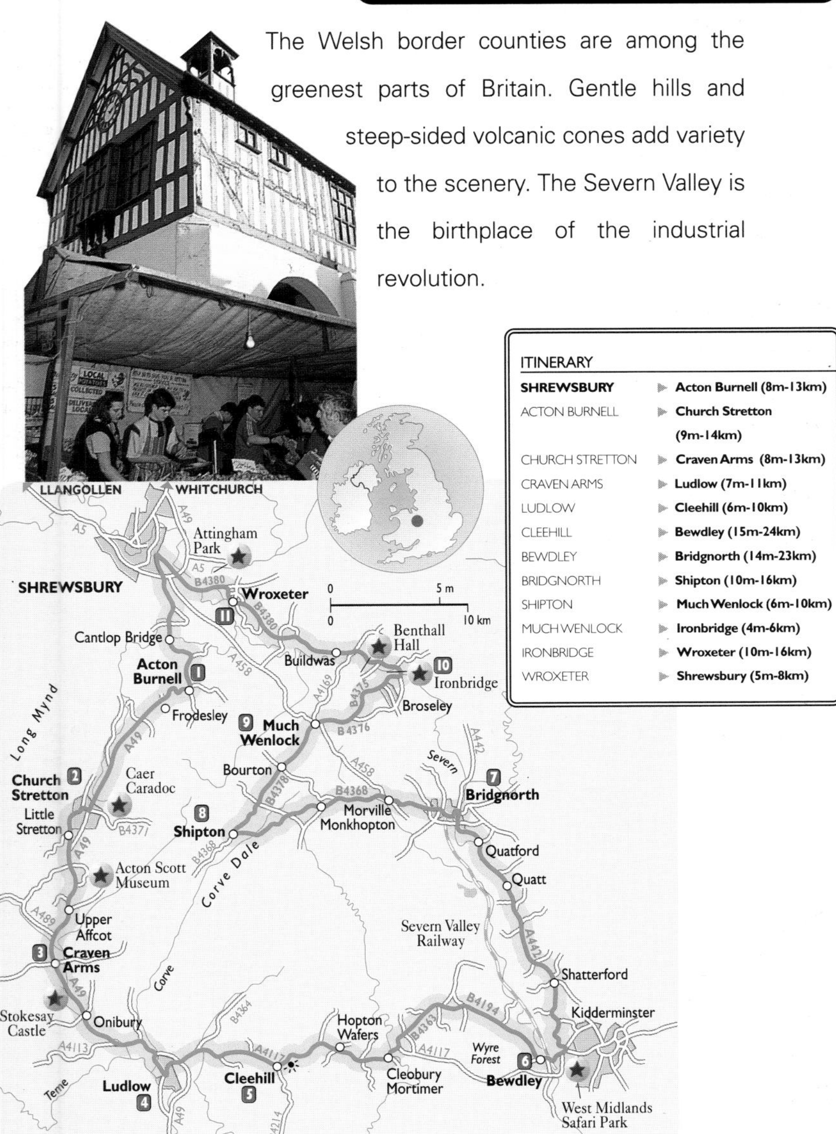


| ITINERARY | |
|---|---|
| **SHREWSBURY** | ▶ **Acton Burnell (8m-13km)** |
| ACTON BURNELL | ▶ **Church Stretton (9m-14km)** |
| CHURCH STRETTON | ▶ **Craven Arms (8m-13km)** |
| CRAVEN ARMS | ▶ **Ludlow (7m-11km)** |
| LUDLOW | ▶ **Cleehill (6m-10km)** |
| CLEEHILL | ▶ **Bewdley (15m-24km)** |
| BEWDLEY | ▶ **Bridgnorth (14m-23km)** |
| BRIDGNORTH | ▶ **Shipton (10m-16km)** |
| SHIPTON | ▶ **Much Wenlock (6m-10km)** |
| MUCH WENLOCK | ▶ **Ironbridge (4m-6km)** |
| IRONBRIDGE | ▶ **Wroxeter (10m-16km)** |
| WROXETER | ▶ **Shrewsbury (5m-8km)** |

# Old Volcanoes & Bridges in Shropshire

*i The Square, Shrewsbury*

▶ *Take the **A458** as far as the ring road where unclassified roads lead to Cantlop Bridge and Acton Burnell, 8 miles (13km).*

**1 Acton Burnell,** Shropshire
On the edge of this picturesque village, with its timber-framed black-and-white cottages and grey-green stone buildings, is a cast-iron bridge, built in 1810 to a design by Thomas Telford. Acton Burnell Castle is a red sandstone ruin, which dates from the 13th century; it is said the first English Parliament met here in 1283. The Church of St Mary is almost entirely 13th-century, apart from its Victorian tower, and contains memorials to the Burnell family who held the manor in 1183. It also houses memorials to the Lees family, who owned the village in the 17th century and who were ancestors of General Robert E Lee, chief commander of the Southern forces in the American Civil war.

▶ *Follow unclassified roads via Frodesley then the **A49** to Church Stretton, 9 miles (14km).*

**2 Church Stretton,** Shropshire
Church Stretton is in fact three settlements. All Stretton lies to the north of the main town, and Little Stretton stands 1½ miles (2.5km) south. The town's medieval remains are in the High Street, along with its 18th- and 19th-century buildings. The Church of St Laurence is partly 12th-century Norman with a 14th-century roof. In the south transept is a memorial to Sarah Smith, the Victorian novelist who wrote under the name of Hesba Stretton. The town was popular with Victorians who came to sample its natural spring water.

▶ *Continue south along the **B4370**, joining the **A49** to Craven Arms.*

### FOR CHILDREN

Acton Scott Working Farm Museum, near Church Stretton, shows life on a Shropshire farm before the introduction of the internal combustion engine. This is not just a show place but a going concern, and visitors can even lend a helping hand. The farm is stocked with rare breeds – it is one of the few places you can see the Tamworth pig – and has a fishpool, waymarked nature trail, café and paddocks. Strong boots and warm clothing are recommended.

### BACK TO NATURE

The Long Mynd, near Church Stretton, is a rocky plateau covered in moorland. Bracken and bilberry grow on the slopes and boggy areas harbour sundews and butterworts. The open moors are home to red grouse, with ring ouzels and wheatears favouring rocky outcrops. Bleak and dangerous in winter, it is splendid walking country in good weather.

**3 Craven Arms,** Shropshire
This small village was originally the hamlet of Newton, but in the 19th century it developed and was named after a coaching inn. Today it is a centre for livestock auctions, at the foot of Wenlock Edge, a steep out-crop of limestone. Stokesay Castle, ½ mile (1km) along the road, is the best preserved and oldest example of a fortified manor house in England.

▶ *Keep on with the **A49** a further 7 miles (11km) to Ludlow.*

**4 Ludlow,** Shropshire
Ludlow is a pearl in a sea of riches and has been described as 'the perfect historic town', with nearly 500 listed buildings. Two buildings worthy of a visit are Ludlow Castle, which dates from Norman times, and the magnificent sandstone Church of St Laurence. Mainly 15th-century, it is the largest in the county and the ashes of the poet A E Housman lie in its churchyard. Near by are 17th-century Feathers Hotel, and the beautiful black-and-white Reader's House. Ludlow Museum, in Buttercross, tells the story of the town from Norman times, and a major arts festival takes place here in late June and early July.

### FOR HISTORY BUFFS

Before Catharine of Aragon married Henry VIII she was his brother's bride. Prince Arthur, the eldest son of Henry VII, brought Catharine to Ludlow Castle and had the gardens designed in a series of walks for her. Arthur died at Ludlow and his younger brother Henry became king.

*i Castle Street*

▶ *Take the **A4117** going east for 6 miles (10km) to Cleehill.*

Reader's House, Ludlow, has a three-storey Jacobean porch

**5 Cleehill,** Shropshire
East of Cleehill, on the A4117, is an AA Viewpoint which offers amazing views over Tenbury and the Teme Valley, towards the hills in the distance. The strange 'golf ball' on 1,750-foot (533m) Titterstone Clee Hill, north of the village, is part of a satellite tracking station. Further along the A4117, running east, is Cleobury Mortimer, with its remarkable twisted wooden church tower. Hugh de Mortimer built a fortress here in 1160 and its earthworks can still be seen near the church.

▶ *Follow the* ***B4363*** *turning right on to the* ***B4194*** *through Wyre Forest to Bewdley.*

**6 Bewdley,** Hereford and Worcester
This elegant Georgian town was a major port of England in the 17th and 18th centuries. For many years boats were manhandled up the River Severn by a hardy breed of boatmen called 'bow hauliers'. There are pleasant walks in the Wyre Forest, and the Severn Valley Railway runs to Bridgnorth through fields and woods. Near by is West Midlands Safari Park, a leisure park with animal reserves and amusements.

> **BACK TO NATURE**
>
> West of Bewdley is Wyre Forest, all that remains of a vast royal hunting forest mentioned in the Domesday Book. It is an area of mixed heath, scrub and oak woodland, with plantations of Douglas fir and larch, where fallow deer roam and silver-washed fritillary butterflies glide.

[i] *Load Street*

▶ *Take the* ***B4190*** *towards Kidderminster turning left on to unclassified roads towards Shatterford, then turning left on to the* ***A442*** *to Bridgnorth.*

**7 Bridgnorth,** Shropshire
There are two parts to this historic market centre, connected by a winding main road, a cliff railway and a steep flight of steps. The original settlement was in the High Town, where Bridgnorth Castle was built. The only remaining fragment is the leaning tower, which is set at a steeper angle than the Leaning Tower of Pisa. The most graceful building is Italianate St Mary Magdalene's Church, built in 1792 by Thomas Telford. For railway enthusiasts there is not only the Severn Valley Railway, but also the funicular, linking the upper and lower parts of the town. In Low Town is Bishop Percy's House, a fine half-timbered building of 1580.

Stokesay Castle is really a fortified manor house

[i] *The Library, Listley Street*

▶ *Leave Bridgnorth on the* ***A458****, then after 3 miles (5km) turn left at Morville on to the* ***B4368*** *to Shipton.*

**8 Shipton,** Shropshire
Set in the heart of Corve Dale, with views of Brown Clee Hill to the south, this small village sits

The town of Ironbridge, famous for its bridge, took a leading role in the Industrial Revolution

snugly in the midst of the green fields and valley. Shipton Hall is the focal point, a beautiful complex of stone buildings dating from 1587. There is an attractive walled garden, medieval dovecote and old parish church, as well as a fine 18th-century stable block.

► *Take the **B4378** to Much Wenlock*

**9 Much Wenlock,** Shropshire
This charming market town has many half-timbered buildings, notably the Manor House, the Guildhall and Raynald's Mansion. Ruined Wenlock Priory was founded by St Milburga in the 7th century as a convent and destroyed by Danes in the 9th century. It was rebuilt by Lady Godiva and her husband, Leofric, in the 11th century, though it was soon destroyed again by the Normans. Benthall Hall, 4 miles (6km) northeast, is a 16th-century house with fine panelling, a carved oak staircase and mullioned windows.

*i* ***The Museum, The Square***

► *Leave Much Wenlock on the **B4376** turning left on to the **B4375**. In a short distance turn left on to an unclassified road to Ironbridge.*

**10 Ironbridge,** Shropshire
Ironbridge was in the forefront of the Industrial Revolution. Its splendid iron bridge over the River Severn, the first of its kind in the world, was built in 1778 by Abraham Darby to enable traffic to pass across the river without interrupting its navigation. West of Ironbridge, the B4380 brings you to Buildwas, where the bridge over the Severn is a 1906 replacement of Telford's original one. The ruins of nearby 12th-century Buildwas Abbey, now roofless and without its aisle walls, are a striking contrast to the enormous cooling towers of the power station downstream. Stone from the ruin was incorporated in the local church.

*i* *The Wharfage*

▶ *Continue for 2 miles (3km) on an unclassified road to take the **B4380** to Wroxeter.*

### 11 **Wroxeter,** Shropshire

Near this quiet little village is the Roman town of *Viroconium*, which was the fourth largest town in Roman Britain. A walk round the site reveals the baths, a market hall and fragments of other buildings. The most impressive relic of the baths is the 20-foot (6m) wall, where a square entrance once had double doors leading to the *frigidarium* or 'cooling off' room. A museum displays pottery, painted plaster and coins from the site.

Two miles (3km) northwest on the B4380 is Atcham, where Attingham Park features magnificent gardens woodlands and a deer park. The gardens are open throughout the year, and the house contains a fine collection of early 19th-century English and Italian furniture. Parts of the red sandstone 13th-century Church of St Eata were built with stones from the ruins of *Viroconium*.

▶ *Continue along the **B4380** to return to Shrewsbury, 5 miles (8km).*

#### SCENIC ROUTES

In the Shipton area the scenery is gentle and the B4378 to Much Wenlock runs through Corve Dale with fine views of the River Corve. From Acton Burnell to Church Stretton, along the A49 and the unclassified road, the views are spectacular, with Long Mynd to the west and Caer Caradoc Hill, where it is thought the Romans defeated the British leader Caractacus in AD50, to the east.

#### RECOMMENDED WALKS

The Shropshire Way is a long distance walk from Whitchurch through Shrewsbury to Clun and the Clee Hills. There are several walks around Ludlow, notably across the Teme and on to Whitcliffe Common, which was the town's common land in the Middle Ages, and the Forestry Commission have several attractive, clearly marked walks, such as from the Wyre Forest centre near Bewdley.

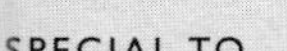

#### SPECIAL TO...

Six miles (9km) of the Severn Valley changed the world as a result of industrial developments in the late 18th and 19th centuries. Here, the past is portrayed in the museums of Ironbridge, Coalbrookdale, Jackfield and Coalport.

The Ironbridge Gorge Museum was one of the first World Heritage Sites in Britain, and one ticket admits you to the bridge, the Darby furnace, Blists Hill, Coalport China Museum, the tile museum, Rosehill House and elsewhere. The ticket is valid indefinitely.

The ruins of Wenlock Priory

# THE NORTH

Dry stone walls at Grassington

The North of England is noted for the old industrial towns of Lancashire and Yorkshire, where communities developed in the wake of the coal mining, engineering, woollen and cotton manufacturing industries. They have become modern thriving towns, while retaining much of historical interest, including relics of the industrial revolution. Surrounding these urban areas are some of the finest expanses of British countryside, especially in the Lake District, which has spellbound the adventurous traveller since the earliest days of tourism, and the Pennines, known as 'the backbone of England'.

Visitors from all over the world are attracted by the scenic beauties of the Lake District, with its mountains, still lakes and villages which seem to have grown out of this rocky landscape. Stone walls can be seen stretching skywards over all but the highest hills, in an area where beauty inspired Wordsworth, bringing walkers and climbers in their droves.

The Lake District villages are generally built of lava or slate, except in Eskdale, to the west, where pink granite is found, but those in the Pennines are quite different: dark and somewhat forbidding in areas of millstone grit, or light and cheery where carboniferous limestone is the local rock. Old quarries and mines are dotted around the hills, and the higher parts of the Pennines became moorland, often bleak and isolated.

Down in the valleys, conditions are kinder to man and animals, and on the lowlands which surround these hill masses there is much rich farming, generally for cattle and sheep, which appreciate the lush grasslands. The larger lowlands, such as the Vale of York, the Lancashire and Cheshire Plain and lowlands of Solway, are where most of the large towns have grown up.

**Carlisle**
The regional capital of Cumbria is a well-placed city, with the Lake District to the south and Hadrian's wall to the north. Carlisle's castle has been a border fortress since Norman times, and its detailed history is portrayed in an exhibition in the keep. A military museum, dedicated to the Border regiments, is also housed here. The cathedral is one of England's smallest, and has remarkable carved choir stalls. Near by is the Carlisle Cross, where servants were once hired, and where Bonnie Prince Charlie stood to claim the throne of England in 1745.

**Morecambe**
This Victorian seaside resort overlooks Morecambe Bay, with its miles of sand, and the Lake District hills are clearly visible to the north. Traditionally a holiday centre for visitors from northern England, Morecambe retains its popularity, and the late weeks of the summer season have the added attraction of 'illuminations'. Marineland, with its displays of marine life and the famous dolphins, was the first oceanarium in Europe.

**Ripon**
Ripon is a busy little town, dominated by its cathedral, one of the oldest in England. An ancient Saxon crypt, thought to date from AD672, lies beneath the cathedral, and inside the fine features include a 16th-century Gothic nave. Another ancient building is the Wakeman's House, built in the 14th century for the man who would 'set the watch' by blowing a horn at 9pm every evening – a practice which continues today. An inscription on the 19th-century Town Hall reminds residents that 'Except ye Lord keep ye cittie, ye Wakeman waketh in vain'. The Prison and Police Museum is well worth a visit.

Ashness Bridge, Derwent Water

**York**
It was the Vikings who established the settlement of Jorvik, which was developed by the Normans as the capital of the north. History lives in every street of this glorious city, which celebrates its 10th-century origins in the time-travelling Jorvik Viking Museum and recreates whole streets from the past in the Castle Museum of Yorkshire Life. But the greatest treasure is York Minster, the largest medieval cathedral in northern Europe, whose grandeur and beauty are unsurpassable. You will need a long stay to see everything of interest in York: medieval houses overhanging the narrow Shambles; the extensive city walls; and the National Railway Museum, a favourite with children and railway buffs, are only a few of its wealth of attractions.

**Macclesfield**
This old textile town made its name from the manufacture of silk, and there are still some of the 18th- and 19th-century mills on the steep streets overlooking the Bollin Valley. The story of silk can be seen in the award-winning Silk Museum, and you can visit the Paradise Silk Mill, a working mill until 1981. Macclesfield's other outstanding attraction is the church, originally founded in the 13th century, which sits high above the town and can be reached by climbing 108 steps.

TOUR
**21**

# The Heart of Lakeland

Leave the soft red sandstones of Carlisle and the Eden Valley to weave through hills of volcanic rocks and lakes carved out during the last Ice Age, before heading into the Pennines, with their different, gentler beauty.

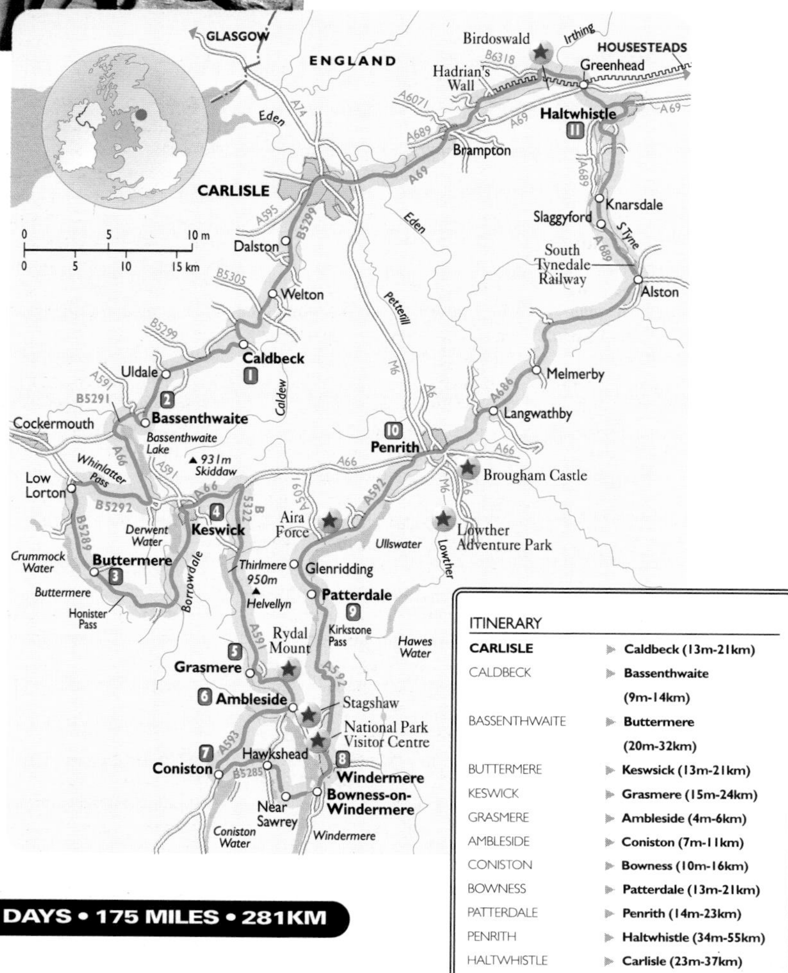


| ITINERARY | |
|---|---|
| **CARLISLE** | ▶ **Caldbeck (13m-21km)** |
| CALDBECK | ▶ **Bassenthwaite (9m-14km)** |
| BASSENTHWAITE | ▶ **Buttermere (20m-32km)** |
| BUTTERMERE | ▶ **Keswick (13m-21km)** |
| KESWICK | ▶ **Grasmere (15m-24km)** |
| GRASMERE | ▶ **Ambleside (4m-6km)** |
| AMBLESIDE | ▶ **Coniston (7m-11km)** |
| CONISTON | ▶ **Bowness (10m-16km)** |
| BOWNESS | ▶ **Patterdale (13m-21km)** |
| PATTERDALE | ▶ **Penrith (14m-23km)** |
| PENRITH | ▶ **Haltwhistle (34m-55km)** |
| HALTWHISTLE | ▶ **Carlisle (23m-37km)** |

**2 DAYS • 175 MILES • 281KM**

[i] *Old Town Hall, Green Market, Carlisle*

▶ *Take the **B5299** south from Carlisle to Caldbeck.*

**1 Caldbeck,** Cumbria
This stone-built village is set in undulating countryside with the Lake District hills to the south. In the churchyard is the grave of John Peel, who was buried here in 1854. The famous huntsman inspired his friend, John Woodcock Graves, to write the song '*D'ye ken John Peel*'. There is a plaque outside the house where Graves composed the song.

▶ *Continue on the **B5299** before branching left on to unclassified roads through Uldale to Bassenthwaite.*

**2 Bassenthwaite,** Cumbria
Bassenthwaite is situated off the A591. 'Thwaite' is a Norse word for a clearing in the forest, and is found in many village names in the area. Bassenthwaite Church, 3 miles (5km) south, was founded in the 12th or 13th century and retains its Norman chancel arch and many Early English features. Nearby Lake Bassenthwaite is a large ice-cut lake, and towering above its western shore is Skiddaw, one of only three Lake District hills higher than 3,000 feet (931m).

▶ *Leave Bassenthwaite on unclassified roads towards the **B5291** round the northern shores of the lake, then take the **A66** south to Braithwaite. Continue on the **B5292** and over Whinlatter Pass to Low Lorton then left on to **B5289** to Buttermere.*

**3 Buttermere,** Cumbria
The tiny village of Buttermere stands in the heart of spectacular landscape. A stiff climb to Whinlatter Pass, beyond the Forestry Commission's Visitor Centre, takes you on to wild moorland. The surrounding hills, Red Pike and High Stile, tower over the flat green valley floor, with impressive waterfalls such as Scale Force. The B5289 takes you through Borrowdale, a valley, which is reached by crossing 1,174-foot (358m) Honister Pass. Dark rocks tower above the skyline and quarries scar the landscape where Borrowdale rock, formed by volcanic activity about 500 million years ago, is extracted. This famous rock is used in buildings as far away as Dallas and Hong Kong, and you can buy small souvenirs from many of the local shops. The southern end of the valley is dominated by the summits of 2,560-foot (780m) Glaramara and 2,986-foot (910m) Great End.

▶ *Take the **B5289** to Keswick.*

Crummock Water, Buttermere

**4 Keswick,** Cumbria
The capital of the northern Lake District now caters for walkers, climbers and holiday-makers, but one of its oldest industries is the manufacture of coloured pencils, which originally used local graphite. The Cumberland Pencil Factory has a museum and among its exhibits is the world's largest pencil.

On a hill to the east of Keswick is Castlerigg Stone Circle, a prehistoric monument in a setting of magical beauty. Cumbrian folklore claims that the famous great stones were once men who were turned into boulders by witches.

[i] *The Moot Hall, Market Square*

▶ *Take the **A66** for 4 miles (6km), then turn right on to the **B5322** through St John's in the Vale and then the **A591** south to Grasmere.*

**5 Grasmere,** Cumbria
Grasmere's hills and lakes are a real tourist magnet. William Wordsworth wrote much of his greatest verse here, and his friends Coleridge, de Quincey and Southey were inspired by the location. Dove Cottage, where Wordsworth lived with his sister Dorothy, is open to the public and contains relics of his

life and times. A few miles further along the A591 is Rydal Mount, where Wordsworth lived from 1813 until his death in 1850. It houses many of the family's belongings and has a beautiful view of tranquil Rydal Water.

*i Redbank Road*

**SPECIAL TO...**

For over a hundred years, Grasmere gingerbread has been made in the village. The recipe is such a closely guarded secret it has to be kept in the vaults of a local bank! The rush-bearing ceremony, held every year, involves the carrying of elaborately decorated bundles of rushes to the church, after which the bearers are rewarded with a piece of delicious gingerbread.

▶ *Continue to Ambleside.*

### 6 Ambleside, Cumbria

Ambleside is a major Lake District centre at the northern end of Lake Windermere. Its many stone houses include Bridge House, the smallest in the Lake District. Built on a tiny bridge over the Stock Ghyll, it is now owned by the National Trust and is open to the public. In the town library are the relics excavated from the Roman site of Galava Fort, at Borrans Park, and the woodland gardens of Stagshaw, just south of the town, have superb views of the lake.

*i The Old Courthouse, Church Street*

▶ *Leave on the **A593** to Coniston.*

### 7 Coniston, Cumbria

Coniston Water is famous as the place where Donald Campbell set a new world record and later died in 1967. The Steam Yacht *Gondola*, an 1859 steam launch, has been restored, and now takes passengers on regular scheduled trips around the lake.

A little further on, at Hawkshead, is the Beatrix Potter Gallery; at Hill House, in Near Sawrey, Potter wrote some of her world-famous children's stories. The house is open to the public.

*i 16 Yewdale Road*

▶ *Take the **B5285** to the Windermere ferry.*

### 8 Bowness and Windermere, Cumbria

The ferry across Lake Windermere to Bowness was restored in 1990 and leads to this small town with its narrow streets and fine 15th-century church.

Windermere, just north of Bowness, is a focal point in the Lake District for sailing and boating. The Steamboat Museum, at Rayrigg Road, has a collection of Victorian and Edwardian boats, many of which still float and are in working order. The lake has 14 islands, including Belle Isle, a privately owned landscaped estate with a round 18th-century mansion house, which can be visited.

*i The Glebe, Bowness; The Gateway Centre, Victoria Street, Windermere*

**RECOMMENDED WALKS**

For a gentle walk, follow the footpath opposite the railway station in Windermere to the top of Orrest Head, 784 feet (239m), where there are fine views of the lake and Belle Isle.

Mysterious Castlerigg Stone Circle

Dove Cottage, Grasmere

**FOR CHILDREN**

The Lake District National Park Visitor Centre is on the eastern shore of Lake Windermere at Brockhole, northwest of Windermere. As well as providing information about the park, it offers a wide variety of attractions, including special family events during school holidays, lake trips in summer, garden tours from May to September, Teddy Bears' Picnics in spring and summer and a children's Squirrel Nutkin Trail.

▶ *Take the **A592** north to Patterdale.*

**9 Patterdale,** Cumbria
Patterdale was named after St Patrick, who is said to have walked here after being shipwrecked on Duddon Sands in AD540. St Patrick's Church, built in 1853, is notable for its tapestries by embroidress Ann Macbeth, who lived here until her death in 1948. This attractive village is at the head of Ullswater, a popular boating lake. A steamer plies from the pier at Glenridding to the opposite end of the lake, and the scenery is dominated by 3,117-foot (950m) Helvellyn. At the foot of the sheer eastern slopes is Red Tarn, a corrie lake in a hollow scooped out of solid rock during the Ice Age. Two miles (3km) from Glenridding is Aira Force, and it was here that Wordsworth was inspired to write of his 'host of golden daffodils'.

*i* *Main Car Park, Glenridding*

▶ *Take the **A592** alongside Ullswater to Penrith.*

**10 Penrith,** Cumbria
Penrith was the capital of Old Cumbria, and there are remains of buildings suggesting its former importance. The 12th-century ruins of Brougham Castle are just outside the town, and remnants of a Roman fort built by Agricola are near by. Beautiful Lowther Park and Adventure Park is a few miles south and is set in 100 acres (40 hectares) of parkland. The Gloucester Arms, dating from 1477, is one of the oldest inns in England, and the Duke of Gloucester, later Richard III, is said to have lived here. The wild, open spaces round Penrith may be bleak, even in summer, and crossing the Pennines can prove difficult in winter.

*i* *Robinson's School, Middlegate*

▶ *Follow the **A686** through Langwathby towards Alston. Turn left on to the **A689** then right along an unclassified road to Haltwhistle.*

**RECOMMENDED WALK**

A popular walk leads up Helvellyn from Patterdale, via Striding Edge, to the summit and returns by way of Swirral Edge. On a clear day the whole circle of Lake District summits can be seen.

**11 Haltwhistle,** Northumbria
This small, grey market town is a good starting point for Hadrian's Wall, built in the 2nd century AD to ward off Scottish tribes. Holy Cross Church, founded in 1178, is a fine example of Early English architecture. There is no tower, and the sanctuary preserves three carved coffin lids which are thought to date from the 14th century. The South Tynedale Railway, England's highest narrow-gauge railway, runs from Alston for a few miles towards Haltwhistle. Further along the A69, at Greenhead, the Roman wall, turret, fort and museum recall life 2,000 years ago.

*i* *Sycamore Street, Haltwhistle*

▶ *From Greenhead take the **B6318** and unclassified roads to rejoin the **A69**. Continue through Brampton to Carlisle.*

**FOR HISTORY BUFFS**

Housesteads, to the east of Haltwhistle, just off the B6318, is the best preserved Roman fort on Hadrian's Wall. Excavations have revealed granaries, a commandant's house, military headquarters, a hospital, baths, latrines and barracks. In the opposite direction, on the way back to Carlisle is the ruined fort of Camboglanna, occupying a ridge-top site near Birdoswald. It was built to guard the Roman bridge carrying Hadrian's Wall over the river at Willowford.

# **Across the** Backbone of England

The green valleys and wild, often windswept moors of Yorkshire provide a rich variety of scenery, with ever-changing views. Curiously weathered rocks add an eerie atmosphere to the landscape of hills and vales, and castles and monastic ruins recall the prosperity of the Middle Ages on this tour.

**2 DAYS • 153 MILES • 246KM**

| ITINERARY | |
|---|---|
| **RIPON** | ▶ **Masham (10m-16km)** |
| MASHAM | ▶ **Middleham (8m-13km)** |
| MIDDLEHAM | ▶ **Leyburn (2m-3km)** |
| LEYBURN | ▶ **Richmond (11m-18km)** |
| RICHMOND | ▶ **Barnard Castle (14m-23km)** |
| BARNARD CASTLE | ▶ **Brough (17m-27km)** |
| BROUGH | ▶ **Sedbergh (19m-31km)** |
| SEDBERGH | ▶ **Hawes (15m-24km)** |
| HAWES | ▶ **Bainbridge (4m-6km)** |
| BAINBRIDGE | ▶ **Buckden (17m-27km)** |
| BUCKDEN | ▶ **Grassington (11m-18km)** |
| GRASSINGTON | ▶ **Pateley Bridge (11m-18km)** |
| PATELEY BRIDGE | ▶ **Fountains Abbey (10m-16km)** |
| FOUNTAINS ABBEY | ▶ **Ripon (4m-6km)** |

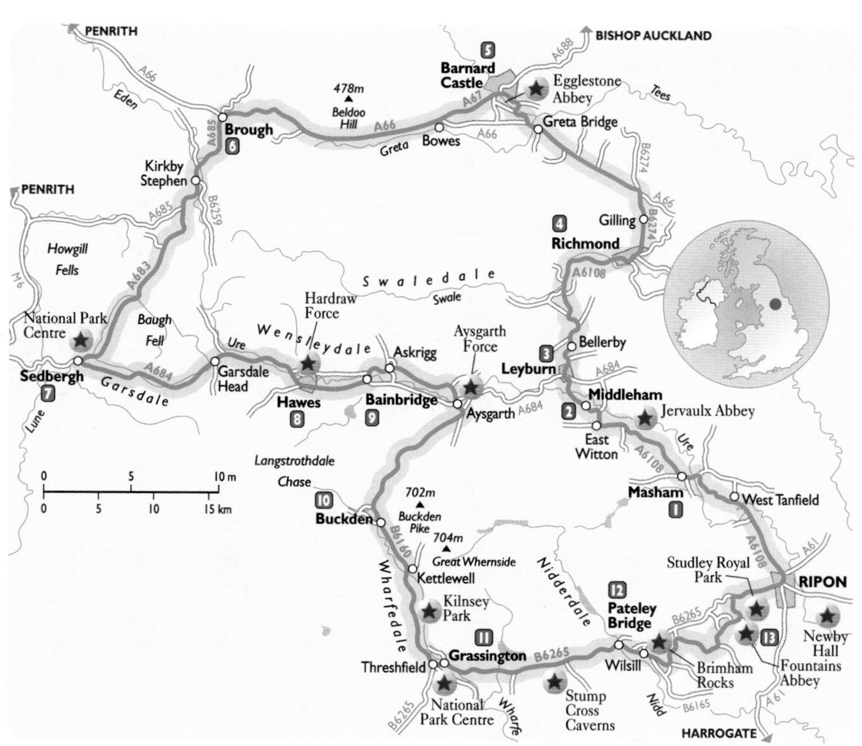

[i] *Minster Road, Ripon*

**FOR CHILDREN**

Four miles (6km) southeast of Ripon is Newby Hall and gardens. The grounds cover about 25 acres (10 hectares) and include thrilling adventure gardens for children, a memorable ride on a miniature train and woodland discovery walks.

▶ *Take the* ***A6108*** *to Masham.*

**1 Masham,** North Yorkshire
Masham's importance as a market town is illustrated by the huge market square, dominated by its Market Cross, which survives even though the market no longer takes place. Masham is full of interesting features: a four-arched bridge over the Ure dates from 1754, and St Mary's Church is older, its 15th-century spire standing on top of a Norman tower. The town is the home of Theakston's brewery, famous for its 'Old Peculier' ale.

Five miles (8km) from town is Jervaulx Abbey, in an attractive riverside setting. This Cistercian abbey was founded in 1156 and later destroyed in the 15th century, though enough of it remains to show how impressive it once was.

▶ *Follow the* ***A6108*** *for 8 miles (13km) to Middleham.*

**2 Middleham,** North Yorkshire
Grandiose building traditions of the past can be seen in the ruins of 12th-century Middleham Castle, a former seat of the Neville family, where some of the walls are 12 feet (3.5m) thick. This was the childhood home of Richard III and its massive keep is one of the largest ever built. The view from the top is magnificent, looking out across Wensleydale over wild but beautiful moorlands. Now an important horse breeding and training centre, Middleham is a good base for exploring Wensleydale.

▶ *Continue north to Leyburn.*

**3 Leyburn,** North Yorkshire
Leyburn has developed into a major trading centre for the area. Its appearance is that of a prosperous late Georgian market town, and even though most shop fronts have become largely modern, some 18th-century houses survive, notably around Grove Square; the Bolton Arms and Leyburn Hall are probably the best examples. This is another good Wensleydale centre, and there are fine views from The Shawl, a 2-mile (3km) limestone scar not far from the town centre.

[i] *Thornborough Hall*

▶ *Keep on the* ***A6108*** *to Richmond.*

**4 Richmond,** North Yorkshire
There is much to see in this capital and gateway to Swaledale, thought to be the finest of all Yorkshire Dales. From every angle Richmond Castle dominates the town. This fine Norman fortress, built on to solid rock, was started in 1071 overlooking the Swale, Britain's fastest river, but was never finished. The large, cobbled market place is surrounded by such architectural gems as the Georgian Theatre Royal, built in 1788, which was restored and reopened in 1962. You can see the home of the original 'sweet lass of Richmond Hill', of whom the famous song was written in 1785, and the award-winning Green Howards Museum covers the history of the regiment, including a unique collection dating from 1688 of war relics, weapons, medals and uniforms. Other interesting sights include Greyfriars Tower, the one surviving feature of an old abbey, and the Holy Trinity Church.

[i] *Friary Gardens, Victoria Road*

**FOR HISTORY BUFFS**

Lead mining helped the growth of Richmond and many of the surrounding villages in the 17th and 18th centuries. There are numerous footpaths leading to the old mine workings, where you can see the crushing floors and other remnants, and perhaps find tiny fragments of lead glistening in the sunlight.

▶ *Take the* ***B6274*** *to the junction with the* ***A66*** *and continue to Greta Bridge. After crossing the River Greta turn right on to unclassified roads to Barnard Castle.*

**5 Barnard Castle,** Durham
Medieval Barnard Castle, after which the town is named is now

Middleham's impressive castle ruins

Bainbridge was the centre of the once-great Forest of Wensleydale

a ruin, but in its great days it stood guard over a crossing point of the River Tees. The town boasts one of the finest museums in Britain, Bowes Museum, in a splendid French château-style mansion which was built in 1869 by John Bowes, son of the Earl of Strathmore. It contains an outstanding collection of paintings, porcelain, silver, furniture and ceramics.

A few miles south, off the B6277, are the ruins of Egglestone Abbey, in a delightful setting on the bank of the Tees, and southwest, along the A67, is the village of Bowes, where the local boarding schools gave author Charles Dickens the idea for Dotheboys Hall in his novel *Nicholas Nickleby*. William Shaw, the unfortunate model for sadistic schoolmaster Wackford Squeers, is buried in the churchyard. The Church of St Giles contains a Roman dedication stone, one of many relics of the Roman invasion in the area. Bowes Castle, like the church, used Roman stone for its building.

*i* *43 Galgate*

▶ *Take the* ***A67*** *to Bowes and follow the* ***A66*** *west along the line of an old Roman route to Brough.*

### 6 Brough, Cumbria

Standing on the site of Roman *Verterae*, Brough Castle, now in ruins, was built by William II and later restored by Lady Anne Clifford in the 17th century. This old settlement was a coaching town in the 19th century and used to hold an annual horse fair, now at Appleby. This area has many miles of good walking.

▶ *Take the* ***A685*** *to Kirkby Stephen, then the* ***A683*** *to Sedbergh.*

### 7 Sedbergh, Cumbria

Sedbergh is an old weaving town, and the Weavers' Yard still exists behind the King's Arms. The town is now more important as a tourist centre, and the rich natural history and beautiful scenery of the area have given rise to the creation of a National Park Centre. The Public School has gained a national reputation for its academic standards sporting traditions. The A684 east takes you through Garsdale, whose only community is a line of houses called The Street.

[i] *72 Main Street*

► *Continue east along the* ***A684*** *to Hawes.*

**8 Hawes,** North Yorkshire
Hawes is a centre for sheep-marketing and a focal point of Upper Wensleydale life. Just off the main street are quaint alleyways and old cottages which have not changed much for 200 years. The National Parks Information Centre is located near the Upper Dales Folk Museum, which is housed in an engine shed of the old railway. Hardraw Force, the highest waterfall in England, is also considered to be the most spectacular, and is accessible only by foot through the grounds of the Green Dragon Inn. The water drops 90 feet (27m) over the limestone Hardraw Scar, into a narrow valley, once the venue for brass band competitions.

[i] *National Park Centre, Station Yard*

► *Take the* ***A684*** *for a further 4 miles (6km) to Bainbridge.*

**9 Bainbridge,** North Yorkshire
This little Dales village, with its lovely stone buildings set round the green, was the former centre of the once great Forest of Wensleydale. Low Mill, on the east side of the green, has been restored and is occasionally open to the public. Brough Hill, a natural grassy hillock to the east is the setting for a Roman fort, and gives fine views of Wensleydale and the village.

A little further along is Askrigg, another charming village, built of local stone and set among hills, valleys and waterfalls. Most of the buildings are 18th- and 19th-century, built as a result of increasing prosperity in the clock-making, lead-mining and textile industries. Waterfalls are numerous, but especially dramatic is Aysgarth Force.

► *From Bainbridge cross the River Ure and turn right, continuing on unclassified roads, then at Aysgarth take the* ***B6160*** *to Buckden.*

**10 Buckden,** North Yorkshire
Buckden, in Wharfedale, is a very popular holiday and walking area. Kettlewell, further down the valley, was formerly part of the estate of the Percy family, ancestors of the Dukes of Northumberland.

This stretch of road passes the imposing limestone outcrop of Kilnsey Crag, one of Yorkshire's most distinctive landmarks, alongside the all-weather attraction of Kilnsey Park, which has been established as a Visitor Centre.

► *Follow the* ***B6160*** *south and turn left at Threshfield on to the* ***B6265*** *into Grassington.*

**SPECIAL TO...**

This area of the Dales was chosen as the location for the successful BBC TV series *All Creatures Great and Small*, the story of a country vet's practice based on the autobiographical books by James Herriot. Cringley Hall, in the centre of the village of Askrigg is 'Skeldale House' and Askrigg itself is 'Darrowby', where the vets have their surgery. For thousands of visitors 'Herriot Country' is every bit as important as 'Brontë Country'.

**11 Grassington,** North Yorkshire
This is Wharfedale's principal village and another National Park Centre, for the North York Moors. Its small passageways, cobbled market place, medieval bridge and interesting old buildings all add to the appeal. There are Bronze and Iron Age settlements at Lea Green, north of the village, and further east, along the B6265, are the underground caverns of Stump Cross. The main cave has been developed into an impressive floodlit show cave, with wonderful stalagmite and stalactite formations.

[i] *Grassington National Park Centre, Hebden Road*

► *Continue along the* ***B6265*** *to Pateley Bridge.*

**12 Pateley Bridge,** North Yorkshire
This pleasant town has been the focus of everyday life in Nidderdale since ancient times. The picturesque ruins of Old St Mary's Church stand above the village on the hillside, and the Nidderdale Museum has fascinating exhibits including the Victorian Room and a replica cobbler's shop. A mile (1.6km) from town is Foster Beck Hemp Mill, now a restaurant, which features a huge 17th-century water wheel, the second largest in the country.

Above and inset: Fountains Abbey, perhaps England's finest abbey

East of town, along the B6165 (turn off at Wilsill) and unclassified roads are Brimham Rocks. These curious rock formations have been sculpted out of the millstone grit by wind and rain over thousands of years, and there are wide views from the surrounding moorlands.

[i] *14 High Street*

▶ *Leave by the* ***B6265*** *turning right after 1 mile (1.6km) on to the* ***B6165****. At Wilsill turn left and follow unclassified roads past Brimham Rocks to Fountains Abbey.*

**13 Fountains Abbey,** North Yorkshire

Founded by Cistercian monks in 1132, Fountains is the largest and perhaps the finest abbey in England. Particularly notable are the tower, nave and lay brothers' quarters. It was acquired by William Aislabie in 1768 and became the focal point of his magnificent landscaped gardens at nearby Studley Royal Park, which contains typical ornaments of the period, such as a lake, a temple and statues. The park's original house burned down in 1945, but there are still estate cottages, huddled round a 19th-century church designed by William Burges. Deer and other livestock can be seen grazing in the park.

▶ *Return to the* ***B6265*** *for the journey back to Ripon.*

### RECOMMENDED WALKS

The various National Park Centres provide a programme of guided walks at Bank Holidays and during July and August. These start at 2pm and usually last 2½ to 3 hours. Local people with a special interest in some aspect of the Dales act as guides. Information about these walks is given in *The Visitor*, a free publication.

### BACK TO NATURE

In the gritstone area of the Yorkshire Dales, above Nidderdale and Swaledale, purple heathers dominate the scene, but in the limestone country round Wharfedale you will find more variety, with the tiny coloured flowers which thrive in the calcite-rich soils. Plants such as yellow pimpernel, giant bell-flower, lily of the valley and ramson grow well in the light shade cast by ash, which grows on the limestone scars, while the unmown roadside verges and hay meadows are favoured by knapweed, sneezewort, early purple orchids and cowslips.

# Over Hills & Plains

Lush green valleys, wild grouse moorland and one of the liveliest seaside resorts in the country are included in this tour which starts at Morecambe, on the edge of the Irish Sea, and climbs to the Pennines, before returning to the coast.

**1/2 DAYS • 152 MILES • 245KM**

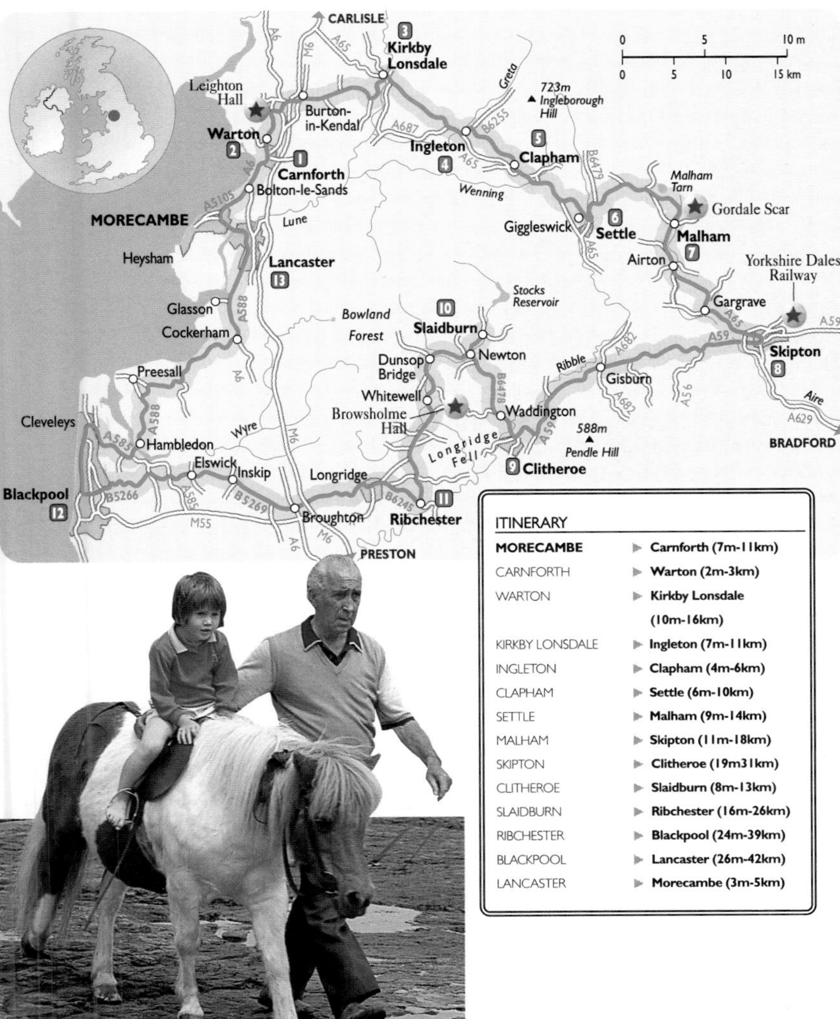


| ITINERARY | |
|---|---|
| **MORECAMBE** | ▶ **Carnforth (7m-11km)** |
| CARNFORTH | ▶ **Warton (2m-3km)** |
| WARTON | ▶ **Kirkby Lonsdale (10m-16km)** |
| KIRKBY LONSDALE | ▶ **Ingleton (7m-11km)** |
| INGLETON | ▶ **Clapham (4m-6km)** |
| CLAPHAM | ▶ **Settle (6m-10km)** |
| SETTLE | ▶ **Malham (9m-14km)** |
| MALHAM | ▶ **Skipton (11m-18km)** |
| SKIPTON | ▶ **Clitheroe (19m31km)** |
| CLITHEROE | ▶ **Slaidburn (8m-13km)** |
| SLAIDBURN | ▶ **Ribchester (16m-26km)** |
| RIBCHESTER | ▶ **Blackpool (24m-39km)** |
| BLACKPOOL | ▶ **Lancaster (26m-42km)** |
| LANCASTER | ▶ **Morecambe (3m-5km)** |

*Station Buildings, Morecambe*

▶ *From Morecambe take the* ***A5105****, then the* ***A6*** *for 7 miles (11km) to Carnforth.*

**1 Carnforth,** Lancashire
Carnforth is a small Victorian market town on the west coast railway line to Scotland. The main attraction is Steamtown, the largest operating railway centre in the country, whose 30 engines include the legendary *Flying Scotsman*. In summer many of them are 'in steam'. Other railway memorabilia include coaches, a coaling plant and working models, and you can take a ride on the narrow-gauge miniature railway.

▶ *Turn left out of Steamtown and follow the unclassified road 2 miles (3km) to Warton.*

The Devil's Bridge at Kirkby Lonsdale is one of the most ancient bridges in the country

**BACK TO NATURE**

**The RSPB reserve at Leighton Moss, 3 miles (5km) northwest of Carnforth, is famous for its reed-beds and wetland wildlife. Otters are regularly seen, and bitterns and bearded tits can be spotted by persistent observers. Arnside Knott, further north, is a limestone outcrop which shows fine examples of limestone pavements. Interesting flowers grow in the cracks and crevices, including several species of ferns and dark red helleborines.**

**2 Warton,** Lancashire
The peaceful village of Warton has an unusual claim to fame. George Washington had ancestors living here, and legend has it that the famous 'Stars and Stripes' come from the family's coat of arms, which can be found in the 14th-century church.

Near Warton is 18th-century Leighton Hall, built on the site of an earlier medieval house. In 1826 the estate was bought by Richard Gillow, a distinguished maker of fine furniture, and the house is a treasure chest of priceless pieces.

▶ *Continue on unclassified roads, across the A6 just south of Burton-in-Kendal then join the* ***B6254*** *at Whittington and follow to Kirkby Lonsdale.*

**3 Kirkby Lonsdale,** Cumbria
Kirkby Lonsdale is a fascinating town to explore. Look out for the three-arched Devil's Bridge spanning the River Lune. Possibly 13th-century, it is one of the finest ancient bridges in the country. John Ruskin, the 19th-century writer and painter, loved this area of the Lune valley. The 'Ruskin Walks', which start near the churchyard, are well signposted. Cowan Bridge, just down the road, has further literary links, for it was here that novelists Charlotte and

St Mary's Church, Ingleton

Emily Brontë endured a harsh boarding school education from 1823 to 1825. Now only a few cottages mark the site of the Clergy Daughters' School, immortalised by Charlotte as Lowood in her novel *Jane Eyre*.

*i 24 Main Street*

▶ *Continue on the **A65** for 6 miles (10km), then turn left on to the **B6255** into Ingleton.*

**4 Ingleton,** North Yorkshire
Ingleton thrives as a centre for visitors to the Yorkshire Dales. The limestone hills to the north are honeycombed with caves, many accessible only to experienced potholers, but White Scar Cave is open to everyone. It is below the heights of 2,373 feet (723m) Ingleborough which, with Whernside at 2,419 feet (737m) and Pen-y-ghent at 2,273 feet (693m), forms the most formidable trio of peaks in the Dales.

*i Community Centre Car Park, High Street*

▶ *Take the unclassified road along the foot of Ingleborough for 4 miles (6km) to Clapham.*

**5 Clapham,** North Yorkshire
Tiny Clapham is the unlikely Fleet Street of the Dales, for it is here that *The Dalesman* magazine is published. The village has a Yorkshire Dales National Park Information Centre, and like Ingleton is a noted potholing centre. To the north of the village is Ingleborough Cave, and the famous Gaping Gill pothole, 378 feet (123m) deep, with a central chamber large enough to hold a small cathedral.

▶ *From Clapham take the **B6480** to the **A65** and follow before branching off left to Settle.*

**6 Settle,** North Yorkshire
Settle is an attractive town, with its picturesque narrow streets, secluded courtyards and Georgian houses. By far the most outstanding building is The Folly (1675), an extravaganza of windows and fine masonry. The 71-mile (114km) railway line from Settle to Carlisle runs through the Ribblesdale valley and is one of the most scenic routes in the country. Just outside the town is Giggleswick Scar, a rock wall caused by massive earth movements millions of years ago. In 1838 the chance discovery of Victoria Cave led to the retrieval of many bones of prehistoric animals long extinct in the British Isles.

*i Town Hall, Cheapside*

▶ *Take the **B6479** north from Settle turning off right at Langcliffe on to unclassified roads to Malham Tarn and Malham.*

**7 Malham,** North Yorkshire
Malham is a focal point for geographers and geologists, and the Yorkshire Dales National Park Interpretation Centre is based here. Stroll up the Pennine Way to Malham Cove, a 250-foot (76m) limestone amphitheatre. It used to be a spectacular waterfall, but the river now crawls out at the foot of the cliff. To the east is Gordale Scar, an almost vertical gorge thought to be a collapsed cavern and boasting a dramatic waterfall.

▶ *Follow the road from Malham to Gargrave, then take the **A65** to Skipton.*

The geological curiosity of Malham Cove lends an other-wordly air to this spectacular area

**RECOMMENDED WALKS**

Malham village is close to the highly dramatic Malham Cove and Gordale Scar. Walk up the steep path to the top of the cove, and continue along the route of the old river, now dried up. You will soon reach the point at which the stream disappears underground through a series of holes. Retrace your steps or turn right and follow the signs to Gordale, where you can scramble down a waterfall and walk through a gorge on the way back to the village.

**8 Skipton,** North Yorkshire
This pleasant market town is dominated by Skipton Castle, one of the most complete medieval castles in England. It was originally built in Norman times and was partly rebuilt in the 1650s after being damaged in the Civil War. Opposite the castle entrance is the Craven Museum, with exhibits on geology and local folk history. Near by, at Embsay, is the Embsay Steam Railway which runs 20 locomotives on its short track.

*i 8 Victoria Square*

▶ *Take the **A59** to Clitheroe.*

**9 Clitheroe,** Lancashire
After the Civil War the small keep of Clitheroe Castle was presented to General Monk, and today it still stands boldly on its limestone knoll overlooking the town. The town itself was once filled with the sound of looms – first wool, then cotton brought prosperity in the last century. Pendle Hill, associated with the trial of several Lancashire women accused of being witches, rises to 1,828 feet (557km) on the east side of Clitheroe.

*i 14 Market Place*

**SPECIAL TO...**

Clitheroe Castle contains a fine collection of carboniferous fossils from the local rocks. Similar fossils can be found in the limestone areas around Malham or Ingleton. Brachiopods look like some of the modern shells you can find on beaches today and there are pieces of coral from a warm ocean floor of 300 million years ago, and crinoids, which look like screws made out of stone.

**FOR HISTORY BUFFS**

A few miles northwest of Clitheroe, just beyond Bashall Eaves, is Browsholme Hall. Pronounced 'Broozum', it is a modified Tudor mansion set in beautiful gardens that were landscaped in honour of the Prince Regent and Mrs Fitzherbert. It contains fascinating collections of tapestry work, armour, furniture and pictures.

▶ *Follow the **B6578** north for 8 miles (13km) to Slaidburn.*

**10 Slaidburn,** Lancashire
The little village of Slaidburn, on the River Hodder, was for centuries the administrative 'capital' of the Forest of Bowland. This wild region of grouse moor and high fells was one of the ancient royal forests of Saxon England. At the centre of the village is an inn called Hark to Bounty. Legend says

Bounty was a foxhound belonging to a local vicar, and that its barking was easily distinguishable from the rest of the pack. Gisburn Forest, northeast of the village, is an extensive coniferous plantation sloping down to Stocks Reservoir, which takes its name from the village drowned to create it during the 1930s.

▶ *Take the **B6478** back to Newton, then branch off on to unclassified roads through Dunsop Bridge, Whitewell and over Longridge Fell to Ribchester.*

**11 Ribchester,** Lancashire
The country round Ribchester was guarded by a Roman fort called *Bremetennacum*, built around AD80. In the 18th century a schoolboy found a Roman ceremonial helmet, and since then its extensive remains have been excavated and you can see many of the finds in the Museum of Roman Antiquities. Two Roman columns support the oak gallery in 13th-century St Wilfred's Church, and the pillars at the entrance of the White Bull Inn are said to come from a Roman temple. The Museum of Childhood, along Church Street, has dolls, toys and models on display.

▶ *Take the **B6245** to Longridge and then the **B5269** west via Broughton and Elswick to join the **B5266** to Blackpool.*

**12 Blackpool,** Lancashire
Blackpool stretches in a long, multicoloured ribbon by the sea, punctuated with three piers and dominated by its 519-foot (158m) tower. Built between 1891 and 1894, Blackpool Tower was for many years the highest building in Britain, and it gives a breathtaking view of the surrounding coast. The heart of Blackpool, the Golden Mile, is more like a quarter of a mile. It is possible to walk the whole length of the sea front between Fleetwood in the north and Squires Gate in the south, but it is more fun to go on one of the trams which still run along the promenade. During autumn evenings, the whole front is ablaze with more than 375,000 bulbs, laser beams, animated displays and tableaux.

*i* *1 Clifton Street and 87a Coronation Street*

▶ *Follow the trams to Cleveleys, before turning inland on the **B5412** then right on to the **A586**. Turn left on to the **A588** to Lancaster via Pilling and Cockerham marshes.*

Blackpool's famous roller-coaster

**FOR CHILDREN**

Blackpool is a paradise for children, with so much to do at every turn, including the Pleasure Beach amusement park, with the first 360-degree 'loop the loop' roller-coaster in Britain, and Sandcastle, the world's greatest 'inside seaside' with tropical fun pools and a 300-foot (91m) water slide.

**13 Lancaster,** Lancashire
This county town was England's chief port for the American trade throughout the 18th century. The elegant Customs House, designed by Robert Gillow of Leighton Hall, is a reminder of its former prosperity. The massive Norman keep of Lancaster Castle now serves to keep people in rather than out: it is the county gaol. It contains a well tower where prisoners languished while awaiting trail – including 10 Lancashire witches convicted and hanged in 1612. On show are grim relics such as the clamp and iron used to fasten a criminal's arm while the initial 'M' (for malefactor) was burned on to his hand. The City Museum in Market Square is also the Museum of the King's Own Royal Lancashire Regiment, and the Judges' Lodgings on Castle Hill contain a Museum of Childhood.

*i* *29 Castle Hill*

▶ *Cross the River Lune on the **A589**, and a short drive takes you back to Morecambe.*

**SCENIC ROUTES**

Spectacular views can be found as you pass through the mountainous spine of England, the Pennines, on the road from Malham to Skipton before it joins the A65. The dramatic form of Ingleborough dominates the landscape, especially from Kirkby Lonsdale and along the A65.

TOUR 24

# Derbyshire's White Peak

This tour of the Peak District explores the gentler southern side, the White Peak, with its high close-cropped sheep pasture, limestone dry walling and pretty wooded valleys, but our route also offers a small glimpse of the Dark Peak – bleaker moorland and angular outcrops of blackened millstone grit.

**1/2 DAYS • 85 MILES • 138KM**

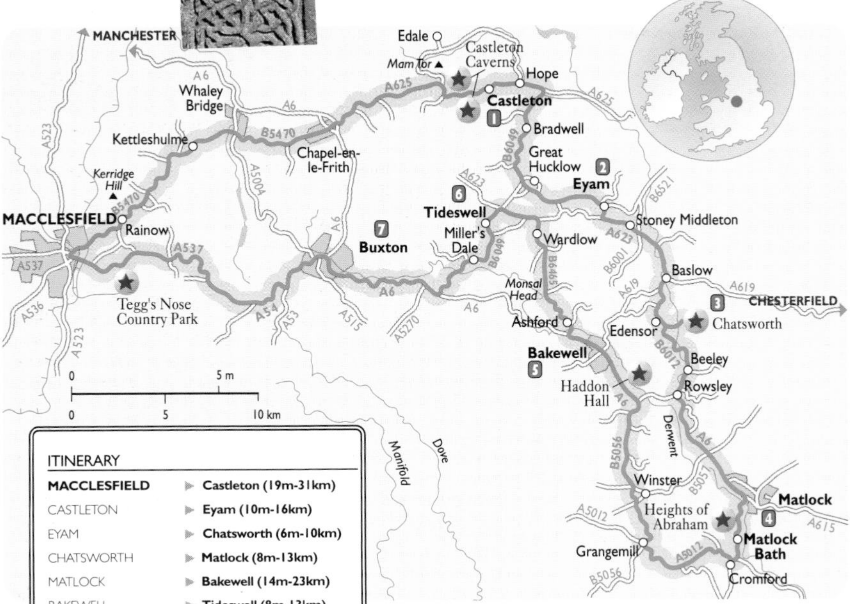

ITINERARY

| | |
|---|---|
| **MACCLESFIELD** | ▶ **Castleton (19m-31km)** |
| CASTLETON | ▶ **Eyam (10m-16km)** |
| EYAM | ▶ **Chatsworth (6m-10km)** |
| CHATSWORTH | ▶ **Matlock (8m-13km)** |
| MATLOCK | ▶ **Bakewell (14m-23km)** |
| BAKEWELL | ▶ **Tideswell (8m-13km)** |
| TIDESWELL | ▶ **Buxton (8m-13km)** |
| BUXTON | ▶ **Macclesfield (12m-19km)** |

Stalactites in Treak Cliff Cave, near Castleton
Left: Saxon cross, Eyam

[i] *Town Hall, Macclesfield*

**BACK TO NATURE**

Situated near Macclesfield, Goyt Valley is an area of bog, moorland, forest and open water. The two reservoirs – Errwood and Fernilee – have wintering wildfowl and species such as red grouse, curlew, lapwing and redshank breed on the open moorland.

▶ *Leave Macclesfield by the* ***A5002*** *to Rainow, then in 4 miles (6km) cross the* ***A5004****, taking the* ***B5470*** *to Chapel-en-le-Frith. Take the* ***A625*** *signed Rushup and Edale, then turn right and shortly left signed Castleton Caverns for Castleton.*

**1 Castleton,** Derbyshire
Dominating this pretty Peak village is Peveril Castle, built by William Peveril, illegitimate son of the Conqueror, and immortalised in Sir Walter Scott's 1825 novel *Peveril of the Peak.* Although roofless, Henry II's huge keep still stands. Castleton has a 200-year history of visitors, who come mainly to see the spectacular caverns in the limestone hills. Follow the stream to Peak Cavern, which has Britain's largest natural cave entrance. You can still see evidence here of the rope makers who lived and worked in the cavern: their speciality was hangman's nooses. There are other local caverns, carved out by miners looking for lead and the lovely Blue John Fluorspar. Treak Cliff, Speedwell (explore it by boat) and Blue John Caverns are all open to visitors.

A trip behind Mam Tor, 'the shivering mountain', leads to nearby Edale, which lies snugly in the Noe Valley and is the starting point of the Pennine Way footpath.

▶ *Go east on the* ***A625****, then turn right on to the* ***B6049****. Soon turn left on unclassified roads to Great Hucklow, through Foolow to Eyam.*

**2 Eyam,** Derbyshire
In 1665, the year of the Great Plague in London, a chest of clothes was sent from the capital to the village of Eyam, high up among the moors. Soon four out of every five villagers were dead. But what made Eyam special was the extraordinary sacrifice that these villagers made. Led by the rector, William Mompesson, they resolved to isolate themselves and prevent the disease from wiping out neighbouring communities. The churchyard's graves reflect this sad story and every August a service is held in a nearby dell, known as Cucklet Church, where Mompesson held his open-air services. Near his wife's grave is a unique sundial, telling the time throughout the world.

▶ *Turn right on to the* ***B6521*** *then left on to the* ***A623****. At Baslow turn right on to the* ***A619*** *then shortly left on to the* ***B6012****. In 5 miles (8km) turn left again at Edensor For Chatsworth.*

**3 Chatsworth,** Derbyshire
Chatsworth is one of the grandest country houses in England, popularly known as the 'Palace of the Peak'. The Elizabethan house, built in 1555 by Bess of Hardwick, was virtually replaced with the 1st Duke of Devonshire's baroque mansion of the late 17th century, finished by the 6th Duke in the 1820s. Although Capability Brown landscaped the grounds, their crowning feature is Joseph Paxton's stunning Emperor Fountain, at 260 feet (80m) the tallest in Britain. When you rejoin the main road, take a look at the golden stone village of Edensor. Before 1839 the village

lay in full view of the big house, so the 6th Duke had Paxton demolish it and rebuild it out of sight!

▶ *Leave Chatsworth and turn left on to the* ***B6012****. At Rowsley turn left on to the* ***A6*** *for Matlock.*

### 4 Matlock and Matlock Bath, Derbyshire

Matlock is the administrative centre of Derbyshire, a busy town built around an ancient stone bridge across the river. Next door is Matlock Bath, a 19th-century spa town, where the water still bubbles up at a constant 20°C, although the Pavilion where Victorians used to take it is now an entertainment centre. Commanding the heights above Matlock Bath are the Victoria Prospect Tower and the strange folly of Riber Castle. Behind its imposing front is a wildlife park for rare breeds and endangered species.

A mile (1.6km) from Matlock is Cromford, an important benchmark in the development of England as an industrial nation. Here, in 1771, Richard Arkwright built the world's first mechanised textile factory. It survives today, with the new village he built for his workers.

*i* *The Pavilion, Matlock Bath*

**FOR CHILDREN**

A spectacular cable car journey takes you from the river at Matlock Bath to the 1,000-foot (305m) Heights of Abraham. At the top, you can climb the Victoria Prospect Tower, and below ground there are two huge caverns to explore, the Great Rutland and the Great Masson.

▶ *Leave Matlock Bath on the* ***A6*** *and at Cromford turn right on to the* ***A5012*** *signed Buxton. Turn right on to the* ***B5056*** *then the* ***A6*** *to Bakewell.*

Bakewell is famous for its puddings

**SPECIAL TO...**

The National Tramway Museum at Crich, just south of Cromford, is unique. Over 40 trams from all over the world, built between 1873 and 1953, are kept here in pristine condition by volunteers, and on any one day several trams run. For the price of admission you can hop on and off as much as you like anywhere along the 1 mile (1.6km) route. Open from April to October.

### 5 Bakewell, Derbyshire

The fine five-arch stone bridge built in 1300 to span the River Wye, is the principal feature of this market town. The Romans came here first for the warm springs; the Saxons named it Bad Quell or 'bath well'. Most of the buildings are 17th- and 18th-century, but the Old House Museum, with its wattle and daub walls, is at least a hundred years older. The town boasts more than 50 shops, including the Old Original Bakewell Pudding Shop. Bakewell Pudding – don't dare call it 'tart' here – is supposed to have originated in the kitchens of the Rutland Arms Hotel, when a cook poured egg on to the jam instead of the pastry.

*i* *Old Market Hall, Bridge Street*

**FOR HISTORY BUFFS**

Haddon Hall, near Bakewell, is reputed to be England's most complete and authentic medieval manor house, and is certainly one of Derbyshire's finest buildings. Unlike many large country houses, it remains very much as it was 300 years ago.

▶ *Go north on the* ***A6*** *from Bakewell. At Ashford turn right on to the* ***B6465*** *and, in 4 miles (6km), left on to the* ***A623****, then turn left into Tideswell.*

### 6 Tideswell, Derbyshire

Tideswell grew with the medieval wool trade – being granted market status as early as the 13th century. Over the intervening years it has become a

sleepy backwater away from the main roads, and little remains to indicate the town's heyday, with one glorious exception. The 14th-century Church of St John the Baptist, with its soaring tower, is known as the 'Cathedral of the Peak'. Tideswell is a venue for well-dressing, the tradition of decorating wells with flowers, which takes place at the end of June or very early in July.

▶ *From Tideswell go south on the* ***B6049*** *then join the* ***A6*** *heading west to Buxton.*

**7 Buxton,** Derbyshire
At 1,007 feet (307m), Buxton is one of the highest towns in England. People have sought the town out since Roman times for its springs of mineral water. Not only is it good for rheumatics, but it tastes nice too. Bring a bottle and help yourself, free, from St Anne's Well; you can even swim in warm spa water in the Pavilion's indoor pool. It was in the 18th century that the town took off as a spa resort, thanks to the 5th Duke of Devonshire, who built the beautiful Doric-style Crescent and the huge domed riding school and stables, now the Royal Devonshire Hospital. The town has two golf courses, an elegantly restored Opera House and the lovely Pavilion Gardens. Walks are plentiful; one that offers a panoramic view of the town is the round trip up to Solomon's Temple, a folly on Grinlow.

[i] *The Crescent*

▶ *Leave Buxton on the* ***A53****, going right on to the* ***A54****. Turn right again on to the* ***A537*** *signed Macclesfield and in 5 miles (8km) left on to unclassified roads past Tegg's Nose Country Park into Macclesfield.*

Buxton is a sophisticated and elegant Georgian spa town

### SCENIC ROUTES

The route between Macclesfield and Castleton offers a picturesque introduction to the Dark Peak. The road undulates up hill and down dale between dry stone walls, through gritstone villages whose cottages have been blackened by centuries of industrial smoke. On a clear day there are lovely views across the Cheshire Plain. On your left as you approach Rainow on the B5470 is White Nancy, a curious monument at the end of prominent Kerridge Hill.

# From Vale to Moor

**2 DAYS • 124 MILES • 201KM**

ITINERARY

| | |
|---|---|
| **YORK** | ▸ **Malton (18m-29km)** |
| MALTON | ▸ **Pickering (8m-13km)** |
| PICKERING | ▸ **Goathland (15m-24km)** |
| GOATHLAND | ▸ **Grosmont (7m-11km)** |
| GROSMONT | ▸ **Danby (11m-18km)** |
| DANBY | ▸ **Rosedale Abbey (10m-16km)** |
| ROSEDALE ABBEY | ▸ **Hutton-le-Hole (5m-8km)** |
| HUTTON-LE-HOLE | ▸ **Kirkbymoorside (6m-10km)** |
| KIRKBYMOORSIDE | ▸ **Helmsley (6m-10km)** |
| HELMSLEY | ▸ **Kilburn (10m-16km)** |
| KILBURN | ▸ **Coxwold (2m-3km)** |
| COXWOLD | ▸ **Wass (2m-3km)** |
| WASS | ▸ **Sutton-on-the-Forest (16m-27km)** |
| SUTTON-ON-THE-FOREST | ▸ **York (8m-13km)** |

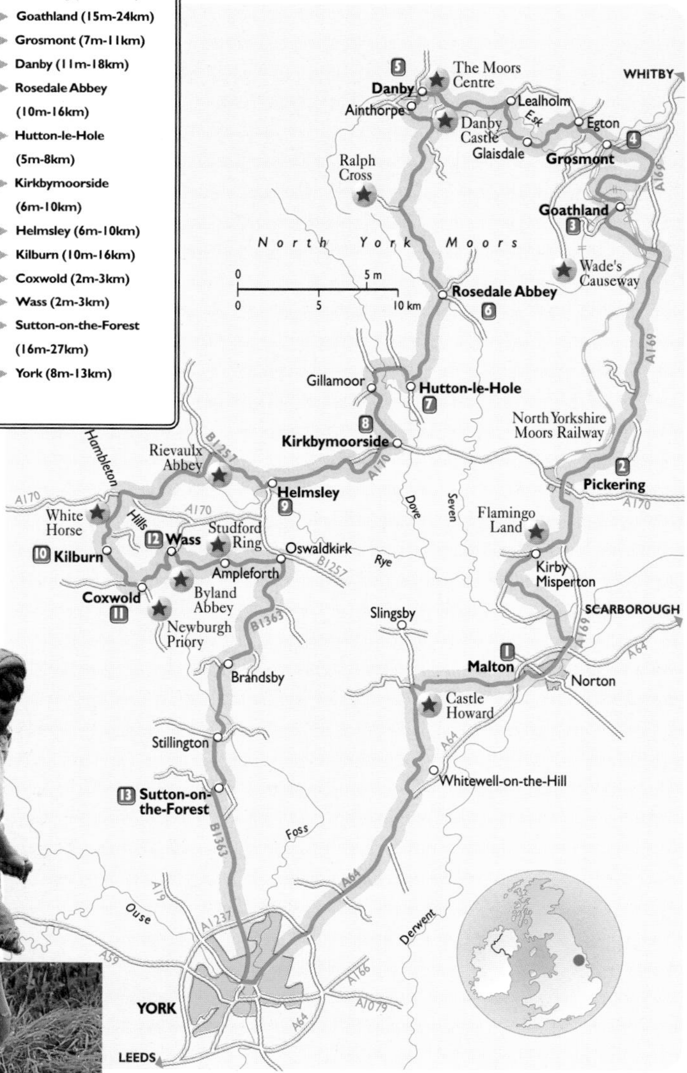

This area of the North Riding extends from the gentle farm lands of the Vale of York to the wild beauty of the North York Moors, taking in delightful villages and evocative ruins.

Castle Howard is one of the architect Vanbrugh's finest works

[i] *De Grey Rooms, Exhibition Square, York*

► *Take the **A64** and turn left on to an unclassified road before Whitewell-on-the-Hill, passing Castle Howard, through Coneysthorpe to Malton.*

**1 Malton,** North Yorkshire
Malton is divided in two by the site of a Roman station. New Malton is the busy market town, and Old Malton, a mile (1.6km) northeast, is a small village. Malton Museum, in the town, contains extensive Romano-British remains from the fort of Derventio and other settlements. Northwards is Eden Camp Military Museum, a former prisoner-of-war camp, where displays include women at war and the rise and fall of the Nazi Party.

Six miles (10km) southwest of Malton, on a signed road, is Castle Howard, a magnificent 18th-century house designed by Vanbrugh. It has been the home of the Howard family for nearly 300 years and notable features include the central dome, the Temple of the Four Winds and Hawksmoor's mausoleum.

[i] *Old Town Hall, Market Place*

**FOR CHILDREN**

**Kirby Misperton, near Malton, is the home of Flamingo Land. Over 1,000 animals include camels and polar bears, many of which have been bred here. Special attractions are organised, such as the parrot and dolphin shows.**

► *Follow the road to Old Malton, cross the **A64** on to the **A169**, turning almost immediately left on to an unclassified road through Kirby Misperton, rejoining the **A169** north to Pickering.*

**2 Pickering,** North Yorkshire
This ancient town is the starting point for the North Yorkshire Moors Railway, which runs between Pickering and Grosmont. Parts of the Church of St Peter and St Paul date from the 11th century and it contains splendid medieval wall paintings, notably *St George and the Dragon*. The ruins of Pickering Castle include a motte which was probably constructed in the days of William the Conqueror, and the Beck Isle Museum of Rural Life, in a fine Georgian building, and is packed with bygones of the Victorian era.

[i] *7 Eastgate Car Park*

► *Continue along the **A169** for about 12 miles (19km) then turn left on to an unclassified road to Goathland.*

**3 Goathland,** North Yorkshire
Goathland is one of the most picturesque villages in the North York Moors. This is a marvellous centre for walking and the area is renowned for spectacular waterfalls, including Nelly Ayre Foss, Mallyan Spout and Thomason Foss.

**SPECIAL TO...**

**Goathland is the home of the Goathland Plough Stots, a sword dance team whose displays originated with Viking raiders over 1,000 years ago. It takes place on Plough Monday, the first Monday after 6 January, when a service is held to bless the Plough Stots ('stot' means bullock).**

► *Return to the **A169** for a short distance, then turn left on to unclassified roads to Grosmont.*

**4 Grosmont,** North Yorkshire
Grosmont is the northern terminus of the North Yorkshire Moors Railway, and its popular-

All aboard the North Yorkshire Moors Railway

ity owes much to the railway. A trip on the Moorsrail will take you back to a gentler and slower age, and the locomotive sheds are worth a visit to see engines being prepared and restored.

▶ *Continue west along unclassified roads to Danby.*

> **FOR HISTORY BUFFS**
>
> **A remarkably well-preserved stretch of an old Roman road, Wade's Causeway, passes near Grosmont. It was built 2,000 years ago as part of a Roman route from Malton to the coast near Goldsborough, and lay hidden until it was rediscovered in 1914.**

**5 Danby,** North Yorkshire
The Moors Centre is located in Danby in a former shooting lodge, with exhibitions and impressive gardens. Southeast of the village are the ruins of 14th-century Danby Castle, where Catherine Parr, Henry VIII's sixth wife, once lived. The route now goes on to the moors past two old crosses Fat Betty, and the Ralph Cross, which is used as the symbol for the North York Moors National Park.

[i] *The Moors Centre, Danby Lodge, Lodge Lane*

▶ *Follow unclassified roads south to Rosedale Abbey.*

**6 Rosedale Abbey,** North Yorkshire
Rosedale's 12th-century Cistercian abbey no longer exists: only a few stones remain in the village. Ruins of railways and kilns at Chimney Bank Top are reminders of the old 19th-century ironstone industry. The famous chimney, once visible for miles, was demolished in 1972 when it was declared unsafe.

▶ *Continue to Hutton-le-Hole.*

**7 Hutton-le-Hole,** North Yorkshire
Hutton-le-Hole's Ryedale Museum, in an ancient cruck-type building, features a marvellous collection of farm equipment, and reconstructed buildings. There are two 3½-mile (6km) walks signposted from the centre of the village into the countryside.

[i] *Road Ryedale Folk Museum*

▶ *Continue on unclassified roads, crossing the River Dove and through Gillamoor to Kirkbymoorside.*

**8 Kirkbymoorside,** North Yorkshire
Situated at the edge of the moor, this small, peaceful town is just off the main road, with quiet streets and squares. The church dates from the 12th century and retains some fine Norman masonry and fragments of a Saxon cross.

▶ *Take the* ***A170*** *to Helmsley.*

**9 Helmsley,** North Yorkshire
Roads from Cleveland, Thirsk and York converge upon the town square, making Helmsley a busy trade centre. Helmsley Castle, sometimes called Furstan Castle, dates from 1186 and was once inhabited by the Duke of Buckingham, court favourite of James I and Charles I. Two miles (3km) west of Helmsley is Rievaulx, one of the largest Cistercian abbeys in England. The 12th-century ruins are surrounded by wooded hills, and above the abbey wall is Rievaulx Terrace, a beautiful landscaped garden with mock-Greek temples completed in 1758.

[i] *Town Hall, Market Place*

> **RECOMMENDED WALKS**
>
> **Highly recommended is the 3½ miles (6km) from Helmsley to Rievaulx, which runs along the richly wooded valley of the River Rye.**

▶ *Follow unclassified roads from Rievaulx through Scawton to rejoin the* ***A170****, then turn left to White Horse Bank and Kilburn.*

**10 Kilburn,** North Yorkshire
Kilburn White Horse is the only turf-cut figure in the north of England. Almost 314 feet (96m) long by 228 feet (70m) high, it can be seen from the central tower of York Minster, 19 miles (30km) away. The village is well known for its woodcarvings, the work of Robert Thompson, who died in 1955. His trademark, a mouse, is still carved into the items produced by craftsmen at his works.

▶ *Continue on unclassified roads for 2 miles (3km) to Coxwold.*

**11 Coxwold,** North Yorkshire
Coxwold's most outstanding building is the 15th-century octagonal-towered church. In the churchyard is the gravestone of the 18th-century author Laurence Sterne, who named his house Shandy Hall, after the hero of his novel *The Life and*

*Opinions of Tristram Shandy*; today it is a museum devoted to his life and works. Just beyond the village is Newburgh Priory, a 17th- and 18th-century house with a lake and gardens.

▶ *Return to Coxwold, then take an unclassified road to Wass.*

**12 Wass,** North Yorkshire
Wass was partly built from the ruins of nearby Byland Abbey, the largest Cistercian church in the country, with a 26-foot (8m) diameter window dating from the 13th century.

Two miles (3km) west of Wass is Ampleforth, which was chosen as the site of a school by English monks escaping from the French Revolution. Ampleforth College is now England's premier Roman Catholic public school. Nearby Studford Ring is thought to date from the Bronze Age and is probably the finest earthwork enclosure in the area.

▶ *Turn right along the **B1363** and continue east on unclassified roads to Oswaldkirk, where you continue south to Sutton-on-the-Forest.*

**13 Sutton-on-the-Forest,**
North Yorkshire
Set in the undulating Howardian Hills, this is an unusual brick-built village with a stone church. Sutton Park, an early Georgian house, contains antique furniture by Chippendale and Sheraton and a collection of porcelain.

▶ *Return to York via the **B1363**.*

Helmsley nestles beneath the southern rim of the moors

### RECOMMENDED WALKS

The 100-mile (160km) Cleveland Way curves round the edge of the Moors, and certain stretches along it make ideal short walks.

### BACK TO NATURE

The North York Moors are managed primarily to encourage the numbers of red grouse, but birds such as golden plovers, dunlins, curlews and lapwings also take advantage of the varied habitat.

# SCOTLAND

Cross the border from England to Scotland, and you will find that the landscape, architecture and historical emphasis all change. This is part of the United Kingdom which retains its own educational and legal systems, banknotes and established church. Scotland joined the Union in 1707, but many of its castles and historic houses, heroes and battlefields are from the time when England was 'the auld enemy'. Football and rugby internationals retain something of that ancestral rivalry.

The ruined Border abbeys are evidence of the old raiding days. Along the Galloway coast, revenue duties on brandy, wine, silks and other goods were so resented that generations of Solway men made their living by smuggling. This was no casual trade. Several smuggling companies were proper businesses, with shareholders and accurate, if secret, books of accounts. Further north, in the Highland and Grampian glens, it was whisky taxes that were bitterly disliked. Pure mountain water, often flavoured by the peaty ground through which it flowed, was the basis of hundreds of illicit whisky stills. Some respectable modern distilleries happily admit to a raffish past.

Scotland has its own character and its own history. At the turn of the 13th and 14th centuries the story was one of avoiding an English conquest, and Scotland's independence was re-asserted during the reign of Robert I – Robert the Bruce. His descendants founded the dynasty of the Stuart kings and queens, and the story of the Highlands in the first half of the 18th century is largely bound up with the efforts of the Stuarts to regain the British throne. All their attempts were failures, but the history of the Jacobites is still well remembered.

The tours take you to Jacobite country, to the land of the Solway smugglers, to ground fought over in the Border wars, and to lonely northwestern districts, where the people were forced off their holdings by 19th-century landlords wanting the larger rents offered first by incoming sheep-farmers and then by wealthy deer-stalkers. In places you will wonder why the land seems so empty: it was not always so.

Neidpath Castle was battered by Cromwell during the Civil War

Gentle hills slope away from the banks of Loch Lomond

**Inverness**

Inverness is the capital of the Highlands. Industry is confined to one area, and the town can boast some fine old buildings among clumsy modern developments. Inverness makes a feature of its riverside walks, overlooked by a 19th-century castle, and footbridges cross to the Ness Islands. There are cruises on the Caledonian Canal, a good local museum, and the curious claim – which you can judge on Tomnahurich Hill – that the town has the most beautiful burial ground in the country!

**Aberdeen**

Aberdeen is the grey Granite City, the capital of North Sea oil, but the granite of its buildings comes to life and sparkles in the sun. There are excellent museums and galleries, such as Provost Ross's House and Provost Skene's House, golf courses and a long beach, while its parks rival any in Britain. Aberdeen is a regular top prizewinner in the Britain in bloom competition: look for the 100,000 roses planted along one city dual-carriageway.

**Edinburgh**

Even if no longer a seat of government, Edinburgh is obviously a capital city. The New Town is one of the most graceful examples of Georgian planning, and few shopping streets have such an imposing backdrop as Princes Street, dominated by the castle rock. Edinburgh houses Scotland's national galleries and some splendid museums as well as being, every August and September, a world-famous festival city. Within the city limits, look for Dean Village, a remarkable survival of lovely buildings by the Water of Leith, and for Cramond, once an oyster-fishermen's village, where the Almond Water flows into the Forth.

**Dumfries**

Dumfries is the Queen of the South, the principal town in the region which stretches from the English border to the Mull of Galloway. Its museums are varied and impressive, one featuring an old windmill adapted to house a camera obscura. Robert Burns is remembered affectionately in Dumfries, his home in later years. His house is one of the town museums and his favourite pub, the Globe Inn, retains many Burns mementoes.

**Dumbarton**

Dumbarton was once the capital of the Celtic kingdom of Strathclyde. Later, it became an innovative shipbuilding centre and, almost in passing, a pioneer of the helicopter and the hovercraft. It is still an exhilarating experience to climb to the viewpoint summit of Dumbarton Rock, the old Celtic stronghold and later a fortress of the Crown. Although the shipyards have been abandoned, the Denny Experiment Tank, where scale-models of hulls were tested to see how they performed in miniature storms still survives.

TOUR
**26**

# History & Mystery

History and magnificent scenery are ever present on this tour. Just outside town lies Culloden, where Bonnie Prince Charlie's defeat in 1746 ruined the last hope of a Stuart restoration to the British throne. There are glorious sea, loch, island and mountain views, and who knows what may be lurking in Loch Ness?

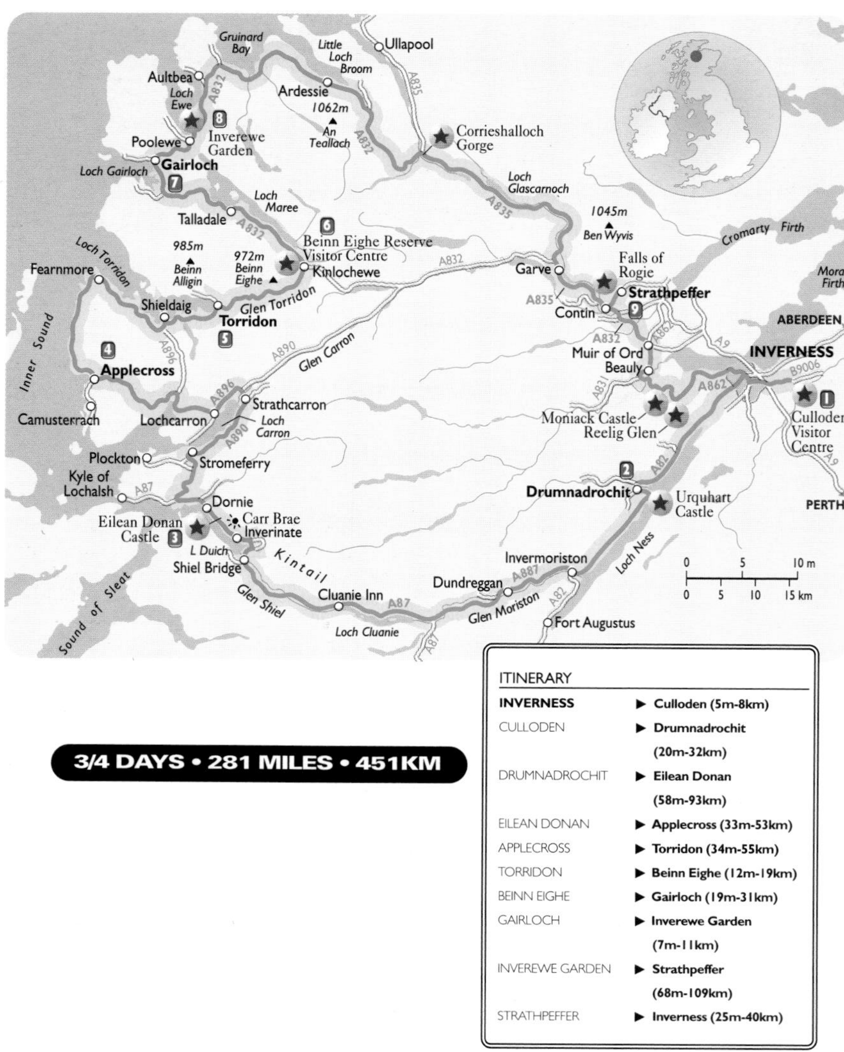


**3/4 DAYS • 281 MILES • 451KM**

ITINERARY

| | |
|---|---|
| **INVERNESS** | ► **Culloden (5m-8km)** |
| CULLODEN | ► **Drumnadrochit (20m-32km)** |
| DRUMNADROCHIT | ► **Eilean Donan (58m-93km)** |
| EILEAN DONAN | ► **Applecross (33m-53km)** |
| APPLECROSS | ► **Torridon (34m-55km)** |
| TORRIDON | ► **Beinn Eighe (12m-19km)** |
| BEINN EIGHE | ► **Gairloch (19m-31km)** |
| GAIRLOCH | ► **Inverewe Garden (7m-11km)** |
| INVEREWE GARDEN | ► **Strathpeffer (68m-109km)** |
| STRATHPEFFER | ► **Inverness (25m-40km)** |

Eilean Donan Castle, built by Alexander II of Scotland in 1220

*Castle Wynd, Inverness*

**FOR CHILDREN**

Before leaving Inverness, pay a visit to Whin Park, one of the finest children's play areas in the Highlands.

*Leave Inverness on the* ***B9006*** *to the battlefield of Culloden.*

**1 Culloden,** Highland
Cared for by the National Trust for Scotland, Culloden Moor is a place of sombre memories. It was here, on 16 April 1746, that the Duke of Cumberland's army crushed the Jacobite rising led by Prince Charles. The battlefield is laid out with plaques showing the disposition of the opposing forces, and in the visitor centre you can follow the story of this last major battle on British soil. Displays illustrate the confusing political climate of the times, when there were Scots – and even different Highland clans – fighting on both sides. The bitter aftermath of the battle, when government troops were sent on a murderous rampage through the glens, is also described.

*Return to Inverness and leave on the* ***A82*** *as for Fort William.*

**2 Drumnadrochit,** Highland
This is the site of the Loch Ness Centre, with its exhibition about the search for the world's most famous monster, said to lurk in the chill waters. You may arrive feeling sceptical, but you will almost certainly leave with the feeling that there is *something* here to be explained. Follow the 'Divach' sign off the A82 to the graceful Falls of Divach, and visit the striking lochside ruins of 13th-century Urquhart Castle, and the roadside monument to John Cobb, the land-speed record holder who was killed on Loch Ness in 1952 trying for the water-speed record.

*Loch Ness Centre*

*Continue on the* ***A82*** *to Invermoriston, then take the* ***A887*** *and go straight on along the* ***A87***. *Continue through Inverinate and turn right up Carr Brae. Go into Dornie and turn left for Eilean Donan Castle.*

**3 Eilean Donan,** Highland
Probably the most photographed castle in Scotland, Eilean Donan was rebuilt on its splendid islet site between 1912 and 1932, after lying in ruins since the Jacobite Rising of 1719. The MacRaes have been its Constables since 1509. Principal apartments open to visitors are the barrel-vaulted billeting room and the small but impressive banqueting hall. In the hall, look for the letter from Bonnie Prince Charlie – 'Being fully persuaded of yr loyalty and zeal for the King's service…' – sent to clan chiefs on behalf of his father, seeking their support in the 1745 Rising.

*Leave Dornie on the* ***A87*** *as for Kyle of Lochalsh, then turn right on to the* ***A890***, *left on to the* ***A896*** *through Lochcarron and Kishorn, and left for Applecross.*

Loch Maree, one of Scotland's most beautiful inland lochs

**FOR HISTORY BUFFS**

Beside the A87 in wild Glenshiel a plaque describes the battle fought there during the short-lived Jacobite Rising of 1719. The defeated Jacobite army included a company of Spanish troops – the last foreign soldiers to fight on Scottish soil.

**RECOMMENDED WALKS**

Lochcarron Environmental Group publishes a guide to 15 hill, coast and forest walks. One, climbs the Allt nan Carnan gorge above three waterfalls, with glorious views over Loch Carron and the Attadale hills.

### 4 Applecross, Highland

If you don't like narrow mountain roads, skip Applecross; if you do you will find a beautifully located crofting village, facing the splendid skyline of the Cuillin Hills on Skye. St Maelrhuba is the local saint, and after his death in AD722, villagers carried soil from his grave on long or perilous journeys. Potter southwards to the lovely rocky bay beyond Camusterrach and take a picnic behind the rippled sandbanks of Applecross Bay. On the lonely road north, look for the pathway which, until a generation ago, was the only land link between the scattered settlements of North Applecross.

[i] *Main Street, Lochcarron, or Applecross campsite*

▶ *Leave Applecross following the 'Shieldaig' sign. Turn left at a T-junction to rejoin the* ***A896****.*

### 5 Torridon, Highland

The Torridon landscape has no peers in mainland Scotland, with shapely Beinn Alligin and its outliers soaring from the sea-loch and, further east, Liathach's seven-peaked pinnacled ridge towering over Torridon village and glen. Both ranges are owned by the National Trust for Scotland, and a classic 9-mile (14km) walk on Trust ground explores the wild country behind Liathach. In summer, the Trust Visitor Centre explains the history, geology and wildlife of this glorious district, and there is an exhibition and audio-visual presentation on red deer near by.

[i] *NTS Visitor Centre*

▶ *Continue on the* ***A896****. Turn left on to the* ***A832****.*

### 6 Beinn Eighe, Highland

This magnificent mountain range, with quartzite summit rocks which give the impression of a permanent dusting of snow, was Britain's first National Nature Reserve. The Visitor Centre on the A832 illustrates the fascinating wildlife of the mountain – warblers and redstarts in the birchwoods, crossbills among the pines, otters and black-throated divers on the margins of Loch Maree. Two waymarked trails – one to 1,700 feet (518m) – offer tremendous views over the loch.

[i] *Aultroy Visitor Centre*

**BACK TO NATURE**

Beinn Eighe National Nature Reserve, near Kinlochewe, has some of the most dramatic scenery in Britain. Remnants of Caledonian pine forest harbour interesting plants such as creeping lady's tresses – an orchid; lesser twayblade orchid, twinflower and chickweed wintergreen.

▶ *Continue on the* ***A832*** *to Gairloch.*

### 7 Gairloch, Highland

Gairloch is really a cluster of crofting settlements on the shores of a very attractive sea-

loch, which has become a resort with fine sands, a fishing harbour and one of the most beautifully located golf courses in Scotland. Gairloch Heritage Museum has fishing boats in its courtyard, an old lighthouse tower installed at ground level, and indoor displays on the fishing, crofting and archaeological history of the heartland of the MacKenzies.

i *Gairloch Community Centre*

▶ *Continue through Poolewe.*

**8 Inverewe Garden,** Highland
This is perhaps the most famous garden in the whole of Scotland. Its Victorian creator transformed a bare, windswept promontory into a pine-sheltered woodland where, helped by the benign effect of the Gulf Stream, a spectacular collection of rhododendrons, primulas, deep blue meconopsis and hundreds of other plants and flowering shrubs now flourishes.

**FOR HISTORY BUFFS**

Turn off the A832 into Aultbea and behind Pier Road is a board describing how, during World War II, the anchorage of Loch Ewe was the gathering-point for Arctic convoys to the Soviet port of Murmansk.

▶ *Continue on the **A832**, turn right on to the **A835** then left at Contin on the **A834**.*

**9 Strathpeffer,** Highland
What was once Europe's most northerly spa remains a fine-looking resort centred on a gathering of sturdy Victorian hotels and villas in wooded grounds. Strathpeffer's redundant station has been restored to house craft shops, and in a pavilion in the square, you can sample some of the mineral-rich waters from local springs. Be prepared for a strong taste of sulphur! In the old days, spa visitors were expected to take vigorous exercise; so there is an excellent golf course, as well as a network of paths in a pleasant pinewood and, on the southern hills patrolled by kestrels and sparrowhawks, to the commanding viewpoint summit of Knock Farril.

i *The Square*

**RECOMMENDED WALKS**

Turn off the A835 after Tarvie for the Falls of Rogie. Footpaths cross a bridge over the rock pools and rapids, and pass a salmon ladder built to allow fish to swim upstream in the spawning season.

**FOR CHILDREN**

At Strathpeffer, ask the children to find the street names in the Victorian heart of the town. Apart from 'The Square', there are none: in its heyday as a spa, house names were the only addresses.

▶ *Return to Contin and turn left on the **A835**. Turn right on the **A832** then right on the **A862** through Beauly. Turn right to Moniack and pass Moniack Castle. Turn right at a T-junction following the Rebeg sign, pass the start of the Reelig Glen forest walk, then continue over a bridge and uphill. Take the first tarred road left, past a house called Kilninver, turn left at a T-junction and immediately first right, then right at a Give Way sign to Inverness.*

**SCENIC ROUTES**

Down Glenshiel, the A87 slices through a landscape of steep green mountainsides. After Inverinate, Carr Brae leads to a wonderful viewpoint, and, later, the A890 opens up dramatic views around Loch Carron.

Inverness Castle: Macbeth is thought to have lived on the site of the first castle here

TOUR
27

# The Castles of Mar

Aberdeen is the gateway to Royal Deeside and to the great spread of historic houses known as the Castles of Mar. The Royal Family's Scottish home is here, where pine and birchwoods line the riversides and heathery grouse moors rise to the skyline hills. Salmon and trout anglers fish the Dee and its companion river, the Don. Gliders soar above Aboyne and Dinnet, while older transport is the fascination at Alford.

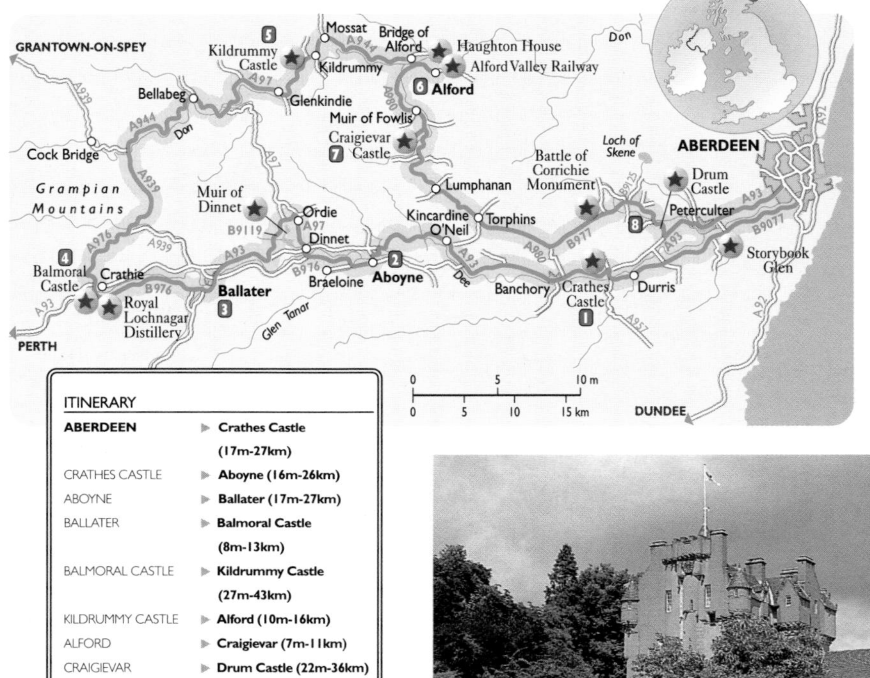


ITINERARY

| | |
|---|---|
| **ABERDEEN** | ▶ **Crathes Castle (17m-27km)** |
| CRATHES CASTLE | ▶ **Aboyne (16m-26km)** |
| ABOYNE | ▶ **Ballater (17m-27km)** |
| BALLATER | ▶ **Balmoral Castle (8m-13km)** |
| BALMORAL CASTLE | ▶ **Kildrummy Castle (27m-43km)** |
| KILDRUMMY CASTLE | ▶ **Alford (10m-16km)** |
| ALFORD | ▶ **Craigievar (7m-11km)** |
| CRAIGIEVAR | ▶ **Drum Castle (22m-36km)** |
| DRUM CASTLE | ▶ **Aberdeen (10m-16km)** |

**3 DAYS • 134 MILES • 215KM**

*i* *St Nicholas House, Broad Street, Aberdeen*

► *Leave Aberdeen on the* ***B9077****. Turn right on the* ***A957****, then left on the* ***A93*** *to Crathes Castle.*

**1 Crathes Castle,** Grampian
Sixteenth-century Crathes Castle was the home of generations of the Burnett family. It is a typical design by the Bells, master masons of Aberdeen and its hinterland, with a tower-like structure and an intriguing ornamented roofline. Look for the lovely painted ceiling of the Nine Nobles Room, and in the Green Lady's Room ponder the story of the Crathes ghost. There are eight splendid individual gardens, and one of their major attractions is the array of massive yew hedges, planted in 1702. Topiarists trim them into sweeping shapes, a task which takes three weeks every year.

**FOR CHILDREN**

Turn left off the B9077 for Storybook Glen, with its tableaux of children's stories, ranging from *Jack and the Beanstalk* and *Little Jack Horner* to the *Incredible Hulk* and *ET*.

► *Continue on the* ***A93*** *to Aboyne.*

**2 Aboyne,** Grampian
Built in Victorian times round a spacious green, Aboyne was previously a base for the 'floaters', the intrepid characters who made rafts of timber, cut up-river, and then steered them down the Dee to Aberdeen. There is a well-kept golf course not far from the water-skiing centre at Aboyne Loch. Anglers fish the Dee, and there are pleasant riverside walks backed by banks of broom. Aboyne Highland Games, held every August on the green, are among the most famous in Scotland.

*i* *Ballater Road Car Park*

**RECOMMENDED WALKS**

After Aboyne, turn left off the B976 at the grand gateway by the Bridge o' Ess into beautiful Glen Tanar. Call in at the interpretive centre at Braeloine for information on the footpath routes beside the Water of Tanar, to forest viewpoints and along part of the Firmounth road, one of the historic rights of way across the Grampians.

**SPECIAL TO...**

Aboyne is just one place which hosts annual Highland Games. Tossing the caber, shot-putting and hill races as well as normal track events are featured at Ballater and further up Royal Deeside. The Lonach Gathering at Bellabeg, on the A944 in Strathdon, is preceded by a march of the green-clad Lonach Highlanders.

► *Leave Aboyne to the south. Turn right on the* ***B976****, left on the* ***A97*** *as far as Ordie. Turn left on to the* ***B9119*** *and left on the* ***A93*** *to Ballater.*

**3 Ballater,** Grampian
Close to the Royal Family's Balmoral estate, this sturdy granite-built town has many shops showing the royal warrant. Golf, angling and walks by the Dee are favourite recreations here, but there are also enjoyable footpaths on Craigendarroch and Craig Coillich, the two wooded viewpoint hills which squeeze the town towards the river. In the now redundant railway station there is a display on the Deeside Line and its most celebrated passengers: the Royal Family used to arrive by train at Ballater and continue by road to Balmoral.

*i* *Station Square*

► *Leave Ballater to the south and turn right on the* ***B976*** *to the car park for Balmoral Castle.*

**SPECIAL TO...**

Single malt whisky is a classic Highland product. Turn left off the B976 before Balmoral for a tour of Royal Lochnagar Distillery, which received its royal warrant after a visit from Queen Victoria.

The baronial elegance of 16th-century Crathes Castle

Craigievar Castle rises six storeys high and is topped by turrets

**4 Balmoral Castle,** Grampian
The Royal Family's Scottish home is their private property, and not one of the great state houses. Prince Albert collaborated closely with the architect commissioned to build the present castle in Scottish Baronial style. From May till the end of July, the beautiful grounds are generally open to visitors. The ballroom houses an exhibition on the history of the estate. Across the river from the car park, Crathie parish church is where the Royal Family worship when they are in residence at Balmoral.

► *Turn left on the **A93**, right on the **B976**, left on the **A939**, right on the **A944** then straight on along the **A97** to Kildrummy Castle.*

**5 Kildrummy Castle,** Grampian
Built in the 13th century, this was the first great stone fortress in the north of Scotland. Even in decay it remains an impressive place. Modern Kildrummy Castle, once a mansion house, is now a hotel. The quarry from which it was built was transformed in Victorian times into a Japanese-style rock and water-garden with woodlands, pools, waterfalls, shrubs and flower beds linked by paths and stairways in a narrow ravine.

FOR HISTORY BUFFS

Kildrummy Castle witnessed a gruesome deed in 1306, when its English besiegers promised to reward the blacksmith who betrayed it to them with gold. They kept their promise by melting the gold pieces and pouring them down his throat to kill him.

► *Continue on the **A97**, then right on the **A944** to Alford.*

**6 Alford,** Grampian
If it runs on wheels, Alford welcomes it. The Grampian Transport Museum houses a fine collection of cars, commercial and farm vehicles, models and transport *memorabilia*. Look for the *Craigievar Express*, a steam wagon built in the 1890s by a local postman; and a Sentinel steam lorry from a distillery, whose wares it advertises as most suitable for medicinal purposes.

Outside, the museum operates a little motor-racing circuit where sprints for modern and vintage cars are held. Close by, the old station has been restored as a railway museum.

*i* *Alford Station*

FOR CHILDREN

From Alford station the narrow-gauge Alford Valley Railway runs into Haughton House country park, where there is an adventure playground in the birchwoods.

► *Return from Alford along the **A944** straight on along the **A980**, then right to Craigievar Castle.*

**7 Craigievar Castle,** Grampian
Although they were not building for fairytales, the Bell family of master masons combined a firm grasp of technique with a glorious lightness of touch. With its profusion of towers and turrets, Craigievar demonstrates this very clearly. Built for 'Danzig Willie' Forbes, who made his fortune in the Baltic trade, it was completed in 1626. Craigievar's five floors of rooms include such features as a grand heraldic fireplace carved from granite, pine and oak panelling, intricate plaster ceilings and the first of the Craigievar gaming tables which had a vogue among 18th-century card players.

► *Continue on the **A980** and go straight on along the **B977** and the **B9125**, then immediately after Flora's Shop, turn right, following the 'Hopeton' sign. Turn right at a crossroads, avoiding a farm road straight ahead, then follow signs to Drum Castle.*

FOR HISTORY BUFFS

On the B977, look to the left for the granite monument to the Battle of Corrichie in 1562. Mary Queen of Scots' army crushed the Gordons, the most powerful family in the northeast, in this battle. The Earl of Huntly, the head of the family, died in the battle, and his corpse was taken to Edinburgh to 'hear' the sentence that forfeited his lands and titles.

**8 Drum Castle,** Grampian
The Irvine family have been lairds at Drum Castle for 24 generations before giving the property to the National Trust for Scotland. They lived in a complex of linked buildings: a 13th-century keep, a Jacobean mansion and Victorian additions. Drum is well furnished with valuable pieces from different centuries. Among the portraits is one of Washington Irving, author of the classic *Rip van Winkle*, whose family left Scotland to live in America.

► *Rejoin the public road, then turn left on to the **A93** to return to Aberdeen.*

# Exploring the Tweed Valley

Hills are an important part of this tour, which visits the Pentlands, the Eildons and the Lammermuirs, and looks south to the Cheviots. But the valley of the River Tweed, one of Scotland's great trout and salmon waters, is the most significant element as the journey reaches the Border country.

**2/3 DAYS • 134 MILES • 216KM**

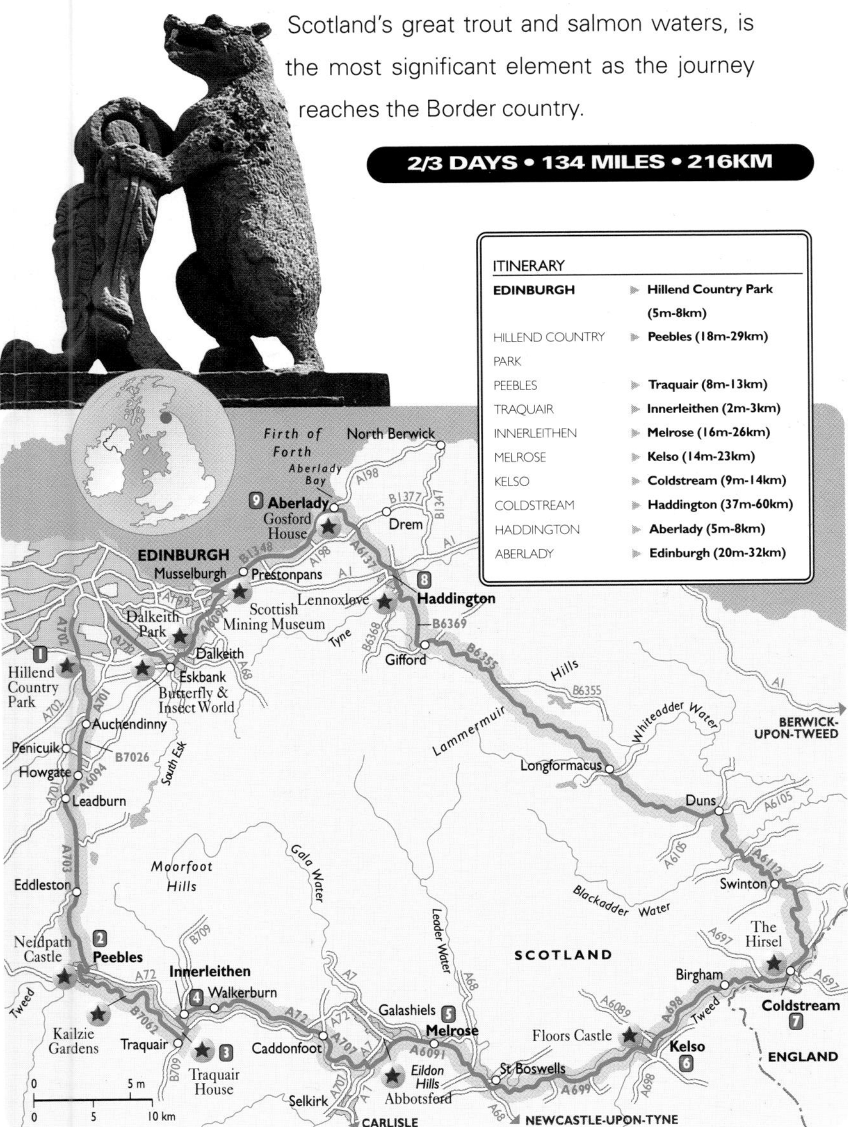


ITINERARY

| | |
|---|---|
| **EDINBURGH** | ▶ **Hillend Country Park (5m-8km)** |
| HILLEND COUNTRY PARK | ▶ **Peebles (18m-29km)** |
| PEEBLES | ▶ **Traquair (8m-13km)** |
| TRAQUAIR | ▶ **Innerleithen (2m-3km)** |
| INNERLEITHEN | ▶ **Melrose (16m-26km)** |
| MELROSE | ▶ **Kelso (14m-23km)** |
| KELSO | ▶ **Coldstream (9m-14km)** |
| COLDSTREAM | ▶ **Haddington (37m-60km)** |
| HADDINGTON | ▶ **Aberlady (5m-8km)** |
| ABERLADY | ▶ **Edinburgh (20m-32km)** |

Edinburgh Castle perches on Castle Rock, possibly the site of an old Iron Age fort

[i] *Waverley Station, Princes Street, Edinburgh*

▶ *Leave Edinburgh on the* ***A702*** *and turn right into Hillend Country Park.*

### 1 Hillend Country Park, Lothian

This is one of two similar parks in the exhilarating Pentland Hills, which rise directly from Edinburgh's southern suburbs. Footpaths climb steeply to the grassy viewpoint summits of Caerketton and Allermuir, the boyhood hills of Robert Louis Stevenson.

These paths link up with others across the rounded passes in the Pentlands, and alongside the many reservoirs which supply the city. Hillend Ski Centre, with its extensive artificial ski-slope, is a year-round mountain resort in miniature.

[i] *Pentland Hills Ranger Service Office*

▶ *Continue on the* ***A702****, then straight on along the* ***A703*** *and follow the* ***A701*** *and* ***B7026*** *through Auchendinny. Take the* ***A6094*** *and the* ***A703*** *again to Peebles.*

**FOR CHILDREN**

**Hillend Ski Centre is the largest of its kind in Europe. Children's courses start for those aged six. On the return to Edinburgh, the Butterfly and Insect World on the A772 houses hundreds of exotic butterflies as well as scorpions, tarantulas and stick insects.**

### 2 Peebles, Borders

No development is allowed to encroach upon Peebles' tree-lined riverside walks by the Tweed, and the town itself has a traditional charm. The Tontine Hotel in the High Street, retains the old front yard where stage-coaches used to sweep to a halt. There is a well-stocked Tweeddale Museum, and the Scottish Museum of Ornamental Plasterwork is close by, where you will be encouraged to don wellies and an apron, and try your hand at the craft. Peebles has extensive public parks and an interesting town walk.

Medieval Neidpath Castle stands dramatically above an up-river wooded curve of the Tweed, to the west of Peebles. Its walls still show signs of the bombardment in 1650 by Cromwell's artillery.

**RECOMMENDED WALKS**

**The Sware Walk at Peebles heads west along the wooded riverbank below Neidpath Castle, crosses Manor Bridge and Old Manor Bridge, then climbs to the wide-ranging Tweeddale viewpoint at Manor Sware.**

[i] *Chambers Institute, High Street*

▶ *Leave Peebles on the* ***B7062*** *and turn left for Traquair House.*

**3 Traquair,** Borders
Twenty generations of Stuart lairds made Traquair House their home, but it dates from well before their time – from 1107 at least – and is the oldest inhabited house in Scotland. Traquair retains mementoes of such famous Stuarts as Mary Queen of Scots and Bonnie Prince Charlie. As well as having valuable collections of glass, porcelain and embroideries, it is famous for its one derelict 18th-century estate brew-house. The present laird restored the copper, the mash tun, the coolers and fermenters, and now brews the rare Traquair Ale in quantities of no more than 210 barrels every year.

▶ *Continue on the **B7062** then turn left on the **B709** to Innerleithen.*

**4 Innerleithen,** Borders
The founder of this little textile town had the idea of using London names so addresses here include The Strand and Bond Street. Cashmere cloth is still woven in Innerleithen's mills, and the National Trust for Scotland has completely restored Robert Smail's Printing Works, closed as a family business only in 1986. A tour of this fascinating place recalls the otherwise lost technology of planers, reglets, quoins and side-sticks, and you may be given the chance to hand-set some type yourself. At a glorious viewpoint high in the town, the little blue-and-white spa pavilion of St Ronan's Wells has also been restored.

**SPECIAL TO...**

After Innerleithen, pause at Walkerburn to visit the Museum of Scottish Woollen Textiles, which illustrates all the processes from sheep-rearing to spinning, weaving and knitting.

▶ *Leave Innerleithen on the **A72**. Bear right on the **A707**, then left on the **B7060**. Turn right on the **A7**, left on the **B6360**, right on the **A6091** as for Jedburgh, and left on the **B6374** into Melrose.*

**FOR HISTORY BUFFS**

Abbotsford, on the way to Melrose, was the home of Sir Walter Scott, author of the *Waverley* novels. He bought the site on which he built Abbotsford in 1811. It took a long time to complete as he kept adding on bits. The tour includes his impressive library and study.

Robert Smail's print shop was started in 1840, when the original press was water-powered

**5 Melrose,** Borders
One of the pleasantest of the Border towns, Melrose is notable for the mellow ruin of its abbey, where the heart of Robert the Bruce is buried, and for Priorwood Garden, in which something like the old monks' orchard has been revived. The restored station houses an exhibition on the disappeared Waverley Line, and there is a small motor museum. Two walks explore the town, and the Southern Upland Way includes a lovely riverside stretch along the meadows by the Tweed.

*i* *Priorwood Garden*

**RECOMMENDED WALKS**

Starting from the B6359 in Melrose, the waymarked Eildon Walk climbs to the 1,325-foot (404m) Eildon North Hill, a magnificent viewpoint where a Roman signal station overlooked the Dere Street route from the Cheviots to the Forth. Here is the legendary resting place of King Arthur and his knights, sleeping under a spell.

▶ *Leave Melrose on the **A6091** as for Jedburgh. Turn right on to the **A68** then left on the **A699** and left on the **A698** into Kelso.*

**6 Kelso,** Borders
Here is a Border market town with a ruined abbey, the oldest cricket club in Scotland, a racecourse and a reputation for providing some of the best angling beats on the Tweed. Kelso has an elegant Georgian centre, and its cobbled square retains a bull ring – a pattern of stones marking the place where bulls were tethered during livestock sales. Turret House is the local museum.

Outside the town, Floors Castle, home of the Duke of Roxburghe, is richly furnished with paintings, tapestries and

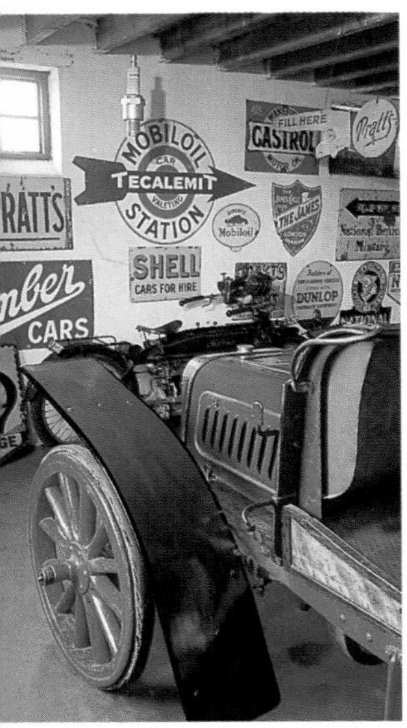


The Myreton Motor Museum at Aberlady

porcelain, and has a window for every day of the year. This huge mansion was built by William Adam between 1721 and 1725.

[i] *Town House Square*

▶ *Leave Kelso on the* ***A698*** *for Coldstream.*

**7 Coldstream,** Borders
This is the closest Scottish town to the English border. The Coldstream Guards, under an earlier name, were stationed in the town in 1660 when they marched south to assist in the restoration of King Charles II to the throne. There is a museum here dedicated to the regiment and its impressive heritage. Just outside Coldstream, the Hirsel estate has a comprehensive museum and a craft centre, several walks and a colourful collection of rhododendrons in Dundock Wood.

[i] *Henderson Park*

▶ *Leave Coldstream on the* ***A6112*** *for Duns, then take the* ***A6105*** *as for Earlston. After leaving Duns, watch for the right turn to Gifford. Turn right to Haddington on the* ***B6369*** *and* ***B6368****.*

**SPECIAL TO...**

In Newtown Street, Duns, the Jim Clark Memorial Room commemorates the great world race-driving champion who won 25 Grand Prix races and the Indianapolis 500.

**FOR HISTORY BUFFS**

Memorials at Gifford recall the Rev John Witherspoon, who signed the American Declaration of Independence and was president of the college which became Princeton university.
Off the B6369, Lennoxlove House is the home of the Dukes of Hamilton. It contains many mementoes of Mary Queen of Scots, including the ring which, on her way to the scaffold, she bequeathed to the Hamiltons.

**8 Haddington,** Lothian
Haddington is famous for the dozens of listed buildings along its streets, lanes and riverside walks. St Mary's Church contains the Lauderdale Aisle, scene of an annual ecumenical pilgrimage. Near by, St Mary's Pleasance is a garden laid out in an old Scottish style. Features to look for in Haddington include the town history display in Lady Kitty's Doocot (dovecote); Jane Welsh Carlyle's House, with its memories of the Victorian writer Thomas Carlyle; the Nungate Bridge; and the statue of two goats fighting. A goat eating grapes is Haddington's unusual coat of arms.

▶ *Leave Haddington on the* ***A6137*** *for Aberlady.*

**9 Aberlady,** Lothian
Once the trading seaport for Haddington, Aberlady is now a residential village with carefully preserved buildings, including a medieval parish church with fine stained-glass windows, and attractive 18th- and 19th-century houses in the High Street. Aberlady's golf course, Kilspindie, shared the ground with a rifle range when it was opened in 1898; hence the names of holes such as the Target and the Magazine. West of the village, Gosford House is the home of the Earl of Wemyss. The magnificent entrance hall houses Gosford's imposing portrait gallery.

**BACK TO NATURE**

The tidal inlet, saltmarsh and dunes at Aberlady Bay Nature Reserve, east of Aberlady, attract great numbers of waders. Regular reports are posted of bird observations: hundreds of sandwich terns, for instance, and godwits, dunlin and plover.

▶ *Leave Aberlady on the* ***A198*** *as for Edinburgh, then straight ahead on the* ***B1348****. Turn left on the* ***A199*** *then right on the* ***A6094*** *through Dalkeith. Turn right on the* ***A772*** *and return to Edinburgh.*

**BACK TO NATURE**

On the return towards Edinburgh, Dalkeith Park nature trails link the River North Esk and the South Esk through extensive estate woodlands.

**SCENIC ROUTES**

The B7062, past Kalizie Gardens, and the A72 follow the Tweed as it winds among woodlands, farms and hillside forests. You can follow a tree-lined road on the B7060 over the shoulder of a hill between two stretches of the Tweed.

# **Along the** Smugglers' Coast

Mountains, forests and beautiful stretches of coastline are the accompaniment to this tour from Dumfries. The huge Galloway Forest Park offers walks and trails, exhibitions, nature reserves and fishing waters. Along the coast, the Solway smugglers once brought contraband from the Isle of Man.

**2/3 DAYS • 119 MILES • 191KM**

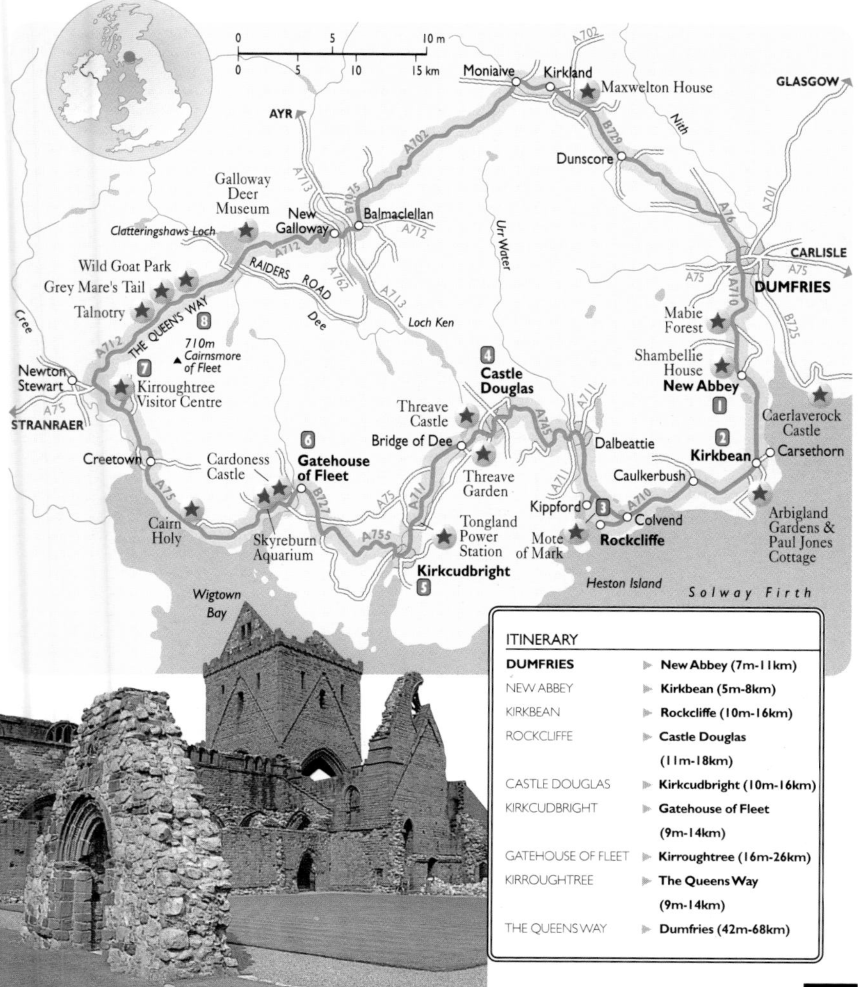


ITINERARY

| | |
|---|---|
| **DUMFRIES** | ▶ **New Abbey (7m-11km)** |
| NEW ABBEY | ▶ **Kirkbean (5m-8km)** |
| KIRKBEAN | ▶ **Rockcliffe (10m-16km)** |
| ROCKCLIFFE | ▶ **Castle Douglas (11m-18km)** |
| CASTLE DOUGLAS | ▶ **Kirkcudbright (10m-16km)** |
| KIRKCUDBRIGHT | ▶ **Gatehouse of Fleet (9m-14km)** |
| GATEHOUSE OF FLEET | ▶ **Kirroughtree (16m-26km)** |
| KIRROUGHTREE | ▶ **The Queens Way (9m-14km)** |
| THE QUEENS WAY | ▶ **Dumfries (42m-68km)** |

TOUR
# 29 **Along the** Smugglers' Coast

*i Whitesands, Dumfries*

**BACK TO NATURE**

The Wildfowl Trust reserve at Caerlaverock, southeast of Dumfries, provides some of the best opportunities anywhere to observe wild barnacle geese and family parties of whooper swans in the winter. Both the sanctuary of the reserve and the supplementary supply of food attract these species along with wigeon, teal and many more. There is a charge for admission (except to members of the Wildfowl Trust).

New Abbey's 18th-century corn mill restored to working order

▶ *Leave Dumfries on the* ***A710*** *to New Abbey.*

## 1 New Abbey, Dumfries and Galloway

Here, 'new' is a relative term. It refers to the lovely ruined abbey of mellow red sandstone which stands on the south side of the village. This is Sweetheart Abbey, new in the 13th century when it was founded by the family which also endowed Balliol College at Oxford. New Abbey also has a splendidly restored 18th-century corn mill. Among the pinewoods at the entrance to the village, Shambellie House is the site of Scotland's Museum of Costume.

▶ *Continue on the* ***A710*** *to Kirkbean.*

## 2 Kirkbean, Dumfries and Galloway

American visitors often come to this attractive village in 'the garden of Galloway' to trace the roots of Paul Jones, organiser and first commander of the Navy, who was baptised John Paul in the parish church here. His birthplace cottage on the Arbigland estate is a museum of his life and exploits, which included raiding his home coast during the American War of Independence! Arbigland itself has attractive sheltered gardens stretching to the Solway shore, where Paul Jones' father was employed.

Also near Kirkbean, Carsethorn is a Solwayside village with salmon stake-nets out on the treacherous tidal sands. Facing the Cumbrian shore, it was built to house the men of a 19th-century coastguard station, in the days when the coastguards' preoccupation was stopping the smugglers.

▶ *Continue on the* ***A710****. Turn left off it, first to Rockcliffe and then to Kippford.*

## 3 Rockcliffe and Kippford, Dumfries and Galloway

These are the principal villages of the Colvend coast, the most beautiful stretch of the Solway Firth. Rockcliffe with its rock flakes in a curving bay, was a Victorian seabathing resort.

Kippford, near the mouth of the River Urr, used to make its living from boat-building and quarrying. Now it is the main sailing centre on the Solway. Almost all the land between the villages is owned by the National Trust for Scotland. Both offer outstanding views over the wooded peninsulas around Rough Firth.

Above Rockcliffe stands the Mote of Mark, site of a 6th-century settlement on a granite outcrop and now a glorious viewpoint.

*i Colvend Post Office, A710*

**RECOMMENDED WALKS**

For one of the most beautiful walks in Scotland, leave Rockcliffe by the Jubilee Path with its gorgeous views over the estuary.
At Kippford, turn left by the post office along the shore road, then return to Rockcliffe by grassy pathways.
Except in May and June when the terns and oystercatchers are nesting, you can extend the walk – with care – along the tidal causeway to Rough Island.

**FOR CHILDREN**

Take the children for a boat trip from the floating jetty at Kippford, and let their imaginations run riot as they sail the smugglers' waters around Rough Firth and Hestan Island, a place honeycombed with 'brandy holes' and contraband hideaways.

▶ *Continue on the* ***A710****, then follow signs for Castle Douglas on the* ***A711*** *and* ***A745****. Turn left at a roundabout and go through the town centre, 11 miles (18km).*

The estuary of the Dee in Kirkcudbright at dusk

**4 Castle Douglas,** Dumfries and Galloway

A light and lively market town, Castle Douglas is lucky in having, as its principal public park, the land around Carlingwark Loch. Here you can hire a rowing boat to potter round the wooded islets and reed-beds where swans and great crested grebes nest and raise their young.

West of the loch, watch for the road on the left to Threave Garden. A property of the National Trust for Scotland, it features springtime daffodil displays as well as herbaceous borders, peat, woodland and rock gardens. Threave House is the Trust's School of Horticulture, and the whole 60 acres (24 hectares) are impeccably kept.

*i Market Hill*

FOR HISTORY BUFFS

At the roundabout after Castle Douglas, take the second exit for the walk and short ferry trip across the Dee to Threave Castle, the ruined island fortress of the Black Douglases, rebels against the crown, in the River Dee.

▶ *Turn left at a roundabout, go along the* ***A75****, then turn left on to the* ***A711*** *to Kirkcudbright.*

**5 Kirkcudbright,** Dumfries and Galloway

Built as the county town, this is a place of elegantly proportioned and colour-washed Georgian houses. It attracted turn-of-the-century artists, and their successors still live and work here. Broughton House, an 18th-century mansion, was presented to the town by the painter E A Hornel. It hosts art exhibitions and is well furnished with a fine antiquarian library and features such as a 1920s-style laundry. Outside, you may be surprised to find a Japanese garden; Hornel was influenced by Oriental themes.

Maclellan's Castle, now an ancient monument, is the ruin of a grander and earlier town mansion. The Stewartry Museum holds a fascinating local collection, including a room devoted to Kirkcudbright shipping, in which Paul Jones features strongly.

*i Harbour Square*

▶ *Leave Kirkcudbright on the* ***A755*** *then follow the* ***B727*** *through Gatehouse of Fleet.*

SPECIAL TO...

Phone Kirkcudbright 30114 to book a place on the tour – starting from Kirkcudbright – of Tongland power station, with its audio-visual presentation on the Galloway hydro-electric scheme, followed by visits to the spotless turbine hall and the salmon ladder in the ravine behind.

**6 Gatehouse of Fleet,** Dumfries and Galloway

Gatehouse by the River Fleet is one of the most intriguing country towns in Scotland full of restored buildings from its brief heyday – from 1790 onwards – as a cotton town. Robert Burns visited Gatehouse during the boom years, and it was in a room at the Murray Arms Hotel that he wrote what was to become Scotland's unofficial anthem, *Scots, wha hae.* The town is surrounded by delicious woodland country. Try the Fleet Oakwoods interpretive trail. A shorter open-ground stroll leads to the field-top viewpoint on Venniehill, which identifies the features of Gatehouse and its surroundings. Beyond

Grey Mare's Tail waterfall

Venniehill, Cardoness Castle is an imposingly situated 15th-century tower which was the home of the notoriously hot-tempered McCullochs.

*[i] The Car Park, High Street*

► *Turn right on to the **A75** (heading west) and in Palnure watch for a right turn to Kirroughtree Visitor Centre.*

**FOR HISTORY BUFFS**

Turn right off the A75 for the standing stones of Cairn Holy, overlooking the Solway. On the return to Dumfries, Maxwelton House, on the B729, was the birthplace of the heroine of Scotland's famous love song, *Annie Laurie*.

### 7 Kirroughtree Forest,

Dumfries and Galloway

The oldest South of Scotland plantations of the Forestry Commission cover a landscape of hills and a river valley overlooked by the great bulk of Cairnsmore of Fleet. An audio-visual presentation explains the workings of the forest, and outdoor attractions include a forest garden with plots of more than 60 tree species, from redwoods and monkey puzzles to cypress and rarities such as the Englemann spruce. Four trails explore the upper parts of the forest, visiting hill lochs and viewpoints, and you should follow the separate Papy Ha'bird trail above the Palnure Burn, habitat of warblers, woodpeckers, dippers, goosanders, shelduck, jays and ravens.

*[i] Visitor Centre*

► *Rejoin the **A75**, then go right on to the **A712**.*

### 8 The Queens Way,

Dumfries and Galloway

Several visitor areas of the Galloway Forest Park are concentrated along the stretch of A712 known as the Queens Way. The start is signalled by the hill-top obelisk at Talnotry commemorating Alexander Murray, a local shepherd's son who became the greatest Oriental linguist in early 19th-century Britain.

Look for the Grey Mare's Tail waterfall, the wild goats and their kids in the roadside reserve at Craigdews Hill, the red deer range and the Galloway Deer Museum among a stand of pines above the shore of Clatteringshaws Loch.

*[i] Talnotry campsite or Galloway Deer Museum*

**RECOMMENDED WALKS**

At Talnotry on the Queens Way, marked trails explore the steep forested hills. Do not be misled by the wide path at the start; much of this is roughish going. The trails go to viewpoints and an old lead mine, and follow the 'lost' 18th-century Edinburgh-Wigtown coach road.

**FOR CHILDREN**

Turn off the Queens Way after the red deer range for the Raiders Road forest drive, an old cattle-rustlers' trail beside the Black Water of Dee. Children usually love the bronze otter sculpture at a picnic pool with rocky islets.

► *Continue on the **A712** through New Galloway. Turn right on the **A713**, left on the **A712**, left on the **B7075** and right on the **A702** through Moniaive. In Kirkland, turn right on the **B729** and return to Dumfries.*

**SCENIC ROUTES**

Beyond Dumfries, the A710 gradually comes within sight of the wide Solway sands and, across the water, the faraway Lakeland hills.

After Gatehouse, the A75 offers beautiful high-level views over the bird-watcher's paradise of Wigtown Bay.

After Moniaive, the A702 and B729 follow the Cairn Valley through a fine landscape of farms, woods and stone-dyked fields.

# The Beautiful Western Highlands

**4 DAYS • 246 MILES • 396KM** Some of the most striking seascapes, mountains, forests and moorland scenery in the West Highlands form the landscape of this tour, based on the firmly Lowland town of Dumbarton.

| ITINERARY | |
|---|---|
| **DUMBARTON** | ▸ **Helensburgh (8m-13km)** |
| HELENSBURGH | ▸ **Inveraray (40m-64km)** |
| INVERARAY | ▸ **Crinan Canal (27m-43km)** |
| CRINAN CANAL | ▸ **Kilmartin (7m-11km)** |
| KILMARTIN | ▸ **Easdale (29m-47km)** |
| EASDALE | ▸ **Oban (16m-26km)** |
| OBAN | ▸ **Sea Life Centre (11m-18km)** |
| SEA LIFE CENTRE | ▸ **Port Appin (14m-23km)** |
| PORT APPIN | ▸ **Ballachulish (18m-29km)** |
| BALLACHULISH | ▸ **Glen Coe (5m-8km)** |
| GLEN COE | ▸ **Loch Lomond (50m-80km)** |
| LOCH LOMOND | ▸ **Dumbarton (21m-34km)** |

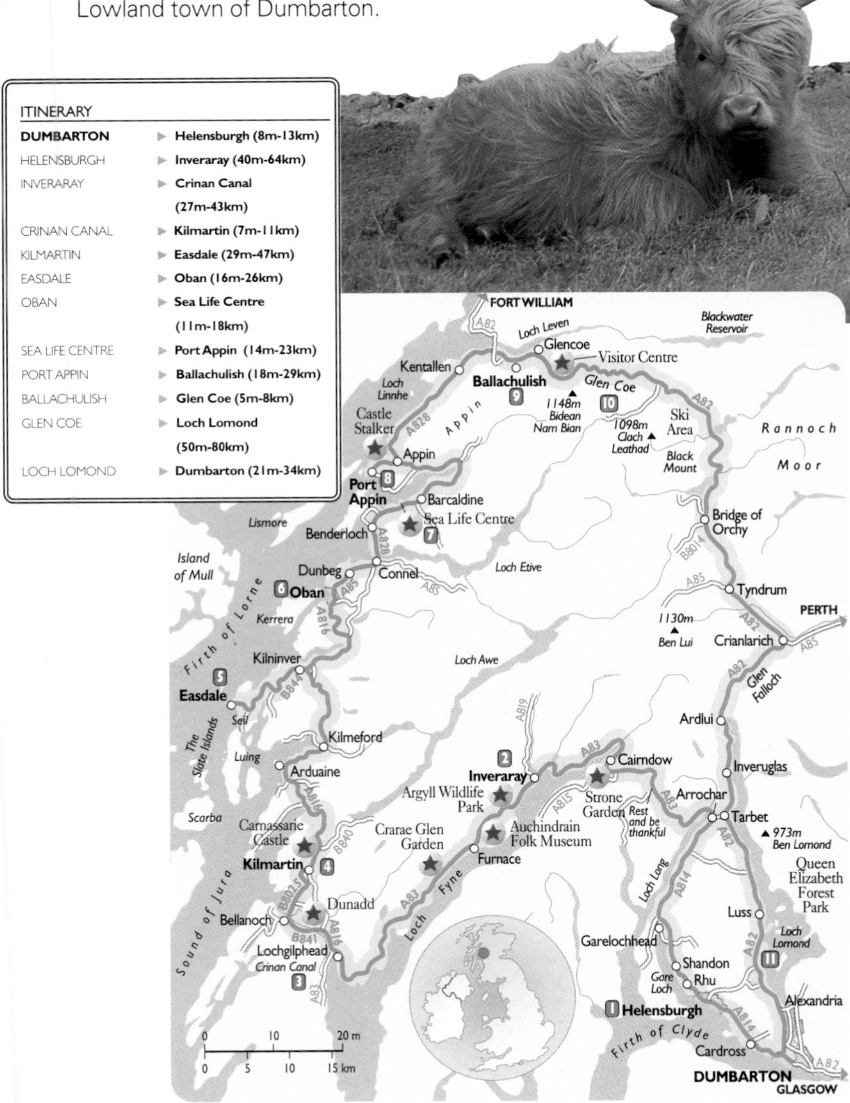

[i] *Milton, by Dumbarton*

▶ *Leave Dumbarton on the **A814** through Cardross, Helensburgh, Rhu and Shandon.*

**1 Helensburgh,** Strathclyde
Think of this residential town rising from the estuary of the River Clyde when you switch on your television. John Logie Baird, the television pioneer, was born here in 1888. Another inventive Helensburgh man was Henry Bell, whose *Comet*, launched in 1812, was the world's first sea-going steamboat. Both men are commemorated in the town.

Charles Rennie Mackintosh, the most famous of Scotland's 20th-century architects, completed The Hill House in 1902. You may share the feelings of many visitors that the elegant interiors, showing Mackintosh's amazing attention to detail, seem to become more rather than less modern as the decades pass.

In summer, ferries sail across the Clyde from Helensburgh. There are sailing races, and dozens of yachts lie moored off Rhu – where the garden of Glenarn is an early-season attraction – and Shandon. After Shandon the road passes the Clyde Submarine Base, home port of Britain's nuclear fleet.

[i] *The Clock Tower*

▶ *Take the third exit from the roundabout, follow the **A814** to Arrochar and turn left on the **A83**. Ignore a left turn for the **A815**, bear left on an unclassified road through Cairndow, and rejoin the **A83** for Inveraray.*

**2 Inveraray,** Strathclyde
Once the county town of Argyll, this gem of 18th-century architecture is reflected in the waters of Loch Fyne near Inveraray Castle, home of the 12th Duke of Argyll. The castle's public rooms include an imposing armoury hall, a tapestry drawing room and a state dining room with elaborate plasterwork. In the grounds, Cherry Park houses a Combined Operations Museum recalling how a quarter of a million troops were trained at Inveraray for seaborne landings of World War II. There are also pleasant woodland walks. If you are fit and sure-footed, try the steep climb through roe deer territory to the viewpoint summit of Dun na Cuaiche.

The town's 20th-century bell tower acts as the Clan Campbell war memorial; and Inveraray Gaol is one of the finest theme museums in Scotland. In the courtroom, sitting among lifelike figures of lawyers and jurymen, you can hear the tape-recorded transcript of an actual trial held in 1850.

**FOR CHILDREN**

South of Inveraray, Argyll Wildlife Park covers 60 acres (18 hectares) of open ground, forest and lochside. There are wildfowl pools as well as badgers, wildcats, foxes, pine martens and deer, and the residents of Owl Avenue stare imperiously down.

The cone-topped towers of Inveraray Castle

*i* *Front Street*

▶ *Continue on the* ***A83*** *to Lochgilphead. Turn right on the* ***A816****, bear left on the* ***B841*** *to cross the Crinan Canal, then go right at Bellanoch on the* ***B8025****.*

**FOR HISTORY BUFFS**

**Beside the A83, Auchindrain is a farming museum. In and around a cluster of restored cottages once lived in by MacCallums, MacCoshams, MacNicols and Munros you can see furnishings and displays of agricultural techniques of generations long gone by.**

**3 Crinan Canal,** Strathclyde
Built to save fishing boats and trading ships the risky journey round the Mull of Kintyre, this 9-mile (14m) waterway is now used mostly by yachts and motor cruisers. To the south of the summit level, spruce plantations clothe the hills where reservoirs store the canal's water supply. From the picnic site at Dunardry a forest walk looks down on the canal, its locks and towpath, and an attractive tree-backed lagoon.

▶ *Bear left on the* ***A816*** *to Kilmartin.*

**4 Kilmartin,** Strathclyde
The lovely Kilmartin valley was the heartland of the 6th-century kingdom of Dalriada, which expanded to become the kingdom of Scotland. The valley also contains Bronze Age burial cairns and standing stones, some set out in a straight linear alignment.

Kilmartin church and churchyard house many medieval grave slabs, and Carnassarie Castle, high above the village, offers a magnificent view, unobtainable from road level, into the narrow canyon which swings down from Loch Awe.

▶ *Continue on the* ***A816****, then left on the* ***B844*** *and follow signs to Easdale.*

Crinan Canal was opened in 1801

**FOR HISTORY BUFFS**

**Few places are as atmospheric, for Scots or descendants of Scots, as Dunadd, south of Kilmartin. With its lovely panoramic views, this hilltop fortress was the capital of the kingdom of Dalriada and the coronation site of the first Scottish kings.**

**5 Easdale,** Strathclyde
The steeply-arched 'bridge over the Atlantic' to Seil joins one of Argyll's Slate Islands to the mainland. Easdale is the name both of the old quarry village on the west side of Seil, and of the smaller offshore island facing it. A deep quarry at Easdale village, breached by the sea during a ferocious storm in November 1881, survives as an open bay.

The village retains its rows of whitewashed quarriers' cottages. In contrast, high walls and a wooded cliff protect the garden of An Cala – with its gentle stream, ponds, herbaceous borders and flowering shrubs – from the salt-laden wind.

Across the narrow sound on Easdale Island, the workings of a now vanished trade and the way the quarry communities created their own lively social life are explained in a fascinating museum.

*i* *Easdale Island Museum*

▶ *Return to the* ***A816*** *and turn left for Oban.*

**6 Oban,** Strathclyde
Oban is a major car-ferry port and hosts several important yacht races. St Columba's, the 20th-century cathedral with carved oak panels showing scenes from the life of the famous Celtic saint, is the heart of the Roman Catholic diocese of Argyll and the Isles.

Elsewhere in the town you can watch glass-blowers and paper-weight-makers at work, and visit the distillery founded in the 18th century. Footpaths climb to outstanding viewpoints such as McCaig's Tower, built in the style of the Colosseum at Rome. Gallanach Road leads south to the little ferry slip for Kerrera, where you can enjoy an exhilarating island walk round a 7-mile (11km) circuit of paths and farm roads.

*i* *Argyll Square*

▶ *Leave Oban on the* ***A85****. At Connel, turn right on the* ***A828*** *as it swings over Connel Bridge.*

**7 Sea Life Centre,** Strathclyde
As you admire the agile seals here you may have the feeling that they are watching the

Fishing boats at Oban harbour

**FOR CHILDREN**

A World in Miniature, on the North Pier at Oban, displays amazingly intricate 1/12 scale model scenes. Look for the pub with its tiny dartboard, the charming music room and the workshop where the miniaturised tools work like their full-scale counterparts.

parade of visitors just as much as the other way round. Similarly, the rays rise up from their low-level tank to look at the tourists. It is intriguing to see the herring shoal swim clockwise round their specially-shaped tank, then suddenly, at a mysterious group signal, all change direction.

▶ *Continue on the **A828** into Appin village then turn left for Port Appin.*

**RECOMMENDED WALKS**

The most spectacular of the Forestry Commission walks around Barcaldine on the A828 starts from Sutherland's Grove. Paths lead up Glen Dubh – the Dark Glen – to a footbridge over the ravine where the river rampages down.

### 8 Port Appin, Strathclyde

On one of the finest stretches of the coast of Argyll, this little village looks out to the long island of Lismore and, beyond it, to the lonely hills of Kingairloch. There is a peninsula walk past a natural archway in the cliffs, and another excursion could start with a ferry trip to the north end of Lismore. Walks there include one to the former limeworkers' village of Port Ramsay. North of Port Appin, look for Castle Stalker, romantically located on a tidal islet.

▶ *Return to the **A828** and turn left. Pass Ballachulish Hotel and turn left on the **A82**.*

### 9 Ballachulish, Strathclyde

The 'Village at the Narrows' used to be well-known for its ferry across Loch Leven, which has been replaced with a modern bridge. A flight of steps after the Ballachulish Hotel climbs to a memorial marking the site of the gibbet where, in 1755, James Stewart of the Glen was hanged for the murder – which he did not commit – of government agent Colin Campbell. After he was dead, Stewart's body was left hanging for three years. The mystery of who really did commit the Appin Murder is still discussed, and Robert Louis Stevenson made it the central theme of his novel *Kidnapped*.

Extensive landscaping has disguised the fact that between 1697 and 1955 Ballachulish was a major centre of the slate industry. A comprehensive display in the visitor centre describes its rise and decline.

*i* *A82 Car Park*

**SPECIAL TO...**

Railway enthusiasts often trace the old line from Oban via Connel Bridge to Ballachulish. It features handsome turn-of-the-century stations, one of which is the Holly Tree Hotel at Kentallen.

▶ *Continue on the **A82**, diverting left into Glencoe village, then return to the main road for Glen Coe itself.*

### 10 Glen Coe and the Black Mount, Strathclyde

Now the tour heads into its most dramatic phase. At the village of Glencoe the informative local museum recalls how, one night

in February 1692, the MacDonalds of Glencoe were slaughtered in their homes by troops billeted on them – an atrocity which has never been forgotten. The story of the massacre is retold in a National Trust for Scotland Visitor Centre a little way up the glen. It also features the wildlife and geology of the district. The northern wall of Glen Coe is a forbidding mountain ridge, while a glorious succession of towers, buttresses, gullies and hanging valleys marches along its southern side. Beyond the isolated Kings House Hotel, desolate Rannoch Moor stretches away to the left.

**RECOMMENDED WALKS**

After the river bridge at Glencoe village, turn left for the Lochan Trail, which circles an ornamental lake backed by Corsican pines. On a calm day it reflects like a mirror the striking outline of Ben Vair – the Peak of the Thunderbolt.

Further on there are tremendous views into the corries of the Black Mount.

*i National Trust for Scotland Visitor Centre, A82*

▶ *Continue on the **A82**.*

### 11 Loch Lomond,

Strathclyde

Having swooped down Glen Falloch, the route reaches Ardlui at the head of Loch Lomond. In the north, the loch fills a narrow glacial trough between crammed-in mountains. Luss, with its low sandstone cottages and fine Victorian church, lies where Loch Lomond broadens out to become part of a gentler Lowland scene with lovely wooded islands. Like Ardlui, Inveruglas, Tarbet, Inverbeg and Balloch, Luss is a port of call for ferries. You can cruise through the islands or cross the loch, walk on the West Highland Way through spruce, larch, birch and oakwoods under the shoulder of Ben Lomond, and sail back to the western shore.

Glen Coe, the most infamous glen in Scotland

*i Main Street, Tarbet*

**SPECIAL TO...**

The most famous but most elusive fish for Loch Lomond anglers is the powan, unique to Scotland. This freshwater herring had to adapt to life away from the sea after glacial debris blocked out the tidal waters.

▶ *Continue on the **A82** and return to Dumbarton.*

**BACK TO NATURE**

Queen Elizabeth Forest Park, near to Loch Lomond, harbours woodland birds, including woodcock and wood warbler, while on the higher ground of Ben Lomond there are golden eagles, ptarmigan and mountain flowers.

# PRACTICAL INFORMATION

## FACTS AND FIGURES

**IDD code:** 44. To call an international number dial '00' followed by the country code, area code and finally number you require.

**Currency:** the unit of currency is the pound (£), divided into 100 pence. Coins are in denominations of 1, 2, 5, 10, 20 and 50 pence and one pound (£1); notes are in denominations of £5, 10, 20 and 50.

**Local time:** the official time is Greenwich Mean Time (GMT). British Summer Time (BST) begins in late March when the clocks are put forward an hour. In late October, the clocks go back an hour to GMT.

**Emergency services:** Police, fire and ambulance tel: 999.

**Business hours –**
**Banks:** generally open 9am-3.30pm weekdays, though times do vary from bank to bank, and some are open on Saturday mornings until noon. In Scotland and Wales, times vary - some banks have different opening times and some close for lunch.
**Post Offices:** Main Post Offices open from 9am-5.30pm, Monday to Friday and 9am-12.30pm on Saturday.

**Credit and charge cards:** these are widely accepted.

**Tourist information:** England: British Travel Centre, 12 Regent Street, London, SW1. English Tourist Board, Thames Tower, Black's Road, Hammersmith, London W6 9EL. Tel: 0181 846 9000. Scotland: Scottish Tourist Board, 23 Ravelston Terrace, Edinburgh, EH4 3EU. Tel: 0131 332 2433. Wales: Wales Tourist Board, Brunel House, 2 Fitzalan Road, Cardiff, CF2 1UY. Tel: 01222 499909.

## MOTORING IN GREAT BRITAIN

### ACCIDENTS

In the event of an accident, the vehicle should be moved off the carriageway wherever possible. If the vehicle is fitted with hazard warning lights, they should be used. If available, a red triangle should be placed on the road at least 165 feet (50m) before the obstruction and on the same side of the road.
If damage or injury is caused to any other person or vehicle you must stop, give your own and the vehicle owner's name and address and the registration number of the vehicle to anyone having reasonable grounds for requiring them. If you do not give your name and address at the time of the accident, report the accident to the police as soon as reasonably practicable, and in any case within 24 hours.

### BREAKDOWNS

Visitors who bring their cars to Britain and are members of a recognised automobile club may benefit from the services provided free of charge by the AA. Car rental companies normally provide cover with one or other of the major motoring organisations in Britain, the AA or the RAC. On motorways there are emergency telephones at the side of the hard shoulder every mile (1.6km).

In the event of a breakdown, the vehicle should be moved off the carriageway wherever possible. If the vehicle is fitted with hazard warning lights, they should be used. If available, a red triangle should be placed on the road at least 165 feet (50m) before the obstruction and on the same side of the road.

### CARAVANS

**Brakes**

Check that the caravan braking mechanism is correctly adjusted. If it has a breakaway safety mechanism, the cable between the car and caravan must be firmly anchored so that the trailer brakes act immediately if the two part company.

**Caravan and luggage trailers**

Take a list of contents, especially if any valuable or unusual equipment is being carried, as this may be required on arrival. A towed vehicle should be readily identifiable by a plate in an accessible position showing the name of the make of the vehicle and the production and serial number.

### Lights

Make sure that all the lights are working - rear lights, stop lights, numberplate lights, rear fog guard lamps and flashers (check that the flasher rate is correct: 60-120 times a minute).

### Tyres

Both tyres on the caravan should be of the same size and type. Inspect them carefully: if you think they are likely to be more than three-quarters worn before you get back, replace them before you leave. If you notice uneven wear, scuffed treads, or damaged walls, get expert advice on whether the tyres are suitable for further use. Find out the recommended tyre pressures from the caravan manufacturer.

## CAR HIRE AND FLY/DRIVE

Drivers must hold, and have held for one year, a valid national licence or an International Driving Permit.

The minimum age for hiring a car ranges from 18 to 25, depending on the model of car. With some companies, there is a maximum age limit of 70. You can arrange to pick up your car in one town and return it in another.

If you are going to hire a car, you can often get a good deal if you arrange a fly/drive package tour.

## CHILDREN

The following restrictions apply to children travelling in private motor vehicles:

Children under 3 years - front seat - appropriate child restraint must be worn - rear seats - appropriate child restraint must be worn if available.

Child aged 3 to 11 and under 1.5 metres tall - front seat - appropriate child restraint must be worn if available. If not, adult seat belt must be worn.

Child aged 12 or 13 or younger child 1.5 metres or more in height - front and rear seats - adult seat belt must be worn if available.

Note: under no circumstances should a rear-facing restraint be used in a seat with an airbag.

## CRASH (SAFETY) HELMETS

Visiting motorcyclists and their passengers must wear crash or safety helmets.

## DOCUMENTS

You must have a valid driver's licence or an International Driving Permit. Holders of permits written in a foreign language are advised to obtain an official translation from an embassy or recognised automobile association. Non-EC nationals must have Green Card insurance.

## DRINKING AND DRIVING

The laws regarding drinking and driving are strict and the penalties severe. The best advice is if you drink don't drive.

## DRIVING CONDITIONS

Traffic drives on the left (it goes clockwise at roundabouts [traffic circles], which crop up frequently at intersections). Speed-limit and destination signs use miles (one kilometre is roughly 5/8 of a mile). Motorways link most major cities; service areas are indicated well in advance. On some motorway stretches, however, there aren't many stopping-places, e.g. the M25 (London's busy orbital route), the M11, M20 and M40.

Tolls are levied on certain bridges and tunnels. Roads in parts of Wales and in the north-west of Scotland are sometimes narrow. On single track roads, pull into passing places only if they are on your left. Stop level with those on your right - the oncoming traffic will make the detour.

## FUEL

Unleaded as well as leaded petrol and diesel is widely available, and an environmental petrol tax means that unleaded is always cheaper. Unleaded petrol has a minimum octane rating of 95, with super octane available from some stations with a rating of around 98.

The most widely available leaded petrol is 'four-star', which has a minimum octane rating of 97. Petrol stations are usually self-service and tend to be situated in and around towns and on the motorways and major roads. Motorway service stations and some service stations on busy major roads and in large towns open round the clock, or at least late into the night. Most petrol stations accept credit cards.

## INSURANCE

Fully comprehensive insurance, which covers you for some of the expenses incurred after a breakdown or an accident, is advisable.

## LIGHTS

You must ensure your front and rear side lights and rear registration plate lights are lit at night. You must use headlights when visibility is seriously reduced and at night on all unlit roads and those where the street lights are more than 185m (600 feet) apart.

## ROADS

Roads in Britain are generally very good, but busy. Try to travel outside the main rush hours of 8-9.30am and 4.30-6pm, especially in built-up areas.

## ROUTE DIRECTIONS

Throughout the book the following abbreviations are used for British roads:

**A** - main roads
**B** - local roads
unclassified roads - minor roads (unnumbered)

## SEAT BELTS

Seat belts are compulsory for drivers and front seat passenger.

Passengers travelling in the rear of the vehicle must wear a seat belt if fitted.

### SPEED LIMITS

Speed limits for cars are 70mph (112kph) for motorways and dual carriageways, 60mph (96kph) for other roads, and 30mph (48kph) in built-up areas unless otherwise indicated.

### TOLLS

Tolls are levied on certain bridges and tunnels.

### WARNING TRIANGLE/HAZARD WARNING LIGHTS

If the vehicle is fitted with hazard warning lights, they should be used in the event of a breakdown or accident. If available, a red triangle should be placed on the road at least 55 yards (50m) before the obstruction and on the same side of the road.

## CAMPING AND CARAVANNING SITES

### Sites

Campsites are abundant in Britain, ranging from small fields with just a single cold tap by way of facilities to large-scale sites with shower blocks and shops. Useful sources of information include the *Freedom* brochures published by the English Tourist Board (for a free copy tel: 01452 413041) and the list published by the Camping and Caravanning Club, East Grinstead House, East Grinstead, West Sussex, RH19 1UA. Tel: 01203 694995. Tourist Information Centres can help with lists of local sites.

### Off-site camping

If you are thinking of camping in the wilds, be aware of all that the British climate can throw at you, and remember that even open moorland is owned by someone - try to ask permission first if possible.

### SITES

The following are located along the routes.

### TOUR 1

**PENZANCE** Cornwall
**Bone Valley Caravan Park** (tel: 01736 60313)
Heamoor TR20 8UJ.
Open March to 7 January.

**ST IVES** Cornwall
**Polmanter Tourist Park** (tel: 01736 795640)
Hasletown TR26 3LX.
Open Whitsun to 10 September.

**Ayr Holiday Park** (tel: 01736 795855)
TR26 1EJ.
Open April to October.

**HAYLE** Cornwall
**St Ives Bay Holiday Park** (tel: 01736 752274)
73 Loggans Road, Upton Towans TR27 5BH.
Open 28 May to 7 September.

**PORTHTOWAN** Cornwall
**Porthtowan Tourist Park** (tel: 01209 890256)
Mile Hill TR4 8TY.
Open July to August.

**TRURO** Cornwall
**Carnon Downs Caravan & Camping Park** (tel: 0187 862283)
Carnon Downs TR3 6JJ.
Open Easter or April to October.

**Summer Valley** (tel: 01872 77878)
Shortlansend TR4 9DW.
Open April to October.

**Tretheak Manor Tourist Park** (tel: 01872 501658)
Veryan TR2 5PP.
Open Easter or April to October.

**FALMOUTH** Cornwall
**Trenmoravah Tent Park** (tel: 01326 312103)
Swanpool TR11 5BA.
Open Mid-May to October.

**MULLION** Cornwall
**Mullion Holiday Park** (tel: 01326 240248/240000)
Lizard Penisula A3083 TR12 7LJ.
Open Easter and May to September.

### TOUR 2

**BODMIN** Cornwall
**Camping & Caravanning Club Site** (tel: 01208 73834)
Old Callywith Rd PL31 2DZ.
Open end of March to early October.

**CAMELFORD** Cornwall
**Juliot's Well Holiday Park** (tel: 01840 213302)
PL32 9RF.
Open March to October.

**LYDFORD** Devon
**Camping and Caravanning Club Site** (tel: 01822 820275)
EX20 4BE.
Open end March to the end September.

**TAVISTOCK** Devon
**Harford Bridge Holiday Park** (tel: 01822 810349)
PL19 9LS.
Open 22 March to 14 November.

**Higher Longford Farm Caravan Site** (tel: 01822 810349)
Moorshop PL19 9LQ.
Open all year.

**LOSTWITHIEL** Devon
**Powderham Castle Tourist Park** (tel: 01208 8272277)
PL30 5BU.
Open April to October.

**ST AUSTELL** Cornwall
**Trencreek Farm Holiday Park** (tel: 01726 882540)
Hewas Water Pl26 7JG.
Open Spring Bank Holiday to 13 September.

### TOUR 3

**LYNTON** Devon
**Camping and Caravanning Club Site** (tel: 01598 752379)
Caffyns Cross EX35 6JS.
Open end of March to the end of October.

**PORLOCK** Somerset
**Burrowhayes Farm and Caravan and Camping Site** (tel: 01643 862463)
West Luccombe TA24 8HU.
Open 15 March to October.

**MINEHEAD** Somerset
**Camping and Caravanning Club Site** (tel: 01643 704138)
Hill Road North Hill TA24 5SF.
Open end March to the end September.

**WATCHET** Somerset
**Doniford Bay Holiday Park** (tel: 01984 632423)
TA23 OTJ.
Open April to mid-October.

**TOUR 4**
**TAUNTON** Somerset
**Ashe Farm Camping & Caravanning Site** (tel: 01823 442567)
Thornfalcon TA3 5NW.
Open April to October.

**CERNE ABBAS** Somerset
**Giants Head Caravan & Camping Park** (tel: 01300 341242)
Giants Head Farm, Old Sherborne Road, DT2 7TR.
Open Easter to October.

**BRIDPORT** Somerset
Binghams Farm Touring Caravan Park (tel: 01308 488234)
Melpesh DT6 3TT.
Open all year.

**CHARD** Somerset
**South Somerset Holiday Park** (tel: 01460 62221)
Howley TA20 3EA.
Open all year.

**TOUR 5**
**SALISBURY** Wiltshire
**Coombe Nuseries Touring Park** (tel: 01722 328451)
Race Plain Netherhampton SP2 8PN.
Open all year.

**Alderbury Caravan and Camping Park** (tel: 01722 328451)
Southampton Rd, Whaddon SP5 3HB.
Open all year.

**WARMINSTER** Wiltshire
**Longleat Caravan Club Site** (tel: 01985 844663)
SP3 4RX.
Open 31 March to 1 November.

**WELLS** Wiltshire
**Homestead Caravan & Camping Park** (tel: 017949 673022) BA9 8BJ.
Open Easter to October.

**PRIDDY** Wiltshire
**Mendip Heights Camping & Caravanning Park** (tel: 01749 870241)
Townsend BA5 3BP.
Open Easter or April to October.

**CHEDDAR** Wiltshire
**Broadway House Holiday Caravan & Camping Park** (tel: 01934 7423304)
Axbridge Road BS27 3DB.
Open end May to September.

**GLASTONBURY** Wiltshire
**Old Oaks Touring Park** (tel: 01458 831437)
Wick Farm, Wick BA6 8JS.
Open March to October.

**TOUR 6**
**SEVENOAKS** Kent
**Camping and Caravanning Club Site** (tel: 01732 762728)
Styrants Bottom Road, Styrants Bottom, Nr Seal TN15 0ET.
Open end March to early November.

**HEATHFIELD** Kent
**Greenview Caravan Park** (tel: 01435 863531)
Broad Oak, TN21 8RT.
Open April to October.

**TOUR 7**
**ASHFORD** Kent
**Broad Hembury Holiday Park** (tel: 01233 620859)
Steeds Lane, Kingsnorth TN26 1NQ.
Open all year.

**FOLKESTONE** Kent
**Little Satmar Holiday Park** (tel: 01303 251188)
Winehouse Lane, Capel Le Ferne CT18 7JF.
Open March to October.

**SANDWICH** Kent
Sandwich Leisure Park (tel: 01304 612681)
Woodnesborough Road, CT13 0AA.
Open March to October.

**CANTERBURY** Kent
**Camping and Caravanning Club Site** (tel: 01227 463216)
Bekesbourne Lane CT3 4AB.
Open all year.

**TOUR 8**
**WINCHESTER** Hampshire
**Morn Hill Caravan Park** (tel: 01962 869877)
Morn Hill SO21 1HL.
Open March to November.

**Tour 9**
**BOURNEMOUTH** Hampshire
Off route. (no tents)
**Chesildene Touring Caravan Park** (tel: 01202 513238)
Chesildene Avenue, BH8 0DS.
Open April to October.

**CHRISTCHURCH** Hampshire
(No tents)
**Grove Farm Meadow Holiday Caravan Park** (tel: 01202 483597)
Stour Way BH23 2PQ.
Open March to October.

**RINGWOOD** Hampshire
**Copper Kettle** (tel: 01425 473904)
266 Christchurch Road, BH24 3AS.
Open March to October.

**BROCKENHURST** Hampshire
**Hollands Wood Campsite** (tel: 01703 283771/282269)
Lyndhurst Road SO42 7QH.
Open Easter to September.

**LYNDHURST** Hampshire
**Denny Wood Campsite** (tel: 01703 283771)
Beaulieu Road SO43 7FZ.
Open Easter to September.

**FORDINGBRIDGE** Hampshire
**New Forest Country Holidays** (tel: 014256 653042)
Sandy Balls Estate Ltd, Godshill SP6 2JZ.
Open all year.

**TOUR 10**
**COLEFORD** Gloustershire
**Christchurch Forest Camping Ground** (tel: 01594 833376)
GL16 8BA.

Open March to October.

**NEWPORT** Gwent
**Tredegar House and Park**
(tel: 01633 816650/815880)
NP1 9YW.
Open Easter to October.

**BRECON** Powys
**Bishops Medow Caravan Park**
(tel: 01874 62205/622392)
Bishops Medow, Hay Road
LD3 9SW.
Open Easter to October.

**BRONLLYS** Powys
**Anchorage Caravan Park**
(tel: 01874 711246/711230)
LD3 0LD.
Open all year.

**HAY-ON-WYE** Powys
**Hollybush Inn** (tel: 01497 847371)
HR3 5PS.
Open Good Friday to October.

**CRICKHOWELL** Powys
**Riverside Caravan & Camping Park** (tel: 01873 810397)
New Rd NP8 1AY.
Open March to October.

**TOUR 11**
**TENBY** Dyfed
**Rowston Holiday Park** (tel: 01834 842178/814090)
New Hedges SA70 8TL.
Open March to mid October.

**Trefalun** (tel: 01646 651514)
Devonshire Drive, St Florence
SA70 8RH.
Open Easter to September.

**Wood Park Caravans** (tel: 01834 843414)
New Hedges SA70 8TL.
Open Spring Bank Holiday to September.

**LAMPHEY** Dyfed
**Freshwater East Caravan Club Site** (tel: 01646 672341)
Little Haven SA62 3UU.
Open Easter to mid-September.

**ST DAVID'S** Dyfed
**Caeefai Bay Caravan & Tent Park** (tel: 01437 72040)
SA62 6QT.

Open Easter to October.

**FISHGUARD** Dyfed
**Fishguard Bay Caravan & Camping Site** (tel: 01348 811415)
Dinas Cross SA42 OYD.
Open March to 9 January.

**LAUGHARNE** Dyfed
**Ants Hill Caravan Park** (tel: 01994 427293)
SA33 4QN.
Open Easter to October.

**TOUR 12**
**ABERYSTWYTH** Dyfed
(No tents)
**Ocean View Caravan Park**
(tel: 01970 828425/623361)
North Beach, Clarach Bay
SY23 3DT.
Open April to October.

**TOUR 13**
**TALSARNAU** Powys
**Barcardy Touring & Caravan Centre** (tel: 01766 770736)
LL47 6YG.
Open Spring Bank Holiday to mid-September.

**BALA** Gwynedd
**Camping and Caravanning Club Site** (tel: 01678 530324 – in season; 01203 694995)
Crynierth Caravan Park, Cefn-Ddwysarn LL23 7IN.
Open end March to early November.

**TYWYN** Gwynedd
**Ynysymaengwyn Caravan Park** (tel: 01654 7106840)
LL36 9RY.
Open Easter or April to October.

**BARMOUTH** Gwynedd
**Hendre Mynach Caravan Park** (tel: 01341 280262)
Llanabar Rd LL42 1YR.
Open March to October.

**TAL-Y-BONT** Gwynedd
**Benar Beach Touring & Caravan Park** (tel: 01341 24751)
LL43 2AR.
Open March to 3 October.

**TOUR 14**
**CAERNARFON** Gwynedd
**Bryan Teg Holiday Park** (tel: 01654 710471)
LL36 9UH.
Open Easter to 14 January.

**BEDDGELERT** Gwynedd
**Beddgerlert Forest Campsite**
(tel: 01766 890288 & 01492 640578)
LL55 4UU.
Open all year.

**PORTHMADOG** Gwynedd
**Tyddn Llwyn Caravan Park & Camping Site** (tel: 01766 512205)
Black Rock Rd LL49 9UR.
Open March to October.

**LLANRWST** Gwynedd
**Bonant Caravan Site** (tel: 01492 640248)
Nebo Road LL26 OSD.
Open March to October.

**Maenan Abbey Caravan Park**
(tel: 01492 660630)
LL26 0UL.
Open March to October.

**CONWY** Gwynedd
**Conwy Touring Park** (tel: 01492 59256)
LL32 8UX.
Open Easter to October.

**TOUR 15**
**WOODHALL SPA**
Lincolnshire
**Bainland Country Park** (tel: 01526 352903)
Horncastle Road LN10 6UX.
Open all year.

**TOUR 16**
**FAKENHAM** Norfolk
**Caravan Club Site** (tel: 01328 862388)
Fakenham Racecourse NR21 7NY.
Open 26 March to 10 October.

**HUNSTANTON** Norfolk
**Searles of Hunstanton** (tel: 01485 534211/532342)
South Beach PE36 5BB.
Open Easter to October.

**SANDRINGHAM** Norfolk
**Camping and Caravanning Club Site** (tel: 01485 542555)
The Sandringham Estate,

Double Lodges, PE36 6EA.
Open end of February to the end of November.

**TOUR 17**
**EAST BERGHOLT** Suffolk
**Grange Country Park** (tel: 01206 298567/298912)
The Grange CO7 6UX.
Open 31 March to October.

**NEWMARKET** Suffolk
**Camping and Caravanning Club Site** (tel: 01638 663235)
Rowely Mile Racecourse CB8 8JL.
Open May to September.

**IPSWICH** Suffolk
**Priory Park** (tel: 01473 727393)
NR33 8EE.
Open April to October.

**TOUR 18**
**OXFORD** Oxfordfordshire
**Oxford Camping International** (tel: 01865 246551)
426 Abingdon Road OX1 4XN.
Open all year.

**CHARLBURY** Oxfordshire
**Cotswold View Caravan Park** (tel: 01608 810314)
Enstone Road OX7 3JH.
Open Easter or April to October.

**CHIPPING NORTON** Oxfordshire
**Camping & Caravanning Club Site** (tel: 01608 641993 & 01203 694995)
Chipping Norton Road OX7 3PN.
Open March to November.

**BANBURY** Oxfordshire
**Barnstones Caravan & Camping Park** (tel: 01295 750289)
Great Bourton OX17 1QU.
Open all year.

**TOUR 19**
**GREAT MALVERN** Hereford & Worcester
**Riverside Caravan Park** (tel: 01684 310475)
Little Clevelode WR13 6PE.
Open March to December.

**EVESHAM** Hereford & Worcester
(No tents)
**Weir Maedow Holiday & Touring Park** (tel: 01386 442417)
Lower Leys WR11 5AB.
Open Easter or April to October.

**BROADWAY** Hereford & Worcester
**Leedon's Park** (tel: 01386 852423)
Childswick Road WR12 7HB.
Open all year.

**CHELTENHAM** Gloucestershire
**Caravan Club Site** (tel: 01242 523102)
Cheltenham Racecourse GL50 4SH.
Open 2 April to mid October.

**GLOUCESTER** Gloucestershire
**Red Lion Camping & Caravan Park** (tel: 01452 730251)
Wainlode Hill, Norton GL2 9LW.
Open all year.

**TOUR 20**
**MUCH WENLOCK** Shropshire
(No tents)
**Presthope Caravan Club Site** (tel: 01746 632634)
Stretton Road TF13 6DQ.
Open all year.

**BRIDGNORTH** Shropshire
**Stanmore Hill Touring Park** (tel: 01746 761761)
Stourbridge Road WV15 6DT.
Open all year.

**TOUR 21**
**CARLISLE** Cumbria
**Orton Grange Caravan & Camping Park** (tel: 01228 710252)
Orton Grange, Wigton Road CA5 6LA.
Open all year.

**KESWICK** Cumbria
**Camping & Caravanning Club Site** (tel: 01768 772392 – in season; 01203 694995)
Derwentwater CA12 5EP.
Open end of January to end of November.

**Derwentwater Caravan Park** (tel: 01768 772579)
Crowe Park Road CA12 5EN.
Open March to 14 October.

**AMBLESIDE** Cumbria
**Skelwith Fold Caravan Park** (tel: 01539 432277)
LA22 OHX
Open March to 15 November.

**CONISTON,** Cumbria
**Park Coppice Caravan Club Site** (tel: 01539 441555)
LA21 8LA.
Open April to October.

**HAWKESHEAD** Cumbria
**Camping & Caravanning Club Site** (tel: 01229 860257)
Grizeldale Hall LA22 OGL.
Open end of March to early October.

**WINDERMERE** Cumbria
**Fallbarrow Park** (tel: 01539 444428)
Rayrigg Rd LA23 3DL.
Open mid March to October.

**Limefitt Park** (tel: 01539 432300)
Open 1 week prior Easter to October.

**POOLEY BRIDGE** Cumbria
**Hill Croft Caravan & Camping Site** (tel: 01768 486363)
Roe Head Lane CA10 2LT.
Open March to 14 of November.

**PENRITH** Cumbria.
**Lowther Caravan Park** (tel: 01768 863631)
Lowther Bridge CA10 2JB.
Open mid March to mid November.

**HALTWHISTLE** Northumberland
**Camping & Caravanning Club Site** (tel: 01434 320106 – in season; 01434 694995)
Burnfort Park Village NE49 OHZ.
Open end of March to early November.

**TOUR 22**
**RIPON** North Yorkshire
**Ure Bank Caravan Park**

(tel: 01765 602964/607764)
Ure Bank Top HG4 1JD.
Open May to October.

**RICHMOND** North Yorkshire
**Brompton-on-Swale Caravan Park** (tel: 01748 824629)
Brompton-on-Swale Dl10 7EZ.
Open Easter or April to October.

**KIRKBY STEPHEN** Cumbria
**Pennine View Caravan & Camping Park** (tel: 01768 371717)
Pennine View, Stratton Road CA17 4SZ.
Open March to October.

**SEDBERGH** Cumbria
**Pinfold Caravan Park** (tel: 01539 620576)
Garsdale Road LA10 5JL.
Open March to October.

**HAWES** North Yorkshire
**Bainbridge Ings Caravan & Camping Site** (tel: 01969 667354)
DL8 3NU.
Open April to October.

**AYSGARTH** North Yorkshire
**Westholme Caravan Park** (tel: 01969 663268)
DL8 3SP.
Open March to October.

**TOUR 23**
**MORECAMBE** Lancashire
**Riverside Caravan Park** (tel: 01524 844193)
Snatchems LA3 3ER.
Open March to October.

**Venture Caravan Park** (tel: 01524 412985)
Langridge Way, Westgate LA4 4TQ.
Open March to October.

**BOLTON-LE-SANDS** Lancashire
**Sandside Caravan & Camping Park** (tel: 01524 822311)
The Shore LA5 8JS.
Open March to October.

**KIRKBY LONSDALE** Cumbria
**Woodclose Caravan Park** (tel: 01524 271597)
Casterton LA6 2SE.
Open March to October.

**CLITHEROE** Lancashire
**Camping & Caravanning Club Site** (tel: 01200 25294 – in season); 01203 694995)
Edisford Bridge, Edisford Road BB7 3LA.
Open end of March to early November.

**BLACKPOOL** Lancashire
**Mariclough Hampsfield Camping Site** (tel: 01253 761034)
Preston New Road, Peel Corner FY4 5JR.
Open Easter to November.

**TOUR 24**
**CASTELTON** Derbyshire
**Losehill Caravan Club Site** (tel: 01433 62036)
Open April to October.

**MATLOCK** Derbyshire
**Darwin Forest Country Park** (tel: 01629 732428)
Darley Moor, Two Dales DE4 5LA.
Open all year.

**BAKEWELL** Darbyshire
**Greenhills Caravan Park** (tel: 01629 813467/813052)
Crow Hill Lane DE45 1PX.
Open all year.

**BUXTON** Derbyshire
**Grin Low Caravan Club Site** (tel: 01298 77735)
Grin Low Road, Ladmanlow SK17 6UJ.
Open April to October.

**TOUR 25**
**YORK** North Yorkshire
**Rawcliffe Manor Caravan Site** (tel: 01094 642244)
Manor Lane, Shipton Road YO3 6TZ.
Open all year.

**Rowntree Park Caravan Club Site** (tel: 01904 658997)
Terry Avenue 9O2 1JQ.
Open all year.

**PICKERING** North Yorkshire (No tents)
**Upper Car Touring Park** (tel: 01751 473115)
Upper Car Ln, Malton Road YO18 7JP.
Open March to October.

**Wayside Caravan Park** (tel: 01751 472608)
Wrelton YO18 8PG.
Open Easter to early October.

**HELMSLEY** North Yorkshire
**Golden Square Touring Caravan Park** (tel: 01439 788269)
Oswaldkirk YO6 5YQ.
Open MArch to October.

**SUTTON-ON-THE-FOREST** North Yorkshire
**Goosewood Caravan Park** (tel: 01347 810829)
YO6 1ET.
Open 22 March to October.

**TOUR 26**
**SHIEL BRIDGE** Highland
**Morvich Caravan Club Site** (tel: 01599 81345)
IV40 8HQ.
Open mid-May to mid-August.

**APPLECROSS** Highland
**Applecross Campsite** (tel: 01520 744268)
IV54 8ND.
Open Easter to October.

**KINLOCHEWE** Highland
**Kinlochewe Caravan Site** (tel: 01445 84239)
IV22 2PA.
Open 2 April to 4 October.

**GAIRLOCH** Dornoch
**Sands Holiday Centre** (tel: 01445 712152)
IV21 2Dl.
Open 20 May to 10 September.

**POOLEWE** Highland
**Camping and Caravanning Club Site** (tel: 01445 7812149)
Iverwe Gardens IV22 2LE.
Open end March to early November.

**TOUR 27**
**ABOYNE** Grampian
**Aboyne Loch Caravan Park** (tel: 013398 86244)
AB34 5BR
Open 31 March to October.

**BALLATER** Grampian
**Anderson Road Caravan Site**

Applecross road

(tel: 013397 557257– in season; 01569 762001)
AB53 5QW.
Open April to mid October.

**ALFORD** Grampian
**Haughton House Caravan Site** (tel: 019755 62107)
AB33 8NA.
Open April to September.

**TOUR 28**
**EDINBURGH** Lothian
**Morton Hill Caravan Park** (tel: 0131 644 153)
38 Morton Hill Gate EH16 6TJ.
Open 28 March to October.

**PEEBLES** Borders
**Crossburn Caravan Park** (tel: 01721 720501)
The Glades, 95 Edinburgh Road EH45 8ED.
Open April to October.

**KELSO** Borders
**Springwood Caravn Park** (tel: 01573 2249576)
TdD 8LS.
Open end of March to October.

**ABERLADY** Lothian
(No tents)
**Gosford Gardens Caravan Club Site** (tel: 01875 870487)
EH32 OPX.
Open 26 March to 25 October.

**MUSSELBURGH** Lothian
**Drum Mohr Caravan Park**
(tel: 0131 665 6867)
Levenhall EH21 8JS.
Open March to October.

**DALKEITH** Lothian
**Fordel** (tel: 0131 663 3046; 0131 663 3046; 0131 660 3921)
Lauder Road EH22 2PH.
Open March to October.

**TOUR 29**
**ROCKCLIFFE** Dumfries & Galloway
**Castle Point Caravan Park**
(tel: 01556 630248)
DG5 4QL.
Open Easter to September.

**KIPPFORD** Dumfries & Galloway
**Kippford Caravan Park** (tel: 01556 620636)
DG5 4LF.
Open March to October.

**CASTLE DOUGLAS**
Dumfries & Galloway
**Lochside Caravan and Camping Park** (tel: 01556 50249; 01557 330291)
Lochside Park DG7 1EZ.
Open Easter to mid-October.

**KIRKCUDBRIGHT** Dumfries & Galloway
**Seaward Caravan Park** (tel: 01557 870267; 01557 331079)
Dhoon Bay DG6 4TJ.
Open April to October.

**TOUR 30**
**INVERARAY** Strathclyde
**Argyll Caravan Park** (tel: 01499 302285)
PA32 8XT.
Open April to October.

**LOCHGILPHEAD** Strathclyde
**Lochgilphead Caravan Site**
(tel: 01546 602003)
PA31 8NX.
Open April to October.

**OBAN** Strathclyde
**Oban Divers Caravan Park**
(tel: 01631 562755)
Glenshellach Road PA43 4QJ.
Open 15 March to 15 November.

**INVERBEG** Strathclyde
**Inverbeg Holiday Park** (tel: 01436 860267; 0131 654 0142)
G83 8PD
Open March to October.

# INDEX

**The Automobile Association**
would like to thank the following photographers and libraries for their assistance in the preparation of this book.

PICTURES COLOUR LIBRARY LTD 5, 7, 52/3;
WOOLSACK COMMITTEE 2;

All remaining pictures are held in the Association's own library (AA PHOTO LIBRARY)
with contributions from the following photographers:
P AITHIE 77; M ALLWOOD-COPPIN 64, 69; A BAKER 89, 110/1, 137; P BAKER 13, 16/7, 19a, 19b, 25, 26, 32, 44, 86/7, 90/1, 130/1; J BEAZLEY 124, 147, 149, 150, 155; A W BESLEY 10; M BIRKITT 84, 85a, 85b, 88, 94, 95, 96, 97, 129; E A BOWNESS 113, 114, 115; P BROWN 40; I BURGUM 58/9, 65, 66, 66/7, 72, 107; D CORRANCE 146, 148; D CROUCHER 50, 57, 76, 81; S L DAY 24, 29, 99, 103, 106, 116, 127, 153; E ELLINGTON 140/1, 165; P ENTICKNAP 49; D FORSS 33, 35, 42, 46, 47, 48, 51, 54, 55; J GRAVEL 63; S GREGORY 135; J HENDERSON 139, 141; A J HOPKINS 59, 71, 128; C JONES 56, 78, 80, 109; A LAWSON 8, 12, 18; S & O MATHEWS 34, 45, 91, 92, 151; E MEACHER 28/9, 70; C & A MOLYNEUX 60, 61; J MORRISON 120/1, 123, 126; R MOSS 11, 15; J MOTTERSHAW 134; R NEWTON 22, 130, 132; D NOBLE 36, 37, 38, 39, 41, 43; K PATERSON 145, 154; N RAY 9, 23, 100/1; P SHARPE 117, 156, 156/7; M SHORT 102, 111; R SURMAN 83; D TARN 112, 119, 122b, 125; M TAYLOR 136; T TEEGAN 14a, 14b; T D TIMMS 73, 74, 75, 79; W VOYSEY 30, 31, 93; R WEIR 142/3, 144; J WELSH 104, 105; L WHITWAM 82, 122a; H WILLIAMS 6, 152; J WYAND 27.

**Contributors**
**Copy editors:** Nia Williams, Dilys Jones **Indexer:** Marie Lorimer